TEXTILES OF RAJASTHAN

AT THE JAIPUR COURT

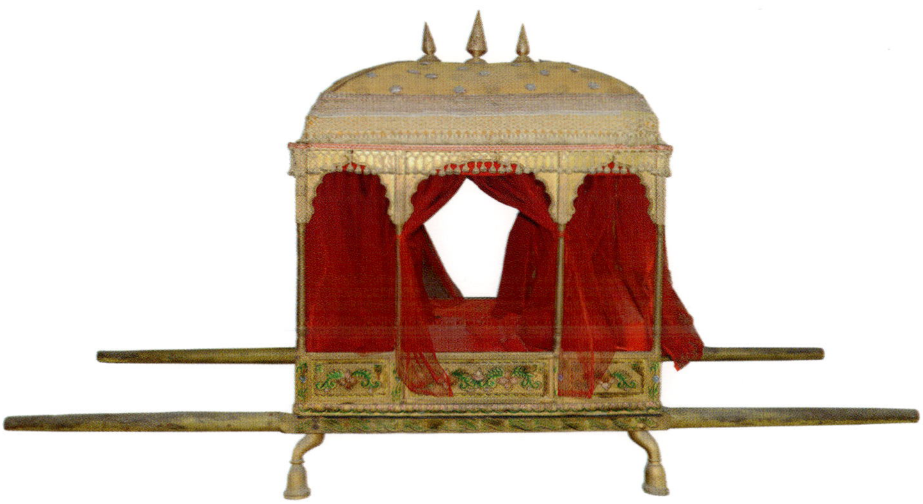

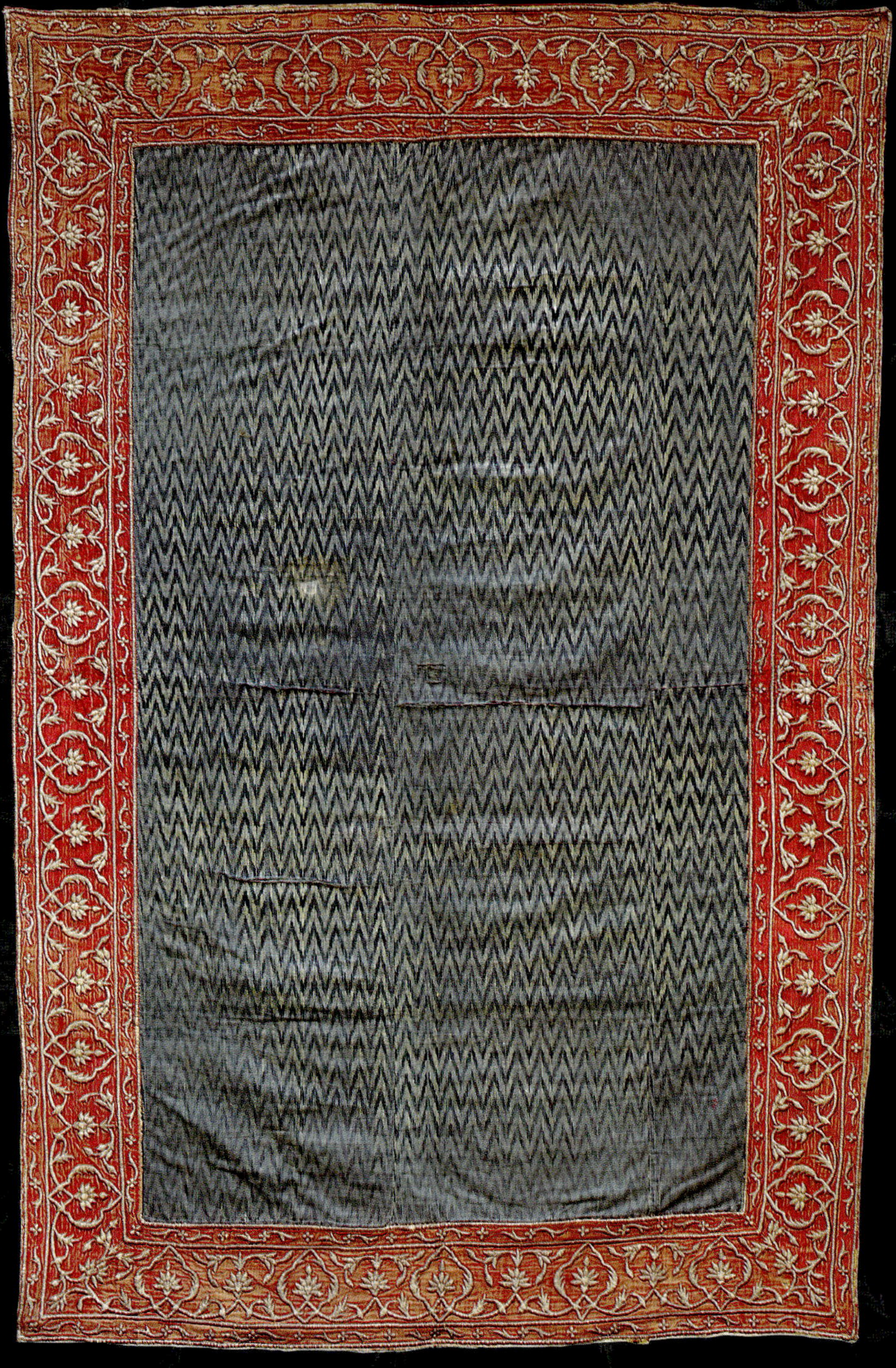

Metal Embroidery
Floor cover
Silk velvet, centre panel patterned with ikat-dyed pile warps; borders embroidered with metal thread.
224 x 145 cm
MSMS II Museum, Jaipur

TEXTILES OF RAJASTHAN

AT THE JAIPUR COURT

VANDANA BHANDARI

NIYOGI
BOOKS

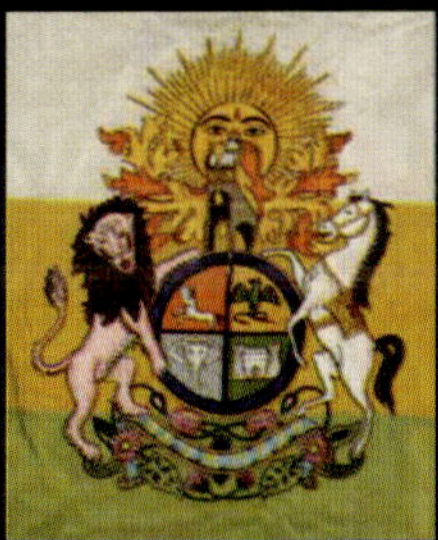

MAHARAJA SAWAI MAN SINGH II MUSEUM TRUST

MAHARAJA SAWAI MAN SINGH II MUSEUM TRUST

Published by
NIYOGI BOOKS
Block D, Building No. 77
Okhla Industrial Area, Phase-I
New Delhi-110 020, INDIA
Tel: 91-11-26816301, 26818960
Email: niyogibooks@gmail.com
Website: www.niyogibooksindia.com

Series Editor: Giles Tillotson
Editor: Arunima Ghosh
Design: Nabanita Das

ISBN: 978-93-89136-61-6
Publication: 2020

Printed at: Niyogi Offset Pvt. Ltd., New Delhi, India

To my parents,
Smt. Shanti and Shree Ballabh Kabra

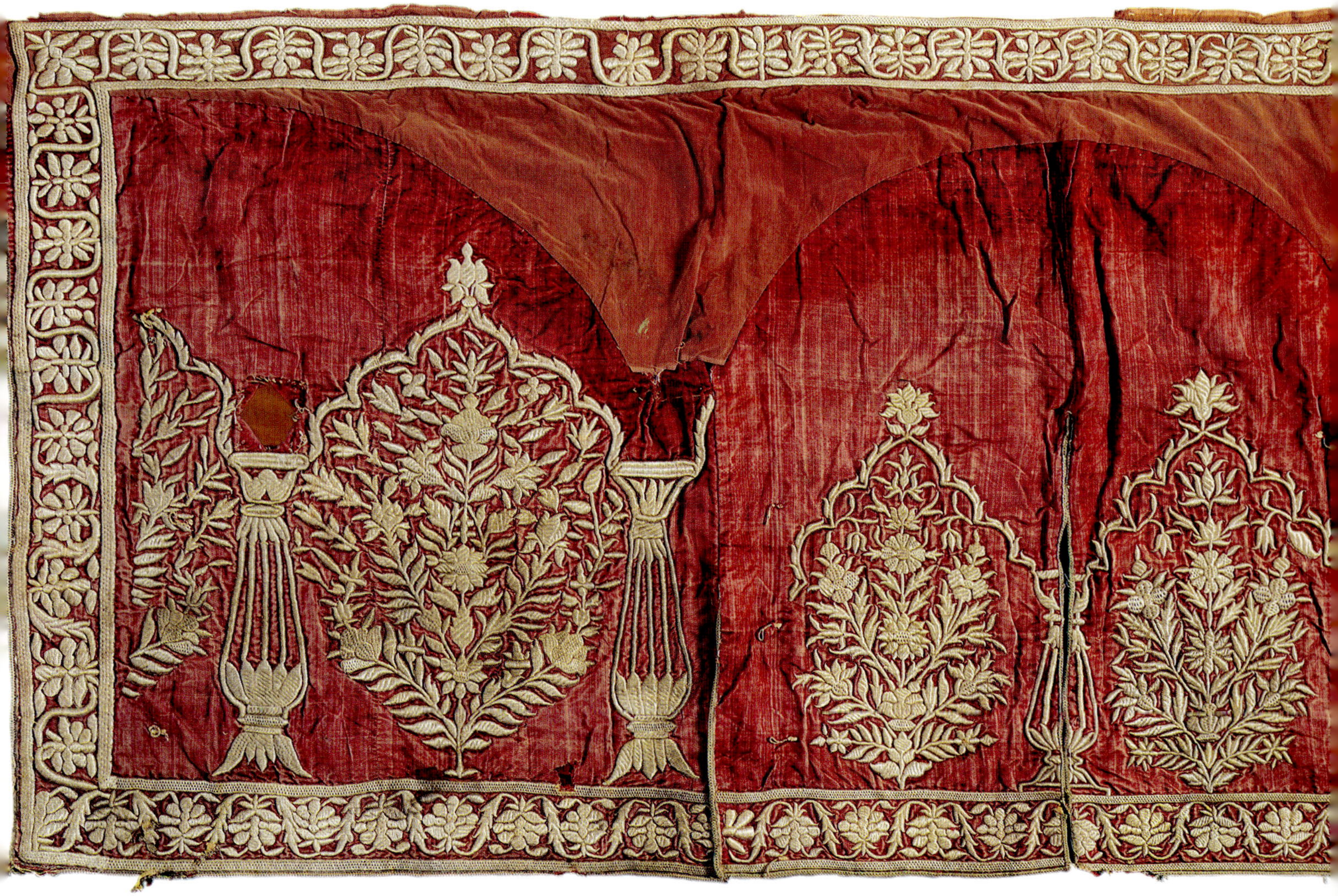

Vasli Embroidery
Fragments of a carriage cover
Silk velvet, embroidered with metal thread. Of the numerous tent and palace furnishings that once belonged to the royal stores of Amber Jaipur, very few remain in the MSMS II Museum collection. Among these are large fragments of a carriage cover of embroidered velvet. This textile may have been produced at a local court shop.
MSMS II Museum, Jaipur
TC.462.73

Half-title page: Varak
Palki
With *varak* and *gota* work on a yellow base on top, the palki is embellished with brocade on the inside.
MSMS II Museum, Jaipur
Reserve collection

CONTENTS

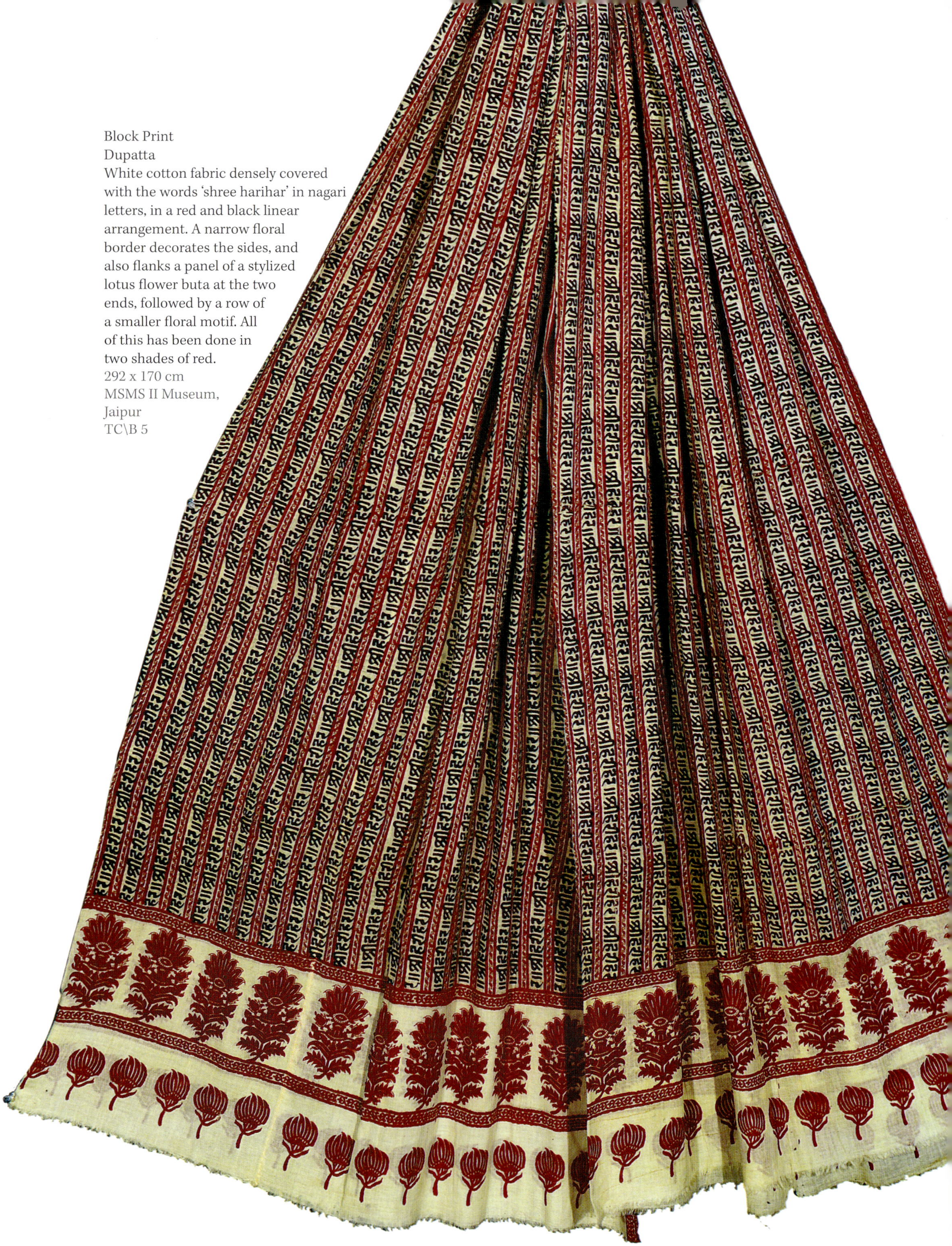

Block Print
Dupatta
White cotton fabric densely covered with the words 'shree harihar' in nagari letters, in a red and black linear arrangement. A narrow floral border decorates the sides, and also flanks a panel of a stylized lotus flower buta at the two ends, followed by a row of a smaller floral motif. All of this has been done in two shades of red.
292 x 170 cm
MSMS II Museum, Jaipur
TC\B 5

FOREWORD

The room in a palace used to store the royal collection of garments and jewellery—traditionally called the *kapad dwara*—was one of the most prized and closely guarded apartments. Of all of the sumptuous arts that contributed to courtly culture, nothing declared the court's wealth and sophistication so clearly as the clothes worn by the members of the ruling family. Descriptions of events at court, such as rituals and ceremonies, composed by court poets, often focus on clothes worn by the principal participants. Visibly splendid as they were, historic garments are also very fragile objects, susceptible to decay. Today, there is a special separate storeroom and a gallery in the museum in the City Palace, where the textile collection is preserved for posterity, and kept for study and display.

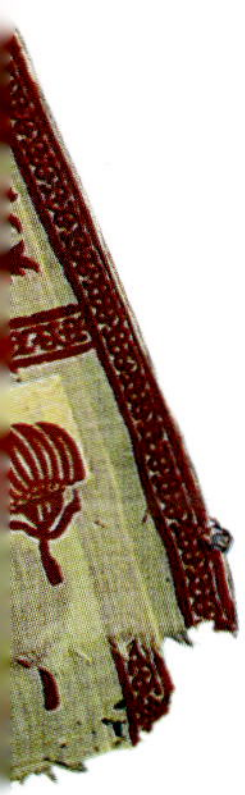

This is the fifth book in a new series of illustrated publications, which we launched in 2014, with the intention of bringing the museum's collections to the attention of a wider audience. One of the earlier books, written by Rahul Jain, considers a selection of the textiles and garments, and ably shows how rich and varied the historic collection once was. The purpose of this second volume on the textiles is slightly different: Dr Vandana Bhandari, a noted expert in the field, focuses especially on textiles that were made locally. Rajasthan has a continuing practice of many different kinds of cloth production, and remains famous for the skilled techniques of its crafts people. From woodblock printing and embroidery to *zardozi*, every type of cloth production and decoration is found here. Each is also well represented in the museum collection as the City Palace was always an ardent patron and supporter of local arts.

I congratulate Dr Bhandari on her book, which lucidly explains and illustrates each of the unique textile techniques in turn. As time passes and taste changes, some of the textile techniques discussed here are endangered. This timely book showcases and celebrates some of our best examples and will help to raise awareness and interest and preserve the legacy of textiles from Rajasthan.

Princess Diya Kumari

Secretary & Trustee

Maharaja Sawai Man Singh II Museum

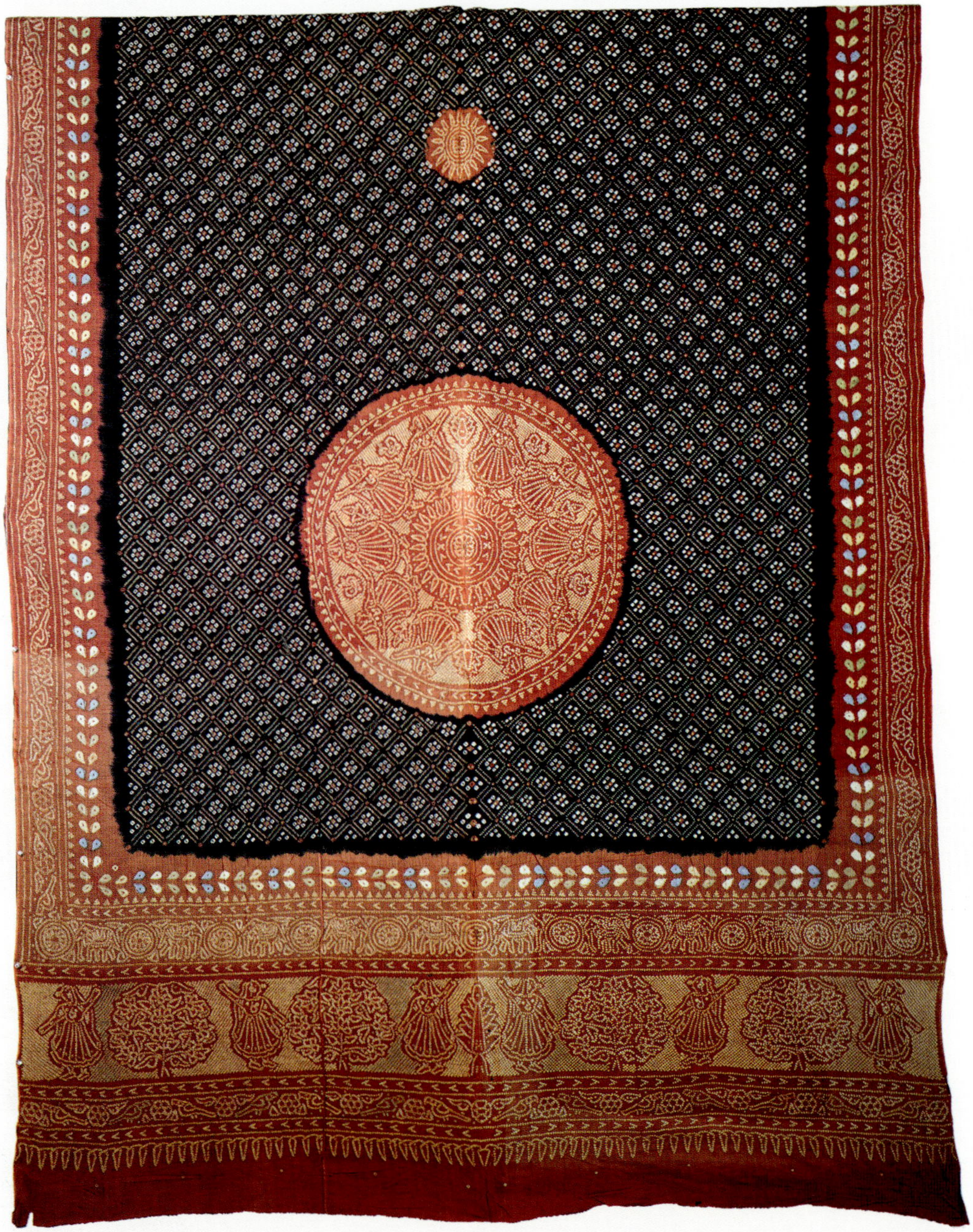

Bandhani
Odhna

Fine black muslin with tie-dyed dotted designs, a checkerboard-like pattern in the centre, comprising three circular motifs of yellow, green, and white dots on a red ground. The small circle represents the sun, and the two large ones carry dancing women, peacocks, and floral motifs. The two ends have elephants, a *boota* design and various trees between two margins, and the extreme sides are bordered with a panel of parrot and flower motifs—all in white and yellow. At the inner edge is a row of small pyramids, followed by two rows of a leaf pattern in white, yellow, blue, and green.

296 X 154.4 cm

MSMS II Museum, Jaipur

TC.537.73

INTRODUCTION

Among the thousands of textiles and garments in the Jaipur royal collection, is an *odhna*, or woman's head covering, with a fine black muslin base and a checkerboard type of design on the central rectangle. There are three circular motifs: the small circle with a red base represents a sun, while the two large circles in the centre depict dancing women with peacocks and floral motifs. The side border has parrots and flowers, while the *pallu* border has elephants and a *boota* design with multiple types of trees and dancing ladies. Royal patronage for textiles such as this led to the development of some of the finest textile techniques in Rajasthan and other parts of India.

The Jaipur court has records of *karkhanas* or ateliers producing different textiles from 18th century onwards. This kind of assimilation and development of textiles was possible because of the existence of strong patronage from the court. The rich and multifaceted textile collection of the Maharaja Sawai Man Singh II Museum in Jaipur

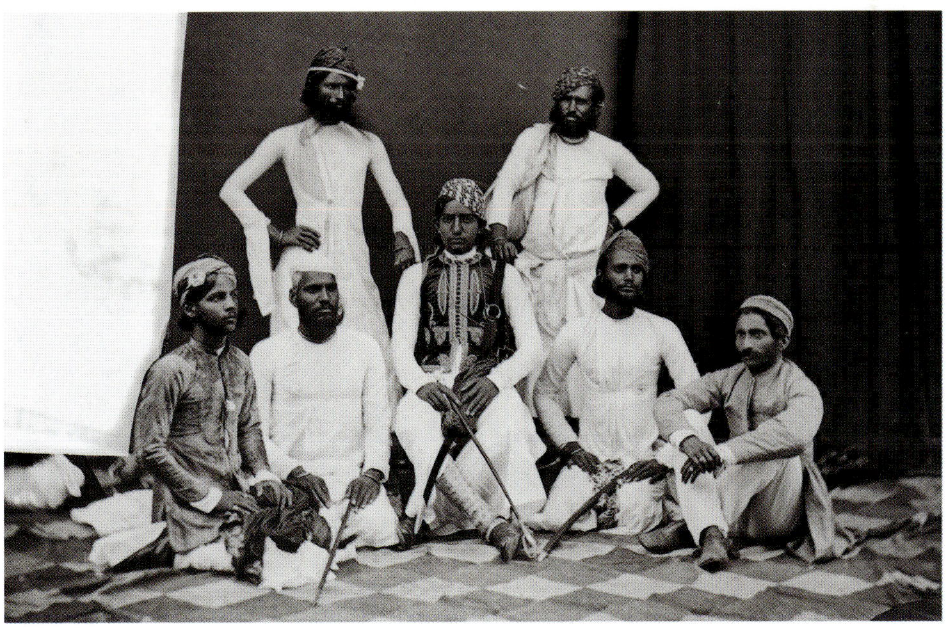

A group of men in the traditional attire of Rajasthan. The turbans of the three men in the centre use a fine tie-dyed fabric known as *leheriya*.
Reserve collection

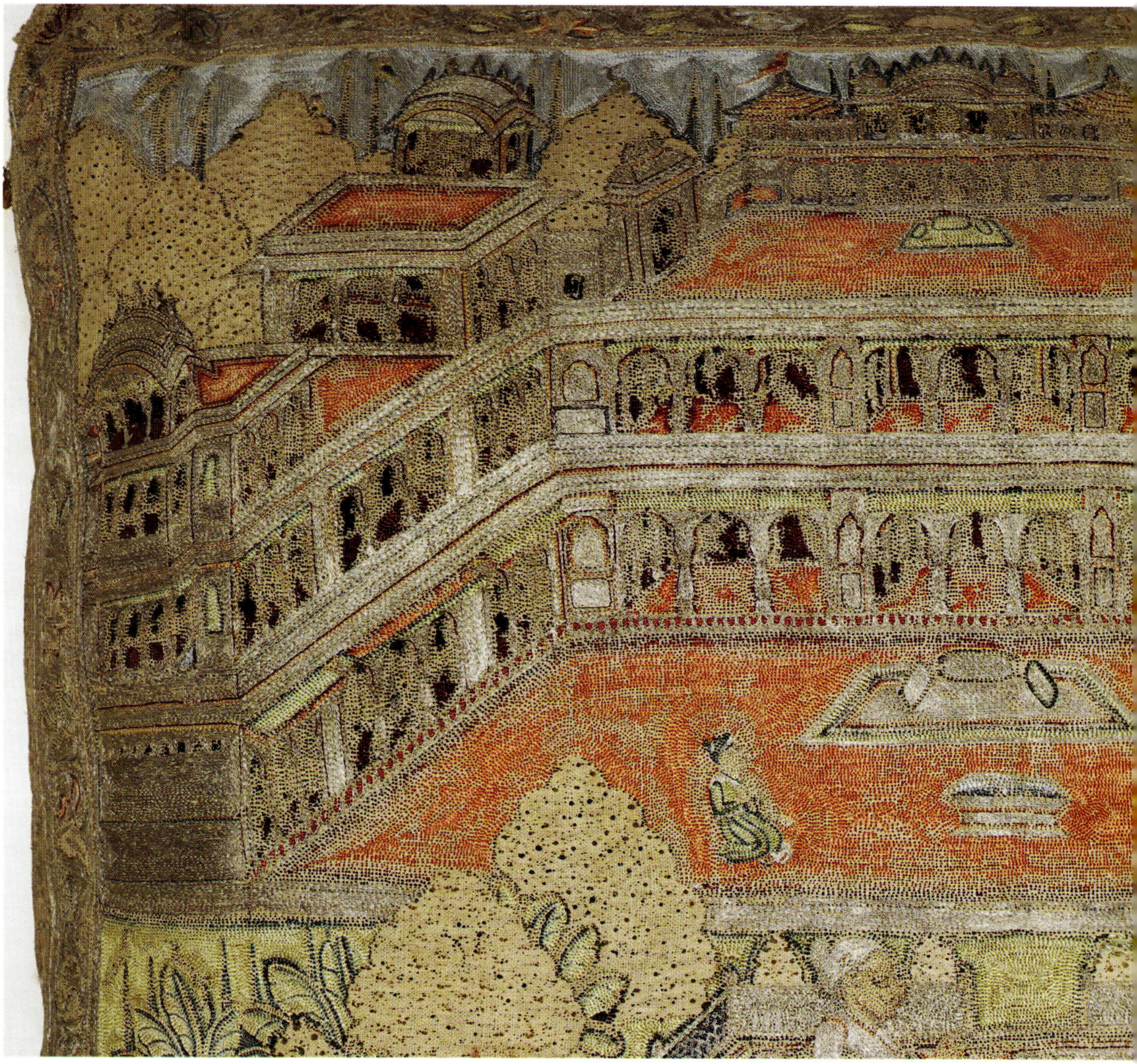

City Palace spans a period of 350 years from the end of the 16th century to the middle of the 20th century. The museum houses over 2500 pieces of textiles, many of which are in pristine condition.

The techniques used to create these textiles were practised across the country and many of them continue to be practised in Rajasthan, especially in Jaipur, even today. Jaipur produces an unmatched array of textiles that are handcrafted using traditional techniques. From the late 20th century, there has been a resurgence of these skills, which has been led

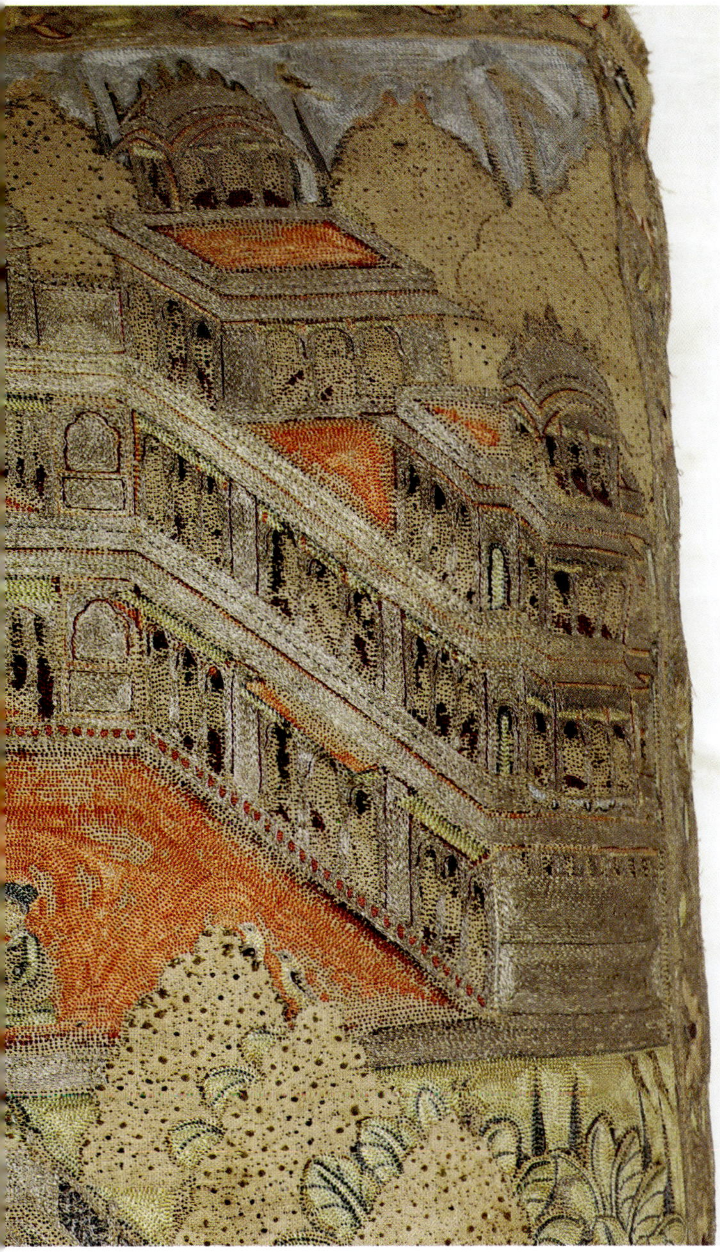

Metal thread embroidery
Cushion cover
Cotton, embroidered with silk and metal thread in chainstitch, this is a partial depiction of a scene of the city with its fortified walls on the cover of a side-cushion (*gao takia*), part of a *gaddi* ensemble.
MSMS II Museum, Jaipur
Tc/D.2

by entrepreneurs, who have, in a sense, acted as patrons for the production and sustenance of fine textiles.

This book looks closely at time-honoured techniques used for textile production in Jaipur and more widely in Rajasthan—a long-standing tradition that finds continuity in the contemporary fashion scenario. It aims to promote an understanding and appreciation of the indigenous craft skills that still prevail in the region and will present masterpieces, which are preserved in the City Palace Museum in Jaipur. The collection features extravagant ornamentation of textiles and dress, spanning over three centuries. The illustrations include photographs from the Sawai Ram Singh archive in the museum's collection, an unparallelled reservoir of immense historic value.

An infinite variety of textiles are produced in Jaipur, each fitting into the social and ritualistic culture of the region. These are produced today in much the same way as they have been for centuries. The book explores their techniques, materials, processes, and design details. The craftspersons producing textiles have done so for generations and, though the context of the products has changed, the techniques remain the same by and large, despite the modernization of raw materials, tools, and methods.

JAIPUR TEXTILES

Literary and archaeological evidence traces the history of Indian textiles to as early as the Indus Valley Civilization c.3000 BCE, when spinning, weaving, dyeing, and patterning were already

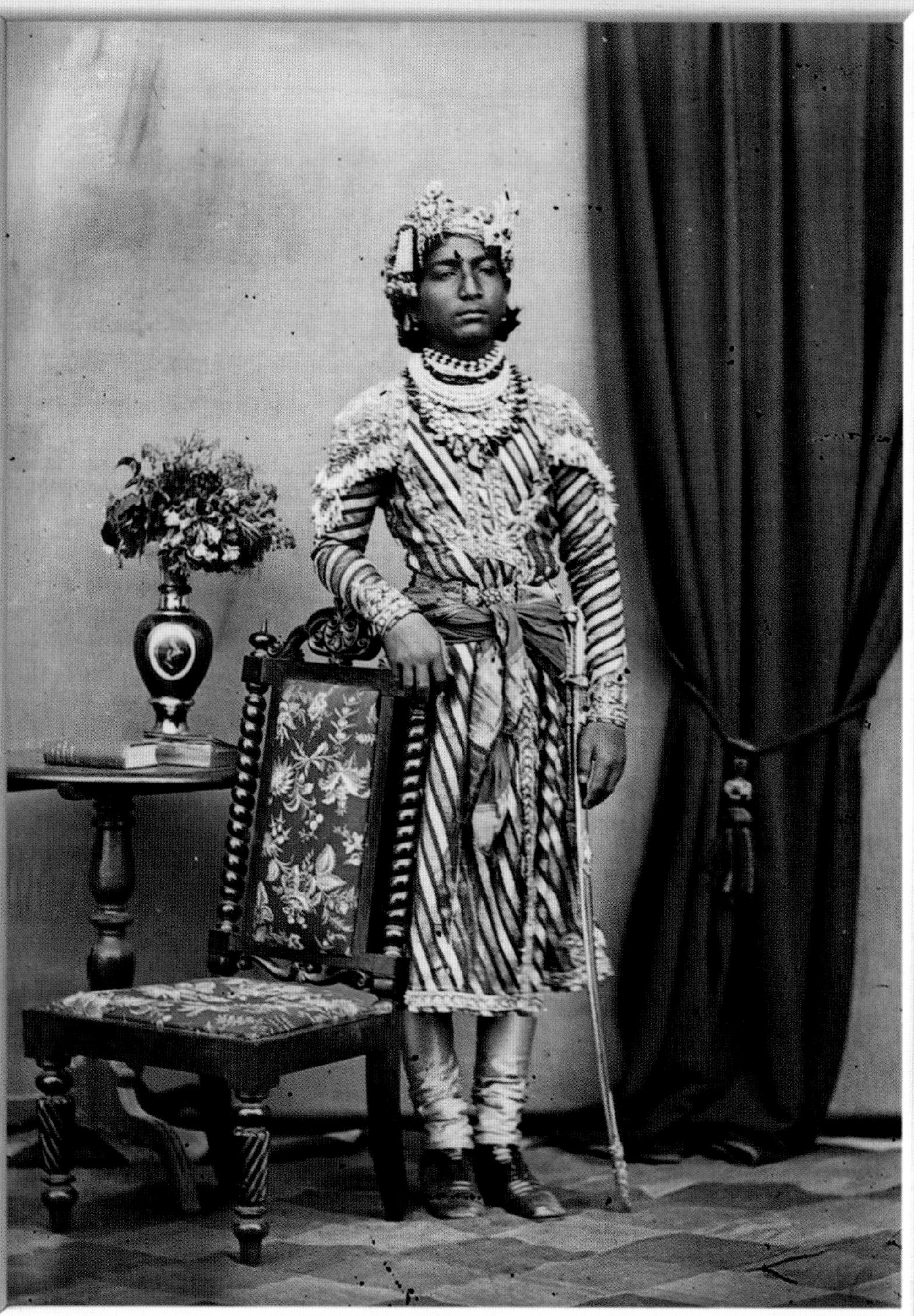

known in India. Later evidence from texts such as the Vedas and *Arthashashtra* also shed light on the finest cloths made of cotton, silk, and wool produced in the country, for domestic use and for trade. Trade was conducted through the silk and spice routes; examples of printed cloth from India have been found in Egypt, while fine muslins have been found to be celebrated in Rome in as early as the 1st century CE. The Ajanta paintings (6th century) are also a rich source of information on embroidery techniques, tie-dye—*bandhani*, *ikat*, and other types of textiles. Bernier, a travel writer of the 17th century, has described the *karkhanas* or court workshops, which were used for production of textiles and other products in the Mughal era.

In Rajasthan, as in other parts of India, royal and temple patronage encouraged master-craftspersons to create the finest panorama of textiles and costumes. The promotion of the crafts in such areas was greatly helped by the dispersal of master craftspersons from the imperial cities such as Delhi with the decline of Mughal wealth in the 18th century. As Kokyo Hatanaka has

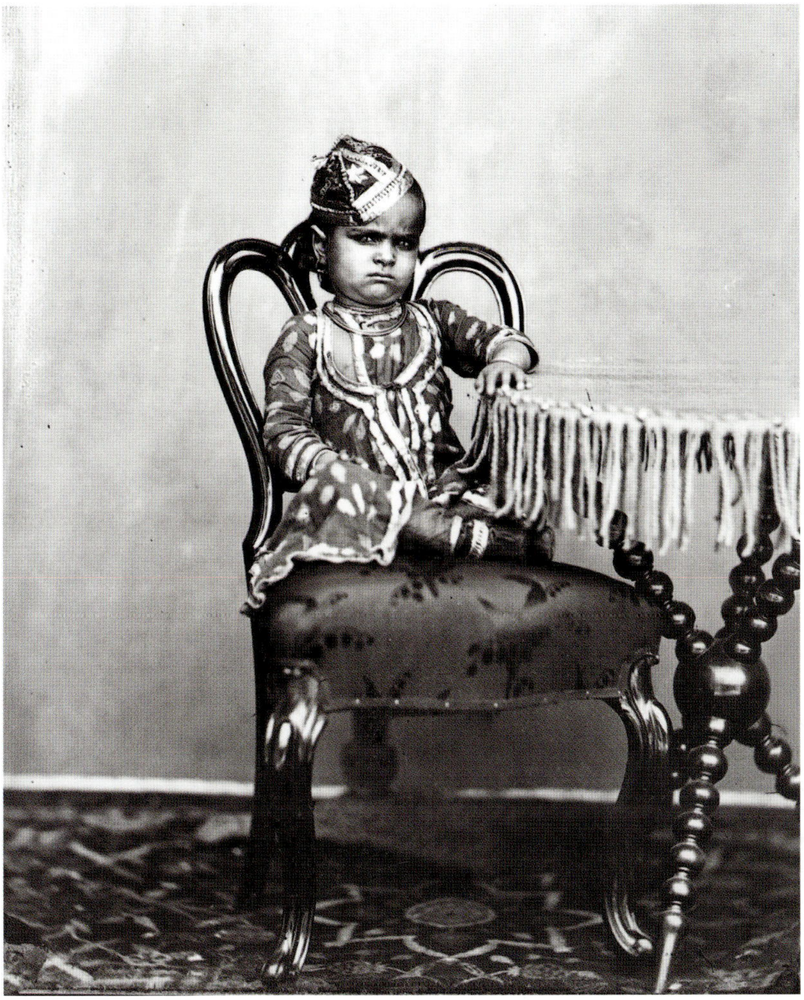

Portrait of a child at court, wearing a *bandhani angarkha*.
MSMS II M 2012.04.0053-0009

Facing page: Portrait of a man wearing a long upper garment with churidar. Heavy embellishment is visible on the shoulders.
MSMS II M 2012.04.0027-0044

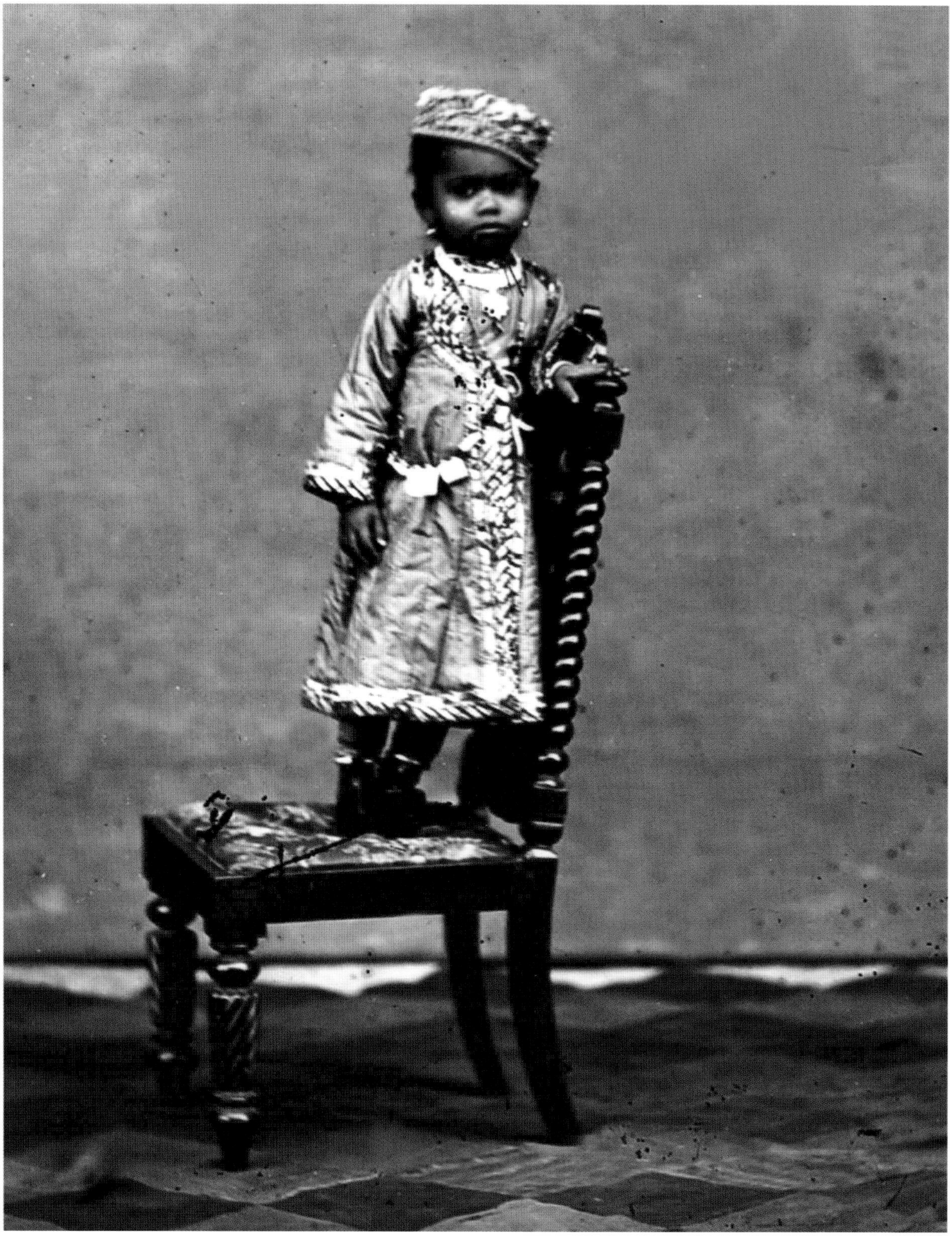

noted (translated by Zahid Sardar), 'When the Mughal courts lost power, the Persian and Hindu artisans that had gathered there dispersed into textile centres such as Gujarat and Rajasthan and their skills permeated the long-standing craft traditions of those areas.'[1] Remarkable diversity of traditional textiles, both in technique and style, has survived to the present day. It forms the basis for further innovation in pattern and design, defining the aesthetics of the region and representing the evolving social and cultural values of its people.

From the foundation of Jaipur in the 18th century, successive rulers have actively supported the textile industry, to boost the city's trading status and to supply the needs of the court. When the city was under construction in the 1730s, certain mohallas in Purani Basti—the north-west corner of the old walled city—were allotted to the weavers, dyers, and cloth printers. These districts include *rangrez walon ka rasta* (dyer's lane) and Mohalla Neelgaran, which are still identified today with similar craft practices. Notable royal patrons include the city's founder, Maharaja Sawai Jai Singh II, the late 18th century ruler Maharaja Sawai Pratap Singh, and the great reforming 19th century ruler, Maharaja Sawai Ram Singh II.

The textiles in the MSMS II Museum collection fall into the following broad classifications: tents and floor coverings, garments for men, women, and children—including both stitched and draped garments—and furnishings and trappings for animals. The collection is strong in textiles made for trade, textiles for use in temples, and textiles made especially for the royal courts. These include printed and painted textiles, *pichhwai*s and ritual scrolls, Kashmir shawls, embroideries and brocades. Folk textiles from different regions of India are also present in the museum. The focus of this book, however, is to discuss those textiles for which of Rajasthan was especially famous.

ENDNOTES

1. Kokyo Hatanaka, *Textile Arts of India*, trans. Zahid Sardar (San Francisco: Chronicle Books, 1996), p. 311.

Facing page: Portrait of a child wearing an *angarkha*, churidar, and cap. The *angarkha* is edged with *magazi* in a striped fabric cut on bias.
MSMS II M 2012.04.0027-0012 (detail)

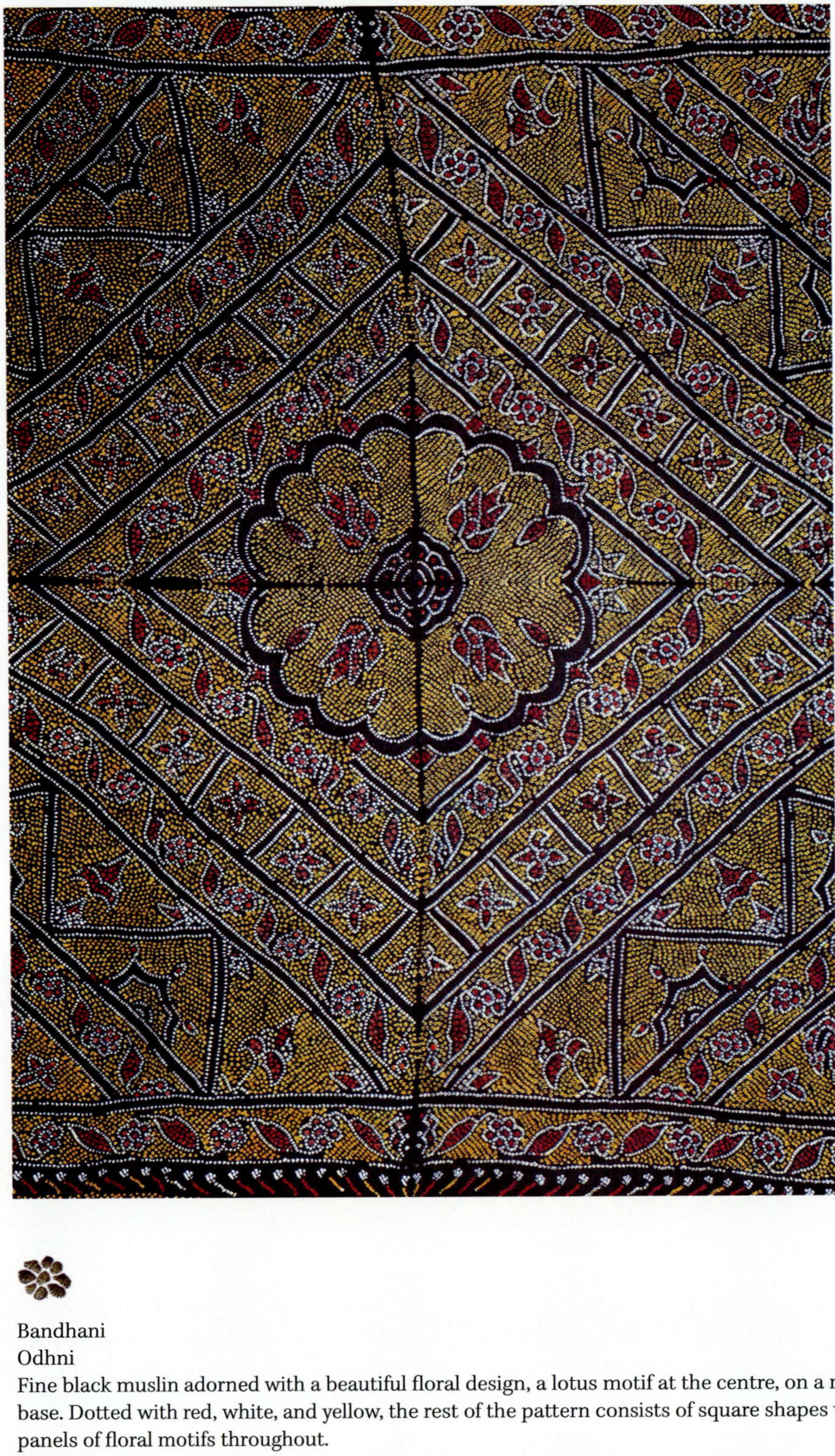

Bandhani
Odhni
Fine black muslin adorned with a beautiful floral design, a lotus motif at the centre, on a red base. Dotted with red, white, and yellow, the rest of the pattern consists of square shapes with panels of floral motifs throughout.
MSMS II Museum, Jaipur
TC-537-73

THE VALUE OF TEXTILES

Textiles have always been valued for multiple reasons, besides serving their tangible purpose as clothing and furnishing. The symbolism of textiles, laid down in tradition, has always been a strong non-verbal language in society. Discussed here are a few social functions which embed textiles in wider social systems.

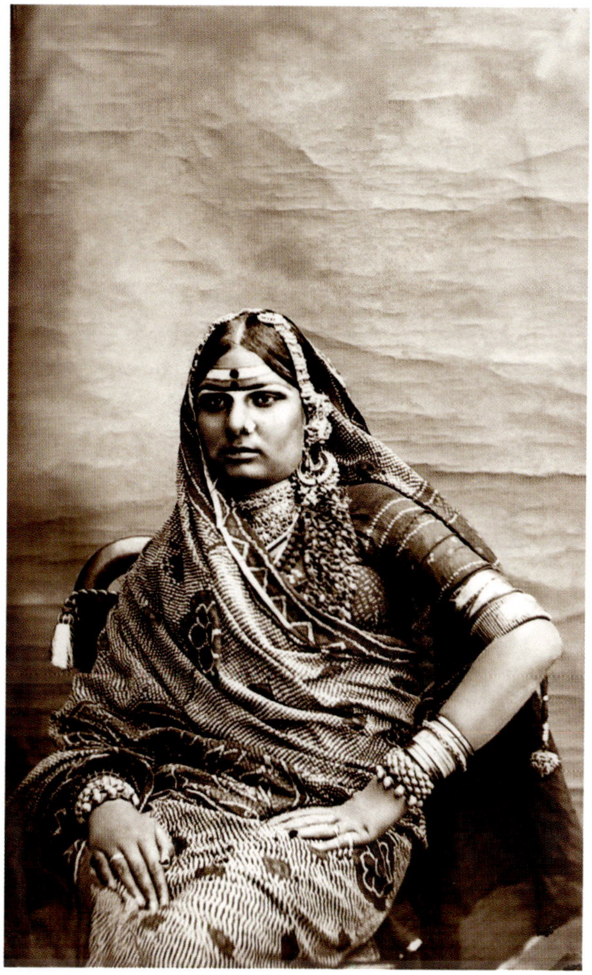

Woman in traditional Rajasthani dress. The dress has an upper garment—*kanchli*, and a finely tie-dyed *bandhani* dupatta.
MSMS II M 2012.04.0004-0006

LIFE CYCLE RITUALS

One type of textile that is central to a woman's everyday life is the *bandhani*. The technique of tie-dye covered the entire span of society and was used across all social strata to mark memories and rituals. The following observation by Chandramani Singh aptly describes the symbolism of textiles. 'The *chunri* is perhaps the most-loved of *odhni*s and is associated with many rituals, festivals and figures in folk songs and lyrics. It symbolizes youth and romance, love and happily married life.'[1]

GIFT GIVING, RELIGIOUS OR SECULAR

Cloth was often gifted to honour a person. It is still customary in India to present a shawl while welcoming guests. A turban tied for a male guest at a wedding is a token of respect. Visiting priests

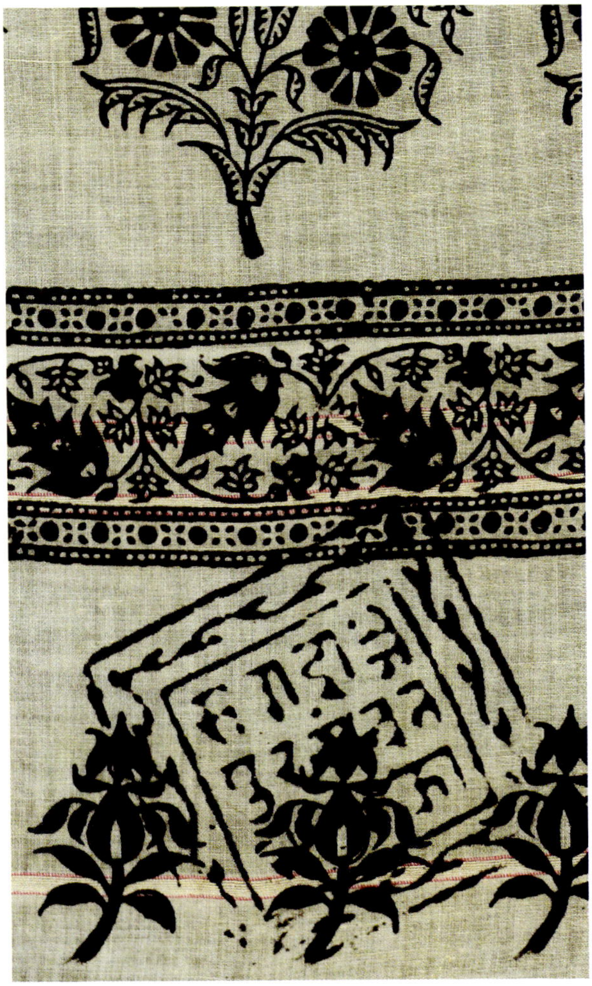

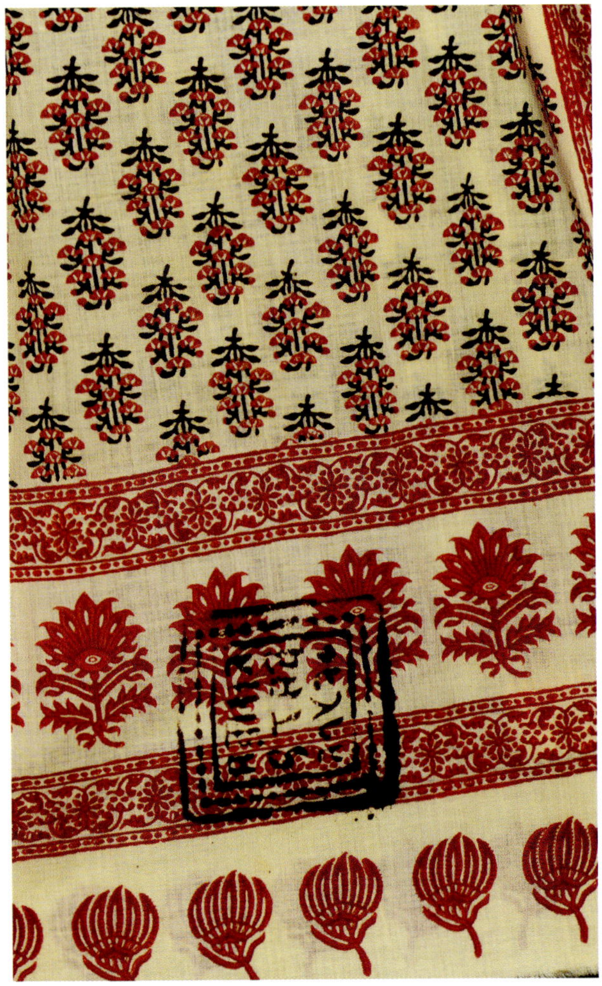

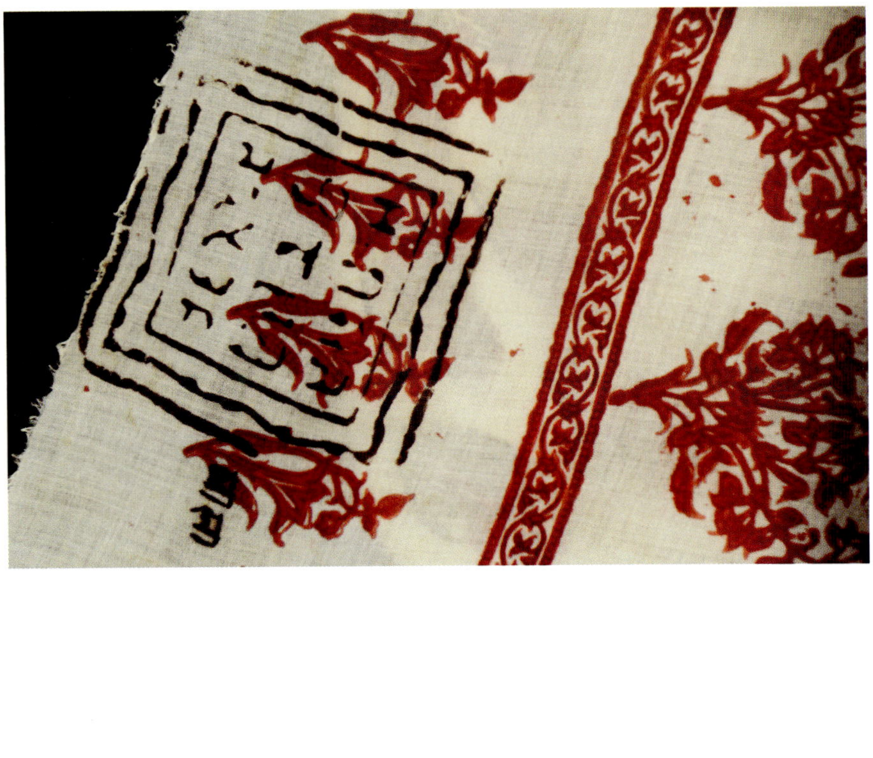

Above left, above right and bottom: Block Print Dupattas
Block printed dupattas displaying the royal seals and stamps that helped to identify the fabrics from Sanganer.
MSMS II Museum, Jaipur
Reserve collection

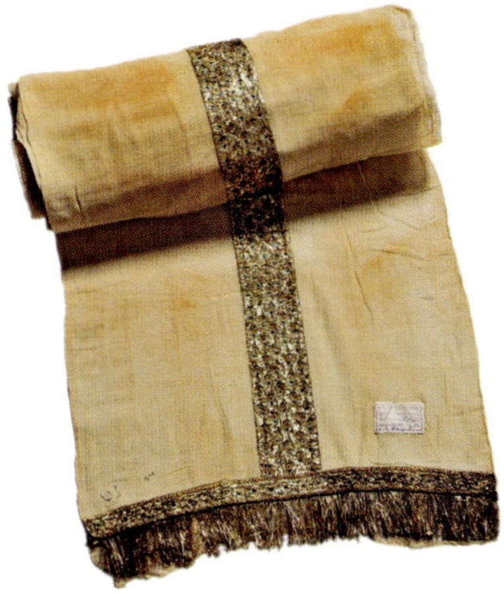

Metallic Embroidery
Pagri
Cotton, yellowing white muslin *pagri* has a broad central panel along its length, embroidered with gold metal plates and *badla*, and green beetle-wing. A similar but narrower border edges one end with a *kinari* to finish it. In a corner is an inscription in Nagari script of a price of '7 rupees' and the number '15' near it.
900 x 41 cm
MSMS II Museum, Jaipur
Tc. 465.75

brought cotton block-printed dupattas or scarves as gifts on festive occasions and others, for the king and his court. A large number of these can be seen in the royal collection. Though people in the royal household rarely wore them, they were kept in store as a mark of respect for the gift. According to Chandramani Singh, 'It was customary for a priest of a temple to present a dupatta and sweets (*prasad*) to the Maharaja. Every year hundreds of such dupattas were received, and they form this collection.'[2]

MARK OF HIGH STATUS AND WEALTH

The finest textiles were produced for and used by the aristocracy and the rich in society. The fineness of a piece was often an indicator of the status of the wearer in society. Textiles using precious metals like gold and silver were associated with high status. 'Literary and historical references emphasise the association of these metals not only with cosmic energy or divine entities, but also with temporal wealth, beauty and power, including the power of healing.'[3]

PATRONAGE FOR LOCAL ARTISANS

Patronage was both the responsibility of a ruler and an emblem of his status. It allowed the fields of arts and sciences to flourish, and bolstered the status and legitimacy of the Maharaja. Trade sustained the development of the new city of Jaipur, which gained popularity for semi-precious stones and textiles among other things.

TEXTILES AS TAXES AND CURRENCY

The textiles, which were created by artisans, were fine and often coveted by the rulers of the states. The high rate of taxes levied on cloth often helped to build textile collections in royal palaces, as the finest textiles could be given in lieu of taxes to the rulers by artisans. The octroi stamps and seals of the ruling kings help to identify the fabrics from Sanganer. A date of the Hindu or Roman calendar on these seals further helps in dating the cloths.

ENDNOTES

1. Aman Nath and Francis Wacziarg, *Arts and Crafts of Rajasthan* (Ahmedabad: Mapin Publishing Pvt. Ltd, 1994), p. 43.
2. In conversation with Chandramani Singh, Jaipur, January 2015.
3. Vandana Bhandari, *Jewelled Textiles: Gold and Silver embellished Cloth of India* (New Delhi: Om Book International, 2015).

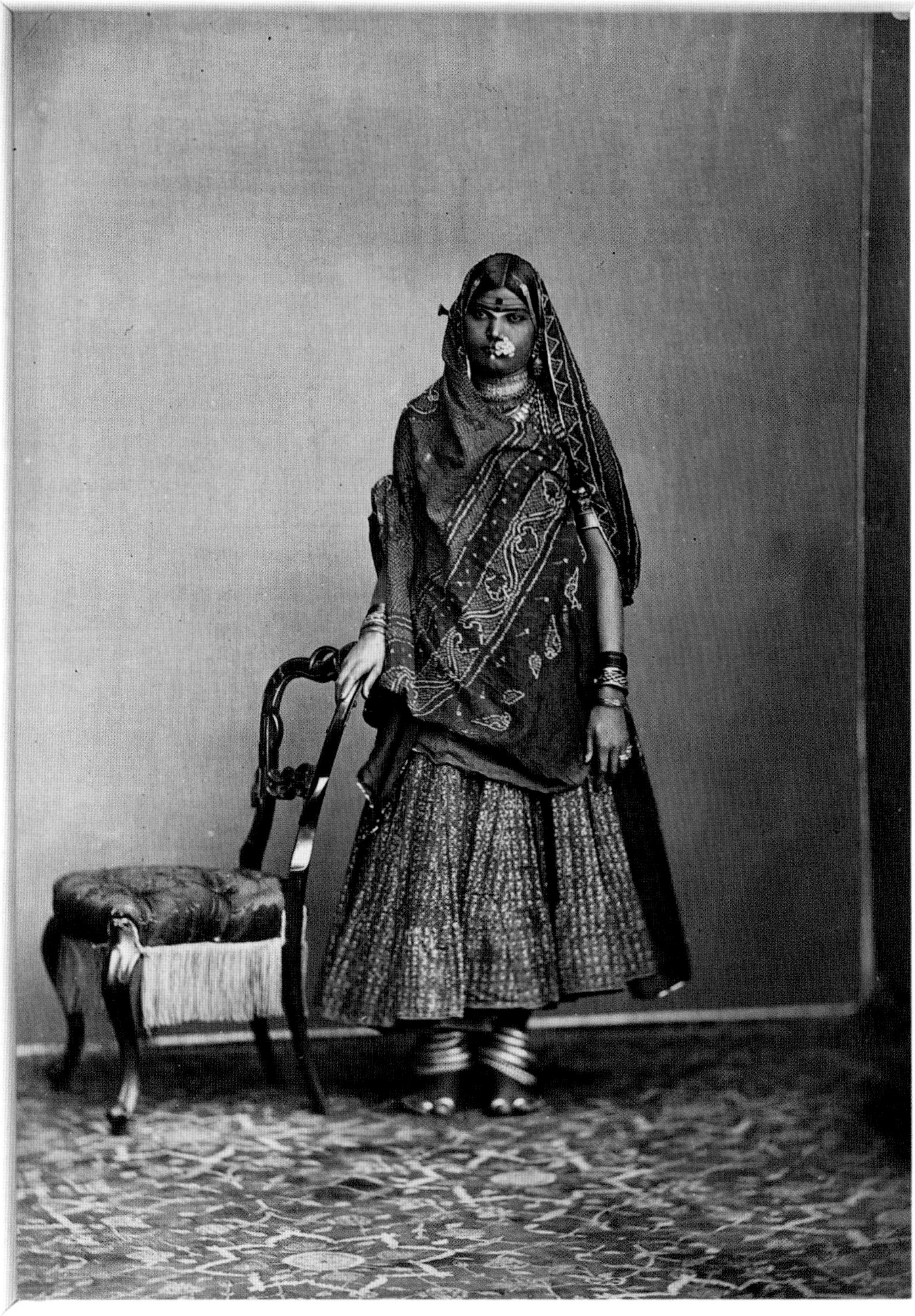

BLOCK PRINTING

Rajasthan has an ancient tradition of intricate and beautiful hand printed cotton textiles. The techniques used for printing have been preserved over centuries and the craft is practised by block printers belonging to the Chhipa community with regional innovations. It is heavily dependent on water and most commercial printing centres developed near water sources. The most famous among these were Sanganer and Bagru near Jaipur, and Barmer, Jodhpur, and Akola near Udaipur.

Jaipur has been known to be a major centre of printing and there is evidence that by the 18th century, it started to develop commercially. Maharaja Sawai Jai Singh II (r: 1699–1743) patronized printers in Jaipur, who produced exquisite printed cloth. As the craft developed, the craftspersons from Jaipur started to relocate outside the city walls. Sanganer, Bagru, and other towns flourished, and each centre developed its own unique design style and techniques. For example, muted colours

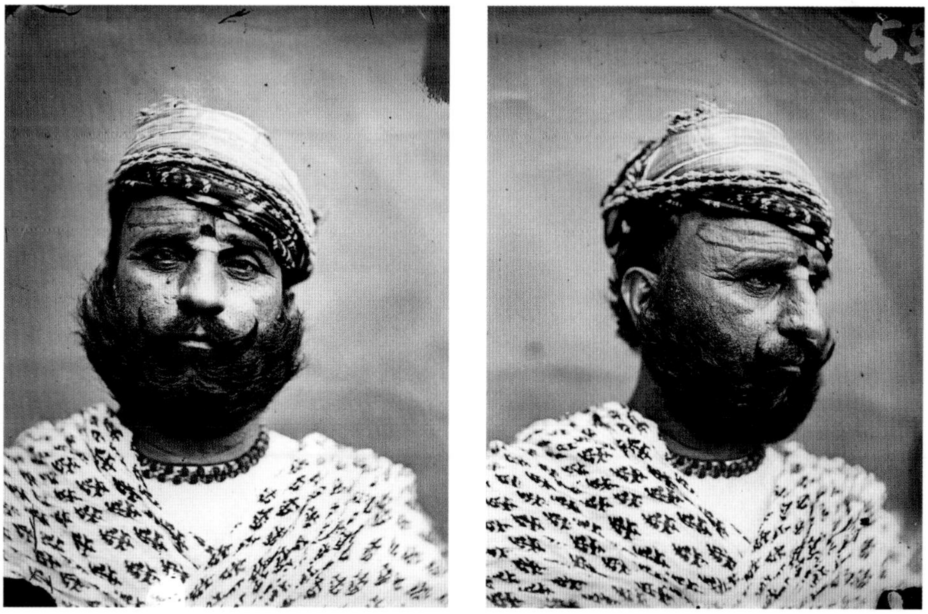

Double portrait of a man with a block printed *angarkha* around his neck and a headgear adorned with a *bandhani* cloth.
MSMS II M
2012.04.0003-0015 (a+b)

Facing page: Woman in *bandhani odhna* and a block printed skirt. Her ankles are adorned with silver *kadas*.
MSMS II M
2012.04.0019-0008

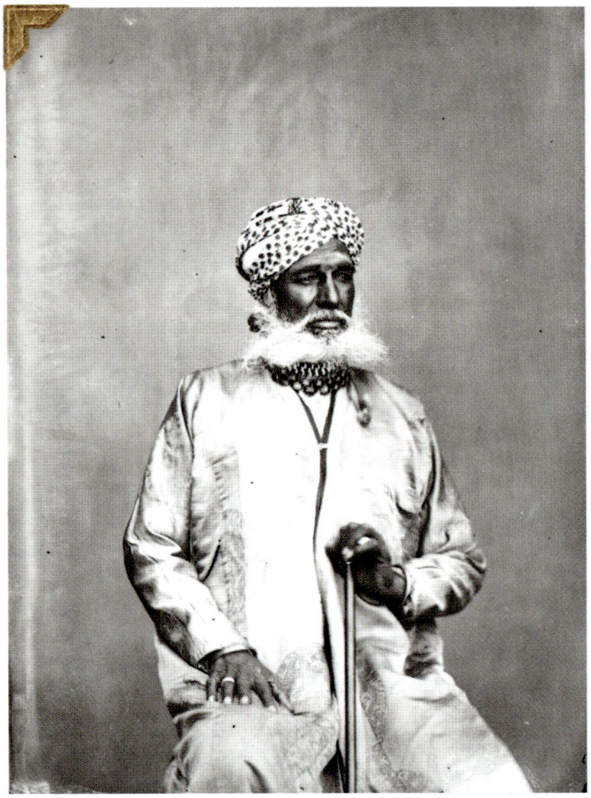

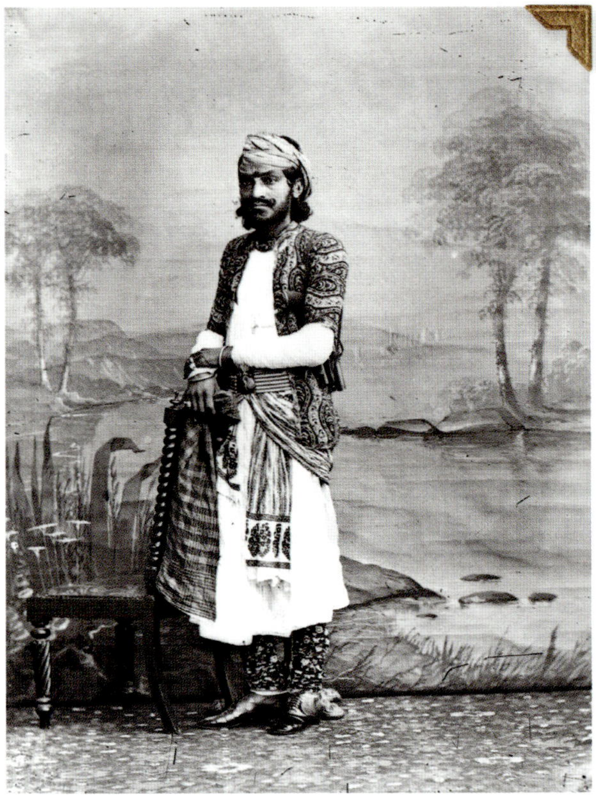

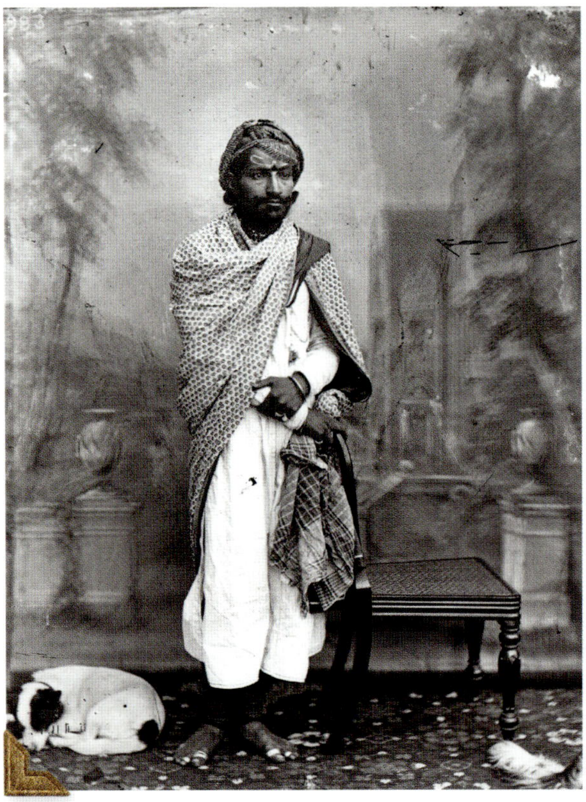

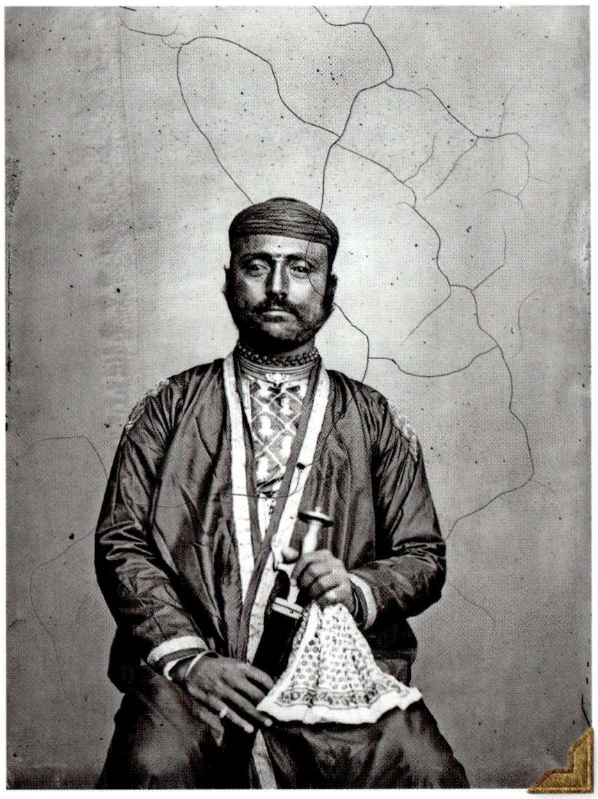

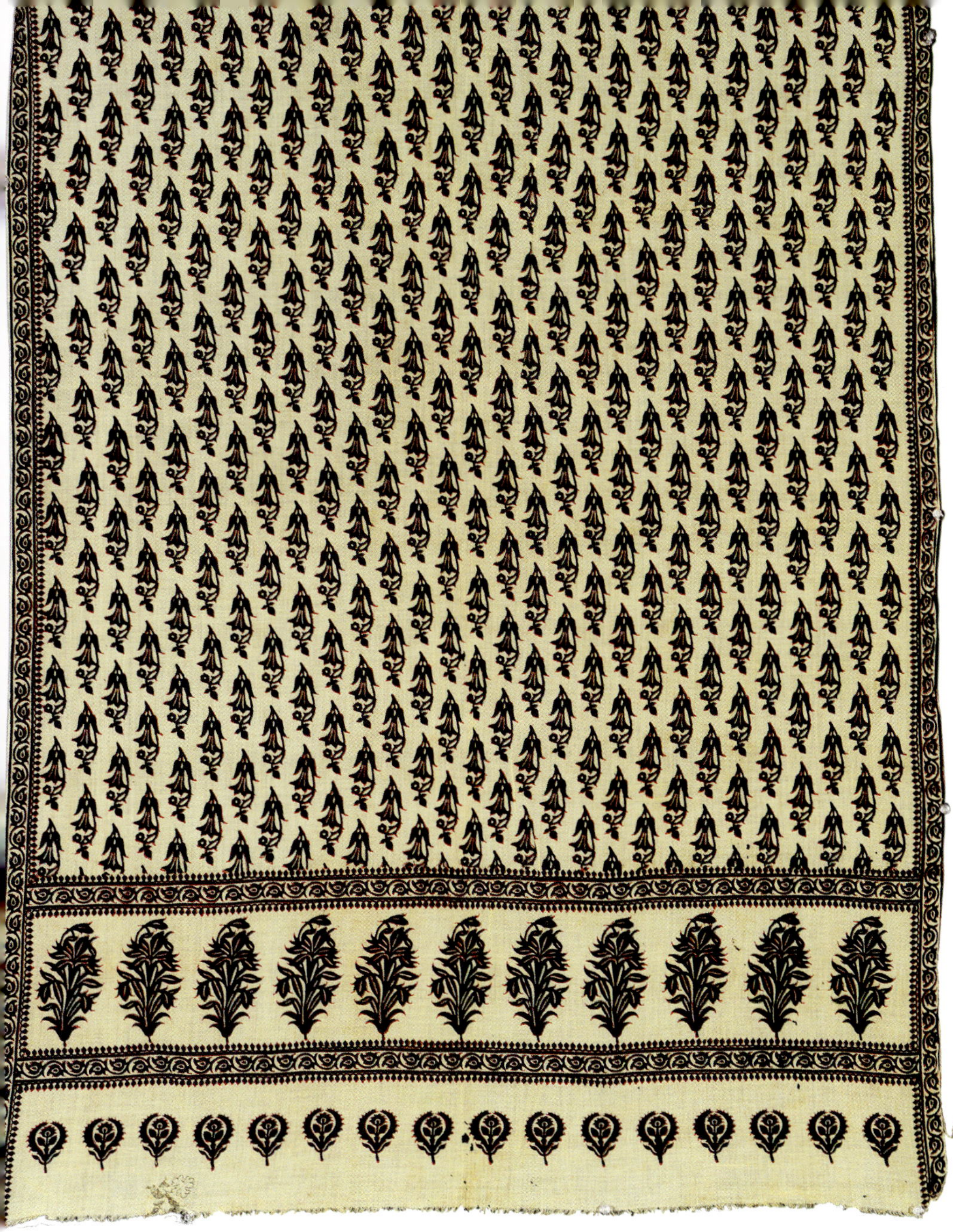

Sanganeri Block Print
Safa
Off-white muslin printed in black and red, with a delicate *dhatura* flower motif in an all-over layout, and a narrow scrolling border with a paisley pattern on the sides. Two rows of the same border can be found at both ends, interspersed with a panel of a large jhar *buta* repeat, and the design has been finished with a row of a small floral motif.
393 x 74 cm
MSMS II Museum, Jaipur
TC/B 68

Facing page: Men of the Jaipur court—including Maharaja Sawai Ram Singh II (top right and bottom left)—are seen using block printed textiles in various forms: as a turban (top left), as a sash made from Namavali cloth (top right), as a dupatta wrapped over a long upper garment and churidar (bottom left), and as a *rumaal* (bottom right).
MSMS II M 2012.04.0072-0017; 0036-0005; 0077-0005; and 0025-0024.

and delicate lines, creating fine motifs like the poppy, rose, and lotus, usually against a fine white background, became characteristic of the fabric printed at Sanganer, which was known as a famous dyeing centre till the 18th century, before it became a centre of printing. In contrast, big and bold motifs on thick cotton *reza* were printed in Bagru, where mud-resist printing was employed as an important process. Wild flowers, buds, and foliage have provided inspiration to the printers of Bagru in a colour palette primarily in indigo blue and deep shades of red, black, and yellow.

According to Sir George Watt, 'The Sanganer town of Jaipur state must, however, be regarded as the very metropolis of the calico-printing craft of India so far as art conceptions and technique are concerned.'[1] The town of Sanganer is said to have been founded in the 16th century by the Kachhwaha Rajput Prince Sangaji. The town flourished, as it was located near the trade

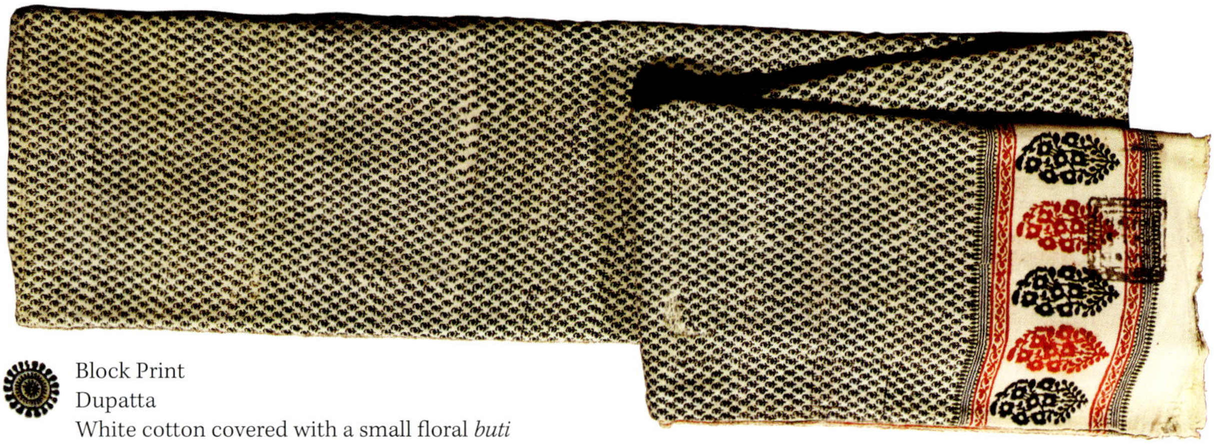

Block Print
Dupatta
White cotton covered with a small floral *buti* in black, and both ends edged with a large *jhar buta*—alternately in black and red—sandwiched between double scrolling borders, one in each of the same colours. Also visible on it is an octroi seal, used for taxation.
251 x 149.5 cm
MSMS II Museum, Jaipur
TC/B 18

routes of the region. There is evidence that by the 18th century, 'printing and dyeing was done using both fast and fugitive colours'. The main contribution of Sanganeri prints to the Indian printing industry are fast colours—meaningful and well proportioned, lyrical motifs designed for dupattas, *odhnis*, dress material, quilts, and upholstery. The sophisticated dyeing and printing techniques were largely used for making cloth used by royalty.[2]

The octroi stamps and seals of the ruling kings also identify the early fabrics from Sanganer. The taxes that were levied on cloth helped to build the textile collections in royal palaces, because the finest textiles could be given in lieu of taxes to the rulers by artisans.

Wooden blocks, mostly made of sheesham wood, are the main printing tools and may have rectangular, square, or circular shapes. They are hand-carved from locally available wood and, usually, the number of blocks per design is equal to the number of colours that are to be used. The depth and fineness of carving blocks is special to Jaipur, especially Sanganer, and results in a sharper print.

The *gad*, *rekh*, and *datta* are three distinct types of blocks that are defined by their different styles of carving and printing effects. The *gad* is carved in intaglio and is used to print large background figures, while *rekh* and *datta* are carved in relief. *Rekh* blocks also mark the outlines of the motif and are often used in conjunction with *gad* blocks, the *rekh* then form fine intricate lines within the imprint made by the *gad* block. *Datta* is carved in bold relief and it complements the designs of both the *gad* and *rekh* blocks. Each of these blocks is used separately or together to produce numerous design variations. The blocks have cylindrical holes drilled in the back to enable the release of air bubbles during the printing process, thereby resulting in an even spread of the dye or pigment. Registration notches

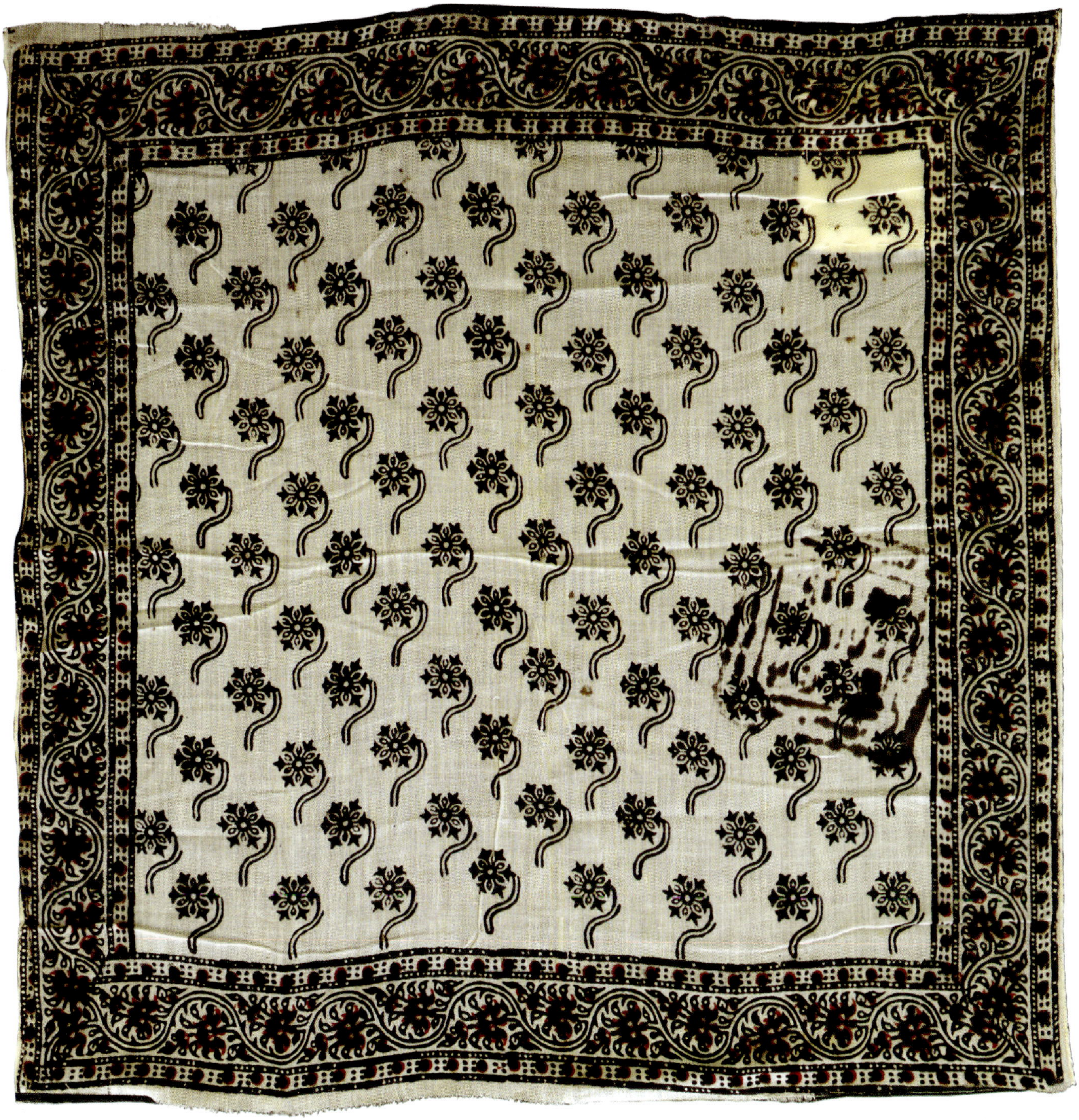

Block Print
Rumal
White muslin printed in black and grey, is filled with rosette *butis* in a half-drop repeat pattern, and edged with a floral scrolling border. A octroi seal has been used.
MSMS II Museum, Jaipur
Reserve collection

are also cut on the side of the blocks to ensure proper alignment for each subsequent colour.[3] Blocks are also made with brass strips inserted in the wood, which create finer lines. These are mostly used for metallic printing—gold leaf printing and khadi work.

The grey or beige fabric to be printed is scoured and bleached to remove starch and other impurities. The processes largely used for the preparation of cloth are dunging, washing, and bleaching; washing in alkaline lye; washing again, galling, drying, mordanting; and application of colour. Traditionally various mixtures were used for de-sizing: oil and *khar* (impure carbonate of soda); cow, sheep, or goat dung with water and milk. Commonly, de-sizing is done by soaking the fabric in a mixture of camel or goat dung, soda ash, sesame oil, and a little water. The fabric is repetitively soaked in the evening in the dung solution, left overnight, and rinsed and dried in sunlight during the day. This laborious and specialized process is carried out locally by washermen to enhance the dye uptake of the fabric. The cotton fibres swell during washing with the mineral rich solution and become absorbent and soft. The fabric is washed and dried and may be given further

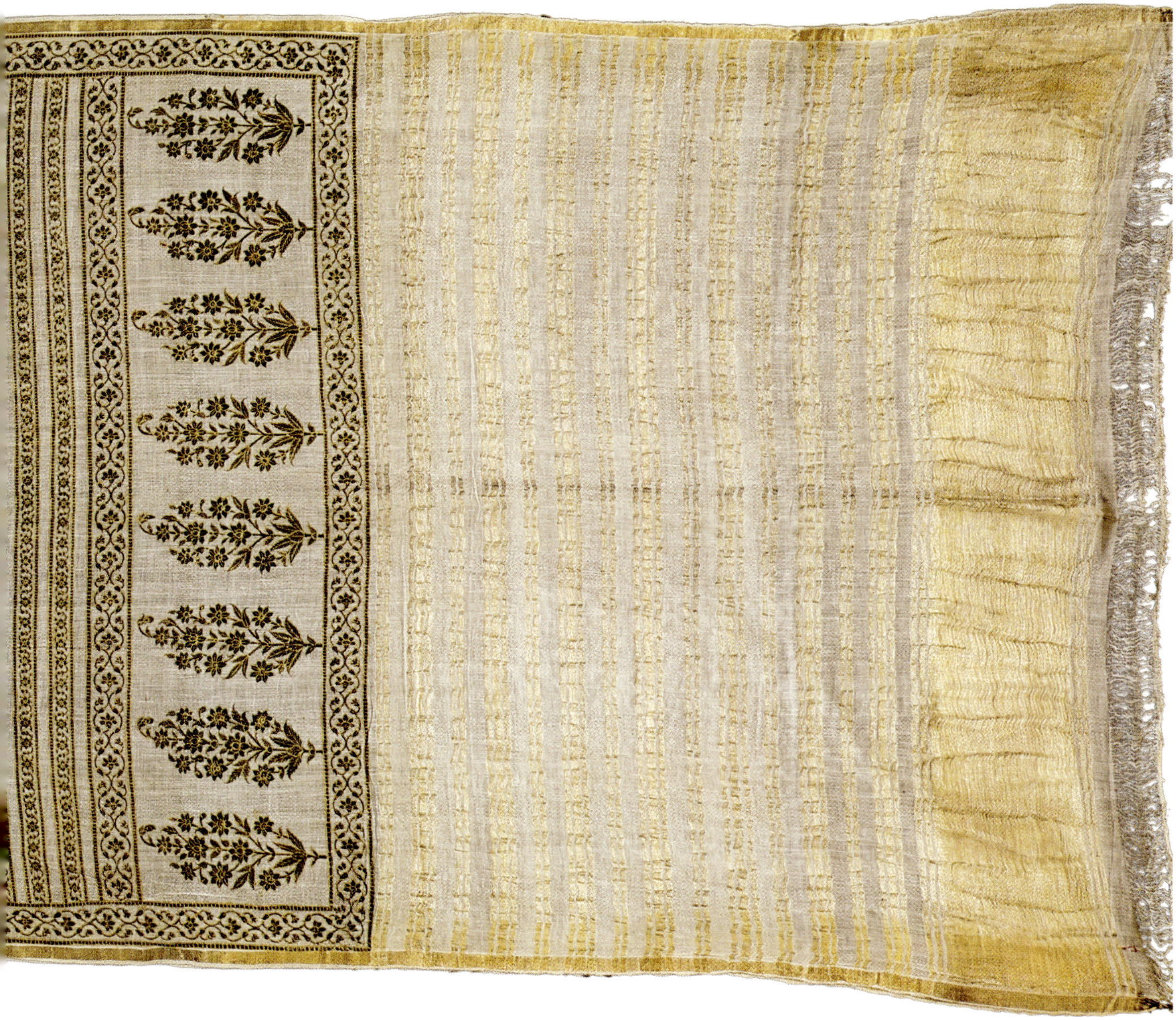

exposure to the sun, while it is moistened with water for whitening it. After the final washing and drying, the *harad* treatment (galling) is done. Cotton has a poor affinity to natural dyes and pre-treatments with metallic mordants assist in the dyeing process and improve the dye fastness.

'Harad', a dried powder extracted from tannin-filled fruit of the *myrobalan* tree (*Terminalia chebula*), is mixed with *mitha tel* (sesame oil) and water. The fabric is soaked in this solution and pounded manually. The fabric is then sun-dried and finally beaten with a wooden mallet, or beaten on stone to remove excess powder. Drying is done in the shade and special care is taken to avoid any contact with iron, after which the fabric is ready for printing.

After *harad* is applied on the fabric, usually red or black outline (*rekh*) printing is done. This

Block Printing with Gold Pigment and a Mordant
Sash / Patka
Off-white cotton has a gold woven border at the two ends, followed by several repeats of a narrower one—the same also edging the sides in a single row. On the inner side, all around, is a scrolling floral border printed in gold and green, with a second row at the two ends sandwiching a panel of large printed *butas*. The innermost ends are embellished with three rows of a narrower gold stripe.
1503 x 63 cm
MSMS II Museum, Jaipur
75.73

may be followed by additional outline printing, locally known as *chirai*. The *datta* (filling) and *gad* (background) block are printed over the outline block depending on the final design to be achieved. The fabric is subsequently washed and dried in the sun, after which it is ready for printing.

Traditionally, the fabric is spread on low tables and the printer sits in front of it. Printing pastes are kept in a tray. Each block is pressed on the printing pad and then stamped on the fabric. Each element of design, like outline and filling, requires printing to be done as a separate process, and for each, an independent tray and block are used.

Some of the printing pastes employed in the printing process are *begar*, *syahi*, and *dabu*. The *begar* paste is prepared by mixing *fitkari* or alum with gum and produces shades of red. Alum acts as a mordant and combines with the colouring substance alizarin to produce colours ranging from pink to deep red on cotton fabrics. Scrap iron is fermented in earthenware vessels with some jaggery and water for a few days to produce an iron-rich solution. This solution is then mixed with a smooth paste of natural gum and water that acts as a binder. The printer uses this *syahi* paste or ink for printing black colour on the fabric. When the iron in the paste reacts with the tannic acid in the *harad* it oxidizes to produce a permanent black dye.

A solution prepared by boiling a mixture of pomegranate rind with water and turmeric gives a yellow colour. This is applied to the cloth by using a woollen fabric and gently rubbing the solution over it. The fugitive yellow coloured piece is dried and then boiled with a solution of water and alum. Shades of green are achieved by over-dyeing an indigo blue fabric with a solution of boiled pomegranate rind and turmeric.

A dye liqour prepared with *dhavdi ka phool* and alizarin powder is used for alizarin dyeing. This kind of dyeing is done on fabric printed with *begar* or *syahi*. The printed fabrics are entered in the dye bath slowly to ensure evenness in colour. The former yields a red colour and the latter a black colour. The *dabu* printed cloth may also be dyed in the vat of indigo dye to obtain a blue colour.

Traditionally, the block printers of Jaipur were renowned not only for their quality, but also for their use of natural dyes. The advent of commercial screen printing in the early 1960s, and new chemical colouration processes have been adopted by the block printers in their printing styles. These printers developed varied colour palettes and gave new dimensions to the story of block printing.

DABU OR RESIST PRINTING

Dabu or resist printing is an additional process, which may be used in block printing. Here, the actual sequencing of the process and different stages of dyeing and printing can vary, depending on the desired pattern. The fabric is printed with a mordant (alum) or a resist (*dabu*) or both. When a cloth printed with mordant is immersed in the dye solution, it reacts with the dye and colour develops in those areas which have been treated with mordant. If the fabric is printed with resist, however, only the areas which are not resisted, but printed with mordant, will accept the dye. The mud-resist is removed by washing after the final design has been achieved.

Dabu is prepared using clay. Different types of *dabu* pastes are used in printing; some of these are *kalidar dabu*, *dolidar dabu*, and *gawarbali dabu*. The most commonly used, however, is the *kalidar dabu*. It is made with *kali mitti* (clay), *chuna* (lime), *bidhan* (wheat flour), and *gaund* (gum), a natural adhesive. The clay is soaked overnight and to this are added wheat flour (soaked in water) and lime solution. These are thoroughly mixed together by the treading of feet, while gum and water are periodically added to this mixture. The gelatinous paste thus produced is strained through a fine muslin cloth to remove any particles which may give an uneven printing quality. The solution is then ready for use in resist printing and, generally, the *datta* or filling blocks are used for printing the *dabu* paste.

WAX-RESIST PRINTING

Another technique unique to the region was the wax-resist printing technique locally known as *mend ki chapai* and it was traditional to Sanganer. Through this technique, printers produced a superior quality and fineness of resisted lines, which was often not possible with the mud-resist method. The wax-resist was prepared by heating a mixture of castor oil (*irandi ta tel*) and beeswax. The *mend* (wax-resist) was applied using a wooden block. The wax was kept in a vessel at a constant temperature and was continuously heated to maintain an even temperature. Thc printer had to be skilled in managing correct temperatures of wax in the container and ensuring application of the heated wax with the block speedily. The printing table (*pattiya*) was also fashioned especially for maintaining temperatures. A wet cloth was kept underneath the fabric on the *pattiya* and sand was spread on it for levelling. The smooth surface and wet cloth ensured that the wax applied on the cloth cooled and hardened evenly.

NAMAVALI TEXTILES

> An object that is created with a certain bhavna, sentiment, concerning a higher power, directed towards an ancestor, or purely as a medium of communication, thereupon emerges as a part of design vocabulary, with its own rules, framework, dimension and freedoms, worthy in itself and capable of giving pleasure to the beholder.[4]

Namavali literally means an object which is inscribed with a name. These names were often religious in nature and, in the context of textiles, could be printed, painted, woven, or embroidered. Such textiles started to be made in the early part of the 18th century and became very popular by the late 18th and early 19th centuries. Examples of woven and printed textiles with calligraphy can be found in Bengal, Gujarat, Orissa, and Rajasthan. Such textiles were worn as saris or scarves, and used as altar cloths—both hung at the back like a curtain and spread as a cover for the throne on which the deity was placed. The altar cloths were often unidirectional, while the

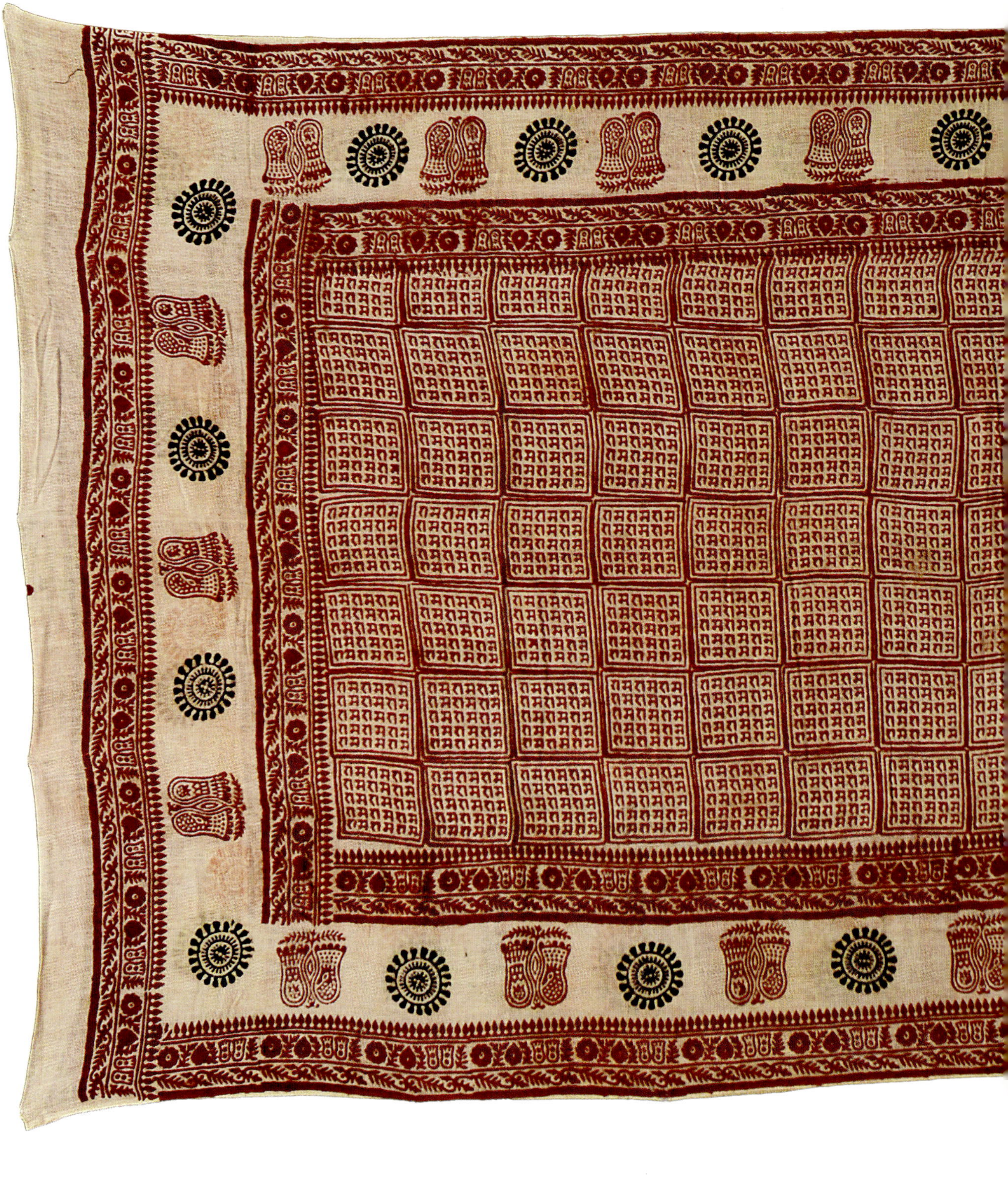

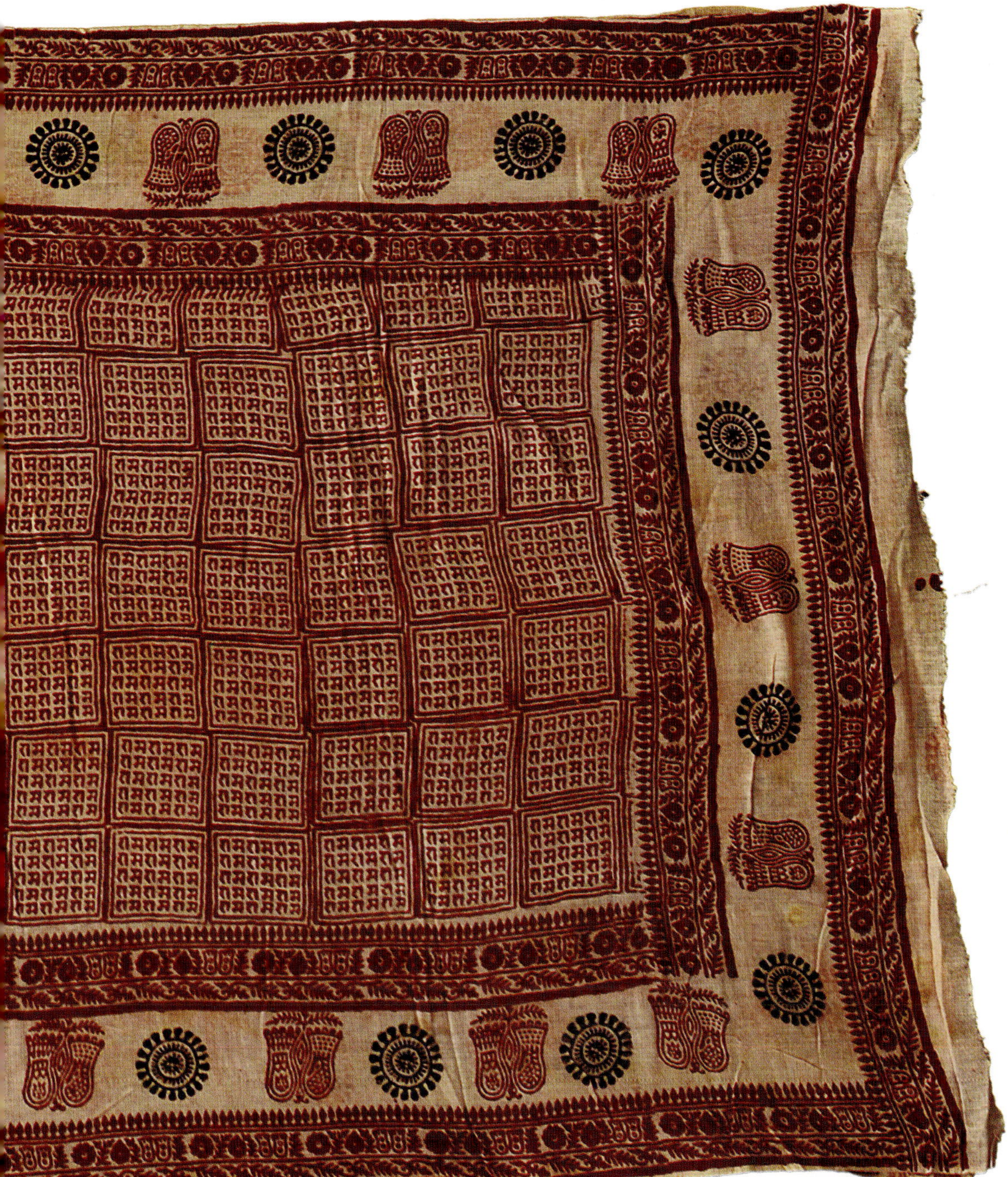

Block Print
Namdhari scarf
Cream coloured cotton with squares of 'Ram' printed all over in red, within which is also included 'shree jamuna ji ki jaya'. The borders display a row of footprint and lotus flower motifs in red and black, between decorative panels in red.
380 x 109 cm
MSMS II Museum, Jaipur
TC 192.73

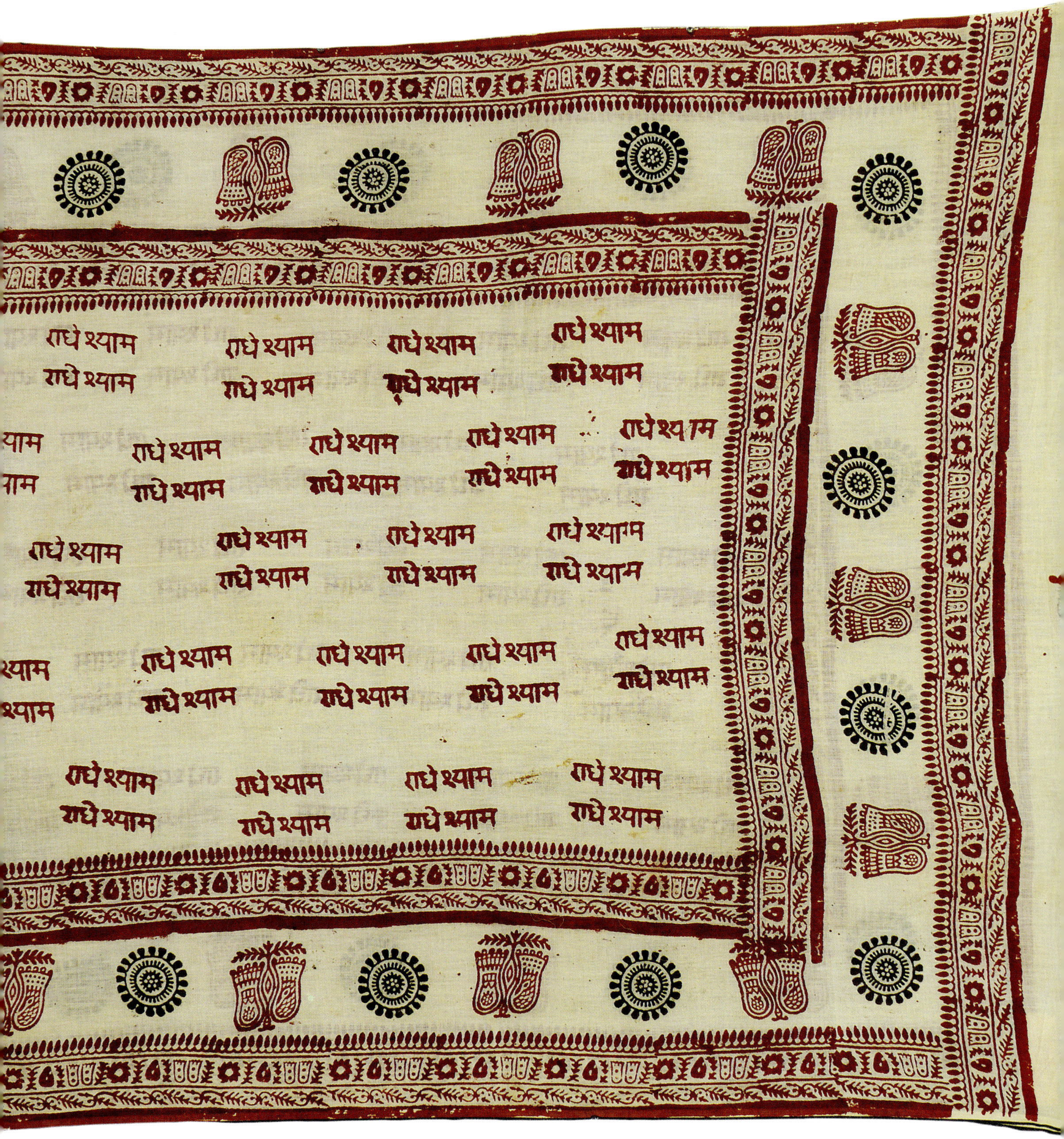
राधे श्याम

dupattas had a symmetrical layout. The same type of printing was also done on *pardas*, which were hung in temples. It was common to see these *pardas* with names and figures of gods and goddesses along with the symbolic motifs in temples of the region. These textiles were considered sacred and used during the Hindu worship ceremonies as offerings to the deities, along with other ritualistic products like flowers and sweets. The priests gave these textiles to the prominent devotees of the deities as a mark of their patronage.

From the artisan who carved the block to the printer and finally the end user of these textiles, all perceived the *namavali* as a source of devotion. Craftsmen from Sanganer and Bagru, who printed these, would rhythmically recite *pancha namaskara* chants, while stamping on the cloth. The act of chanting while doing the printing was a spiritual immersion for the printer. Special care was taken by the printer to maintain a high quality of workmanship as these were produced for ritualistic offerings. These were also known as *saropas*.[5]

The dupattas were made for the purpose of being distributed by devotees and were produced on order especially for patrons and generally not sold in the open market. Red and white dupattas were made for the purpose of distribution to devotees. They seem to have been made in their original form up to the 1950s and some variations of these were produced later. Three well-known experts who produced these textiles in Bagru and Sanganer in the last century were: Ramdas Sadh and Kanji Bhagat from Sanganer, and Ramdas Bhagat from Bagru.[6]

The printing process was simple with the most common colour combination being red on a white muslin cotton base. Red is considered to be an auspicious colour in Hinduism. After the *rangai*, that is, dyeing, *tapai*, or sun-bleaching of the printed cloth was carried out. The yellow colour was obtained by dyeing with flowers of *kasumba* and this process was known as *phool-rangai*. The *kesariya* hue was considered the colour of the gods. The borders were printed with a gad block while the field used blocks which were called *khulla* (embossed with text).

The dupattas were also treated with fragrance and these varied according to the season. *Gulab* was used in summer, *khas* in the monsoons, and *hina* was applied during the winter months. These cloths had sacred symbolism; they were mainly made for followers of Shiva and different sects of Vishnu. Shiva and Vishnu formed two important gods of the Hindu triad and were worshipped in their many avatars.

The motifs and layouts reflected the religion followed by the devotees. The names of gods, anthropomorphic representations of the deities, and holy writings were repeated continuously on the fabrics. Each of these had a mythological

Sanganeri Block Print
Dupatta
White muslin dupatta, received as blessings from a Vaishnava temple, has 'radheyshyam' printed in red in an all-over linear double-dash formation. The border has religious motifs—a stylized lotus and a footprint—alternately in red and black, between two rows of a complex design in red.
134 x 39 cm
MSMS II Museum, Jaipur
TC/B 78

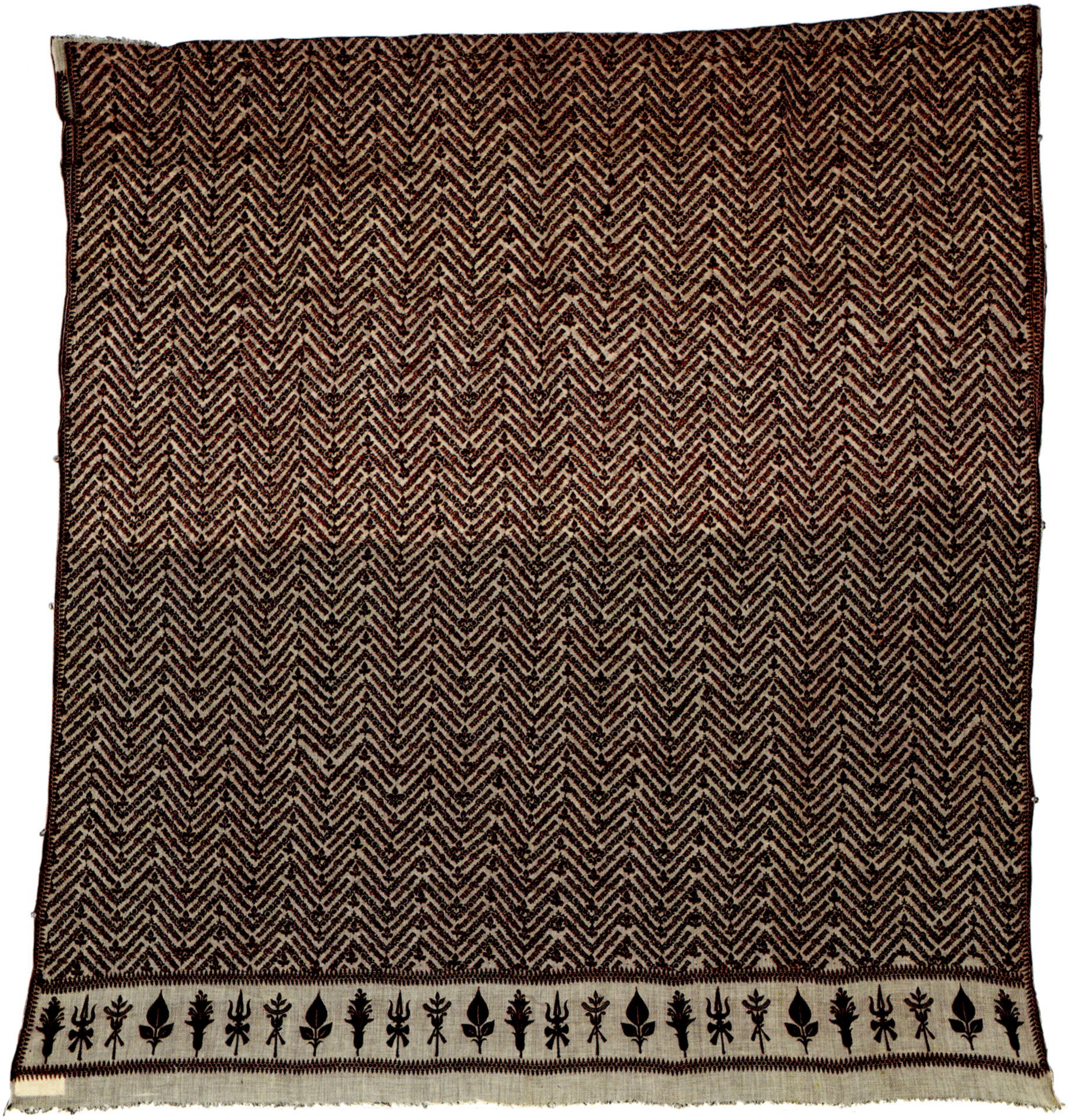

and spiritual association and the *chadar*s became popular by the names of the gods, which were printed on them.

The symbols used to depict Shiva were the conch shell, moon, *trishul*, *bilvapatra*, *dhatura* flower, *rudraskha* beads, *arka* flowers, and stripes with trefoil bel leaves that are sacred to Shiva. The *pallu* would have 'Om' printed, using

Block Print
Dupatta
Off-white muslin, printed in red and black, with an all-over design in an alternating chevron/ *gandadar* pattern, has 'bilvapatra' and 'om namah shivay' written in a continuous manner with a vertical floral strip between them. The two ends exhibit motifs which include Shiva's emblems—the trident and the *dhatura* flower—between two rows of a narrow jagged border.
293.5 x 146 cm
MSMS II Museum, Jaipur
TC 184.73

khulla blocks. The main field would have words in Devanagari, like 'har har gange', 'gangehar', 'shri jamuna ji ki jai', 'om namah shiva', and 'shiv shakti'. These were primarily made for the priests of the Shiva temple.

Among the worshippers of Vishnu were two sects—the Ramanandi and the Radhaballabhi—for whom these dupattas were particularly made. Sacred words like 'sitaram' and 'jaishree sitaram' were printed on the Ramanandi sect dupattas. The shape of the tilak on the border was also unique. *Chitra* or images of Radha-Krishna were also present on the *pallus*. Some inscriptions and symbols printed on these textiles are *vishnupada* or footprints of Vishnu, the lotus, conch shell motifs, Ram, Radheyshyam, Ishwar, and Shree Radhey Bal Govind. The symbols, like the lotus flower pattern, *vishnupada*, conch shell motifs, and *sathiya*, were common among both sects. In the dupattas made for the Radhaballabhi sect, phrases like 'jai shri radha krishna' and 'jai shri radheyshyam' were also printed. A fourth type of dupatta was produced for the Shrihit Harivanshi Sampradaya. These had motifs like *pad* (feet), lotus, 'radhey radhey', and 'shri hari harihant' printed on them.

The dupattas were made both for men and women and it was mandated that they should cover only the upper part of the body. A typical length and width of the dupatta was 250 cm and 115 cm respectively. The Brahmins also wore the printed *namavali* dupattas, which had different colours, inscriptions, and motifs

Sanganeri Block Print
Dupatta
Cream coloured muslin filled with 'sitaram' in a linear red text, and edged with a narrow border. The two ends have a row of a floral *buta* between a patterned stripe on either side—all in red and black.
292 x 170 cm
MSMS II Museum, Jaipur
TC/B 4

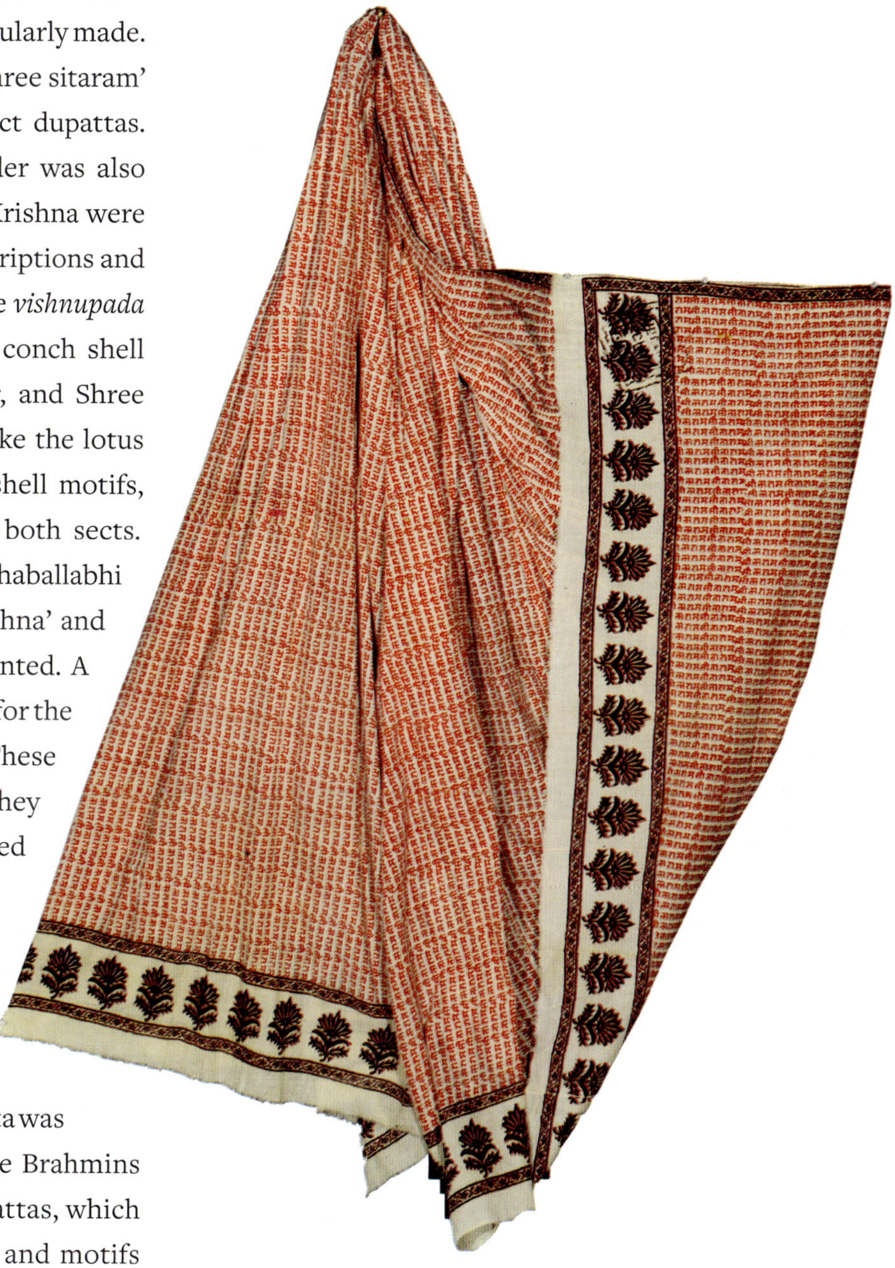

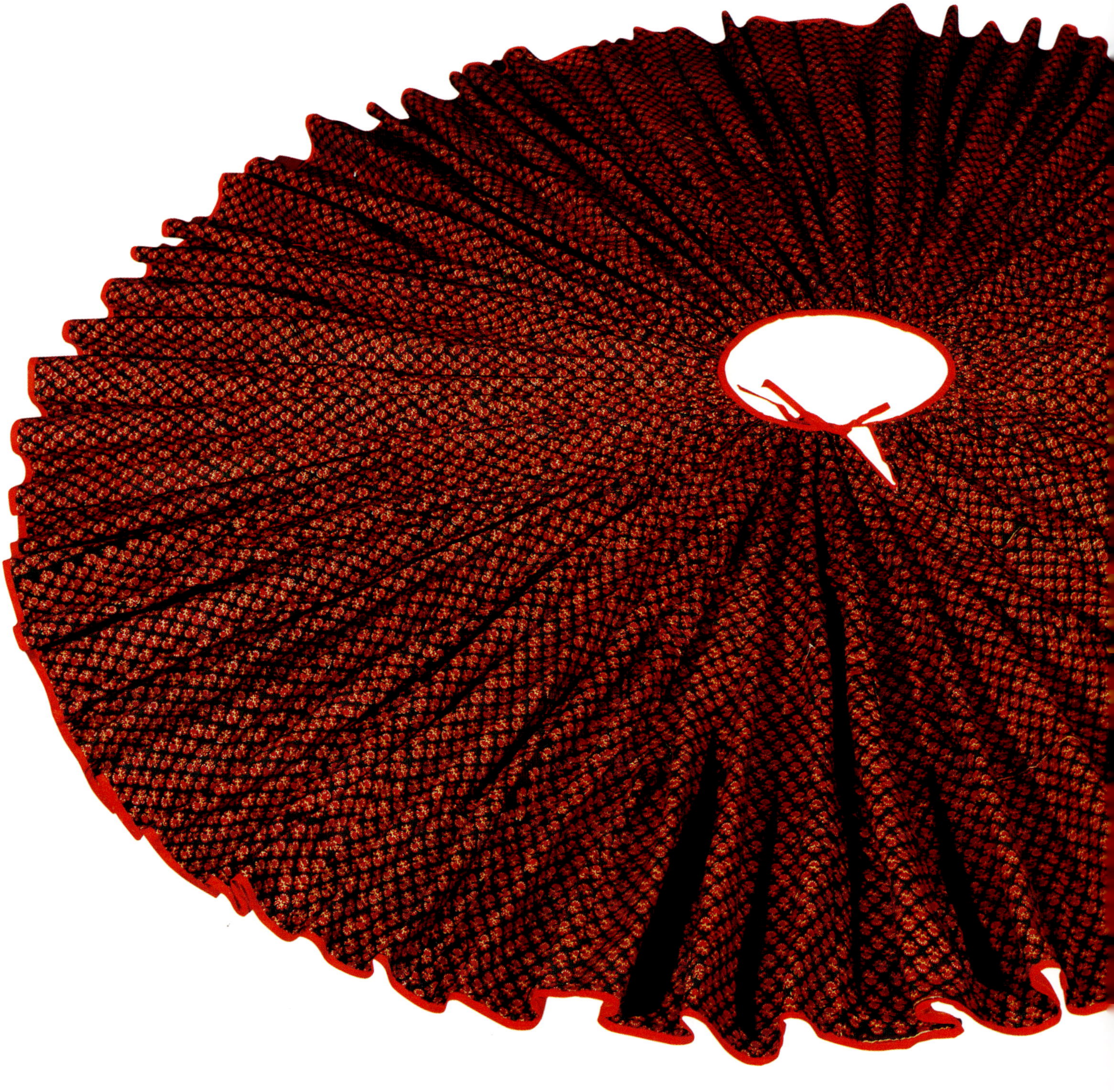

depending on the particular deity whom they worshipped. The cloth that was printed was always used for draping the upper part of the body. In different forms they became an integral part of the hippie movement in the '60s and today are often screen-printed.

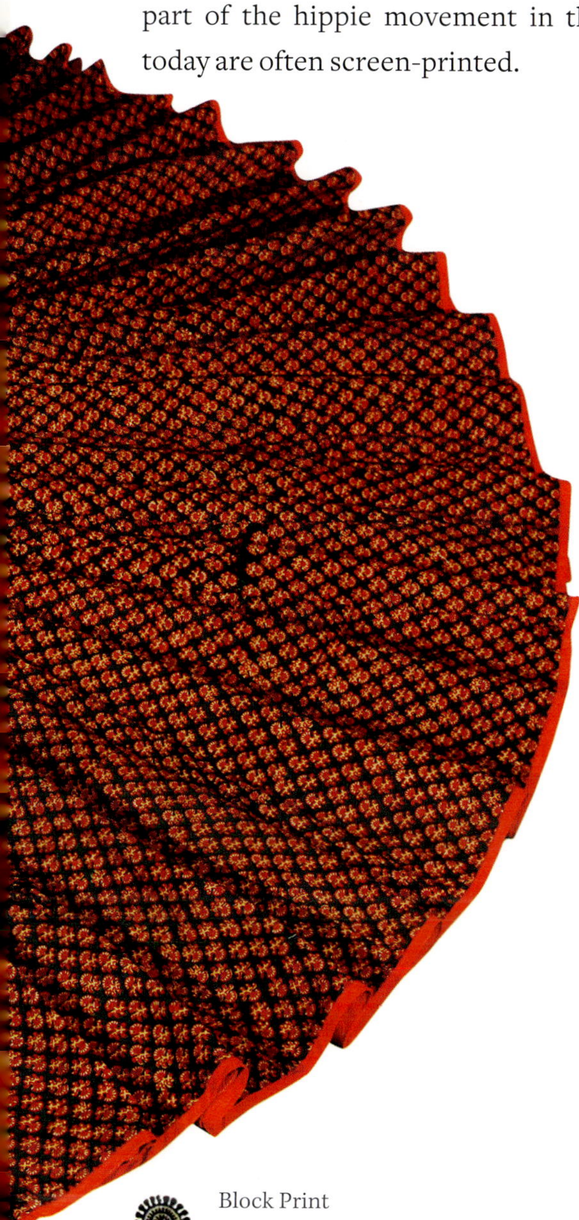

Block Print
Ghaghra
Cotton ghaghra, with an all-over print of small floral *butis* in red and black, has a red piping at the waist and hem.
225 x 33 cm (waist 30 cm)
MSMS II Museum, Jaipur
LA 270

A large number is present in the royal collection of the museum and according to Chandramani Singh, 'it was customary for a priest of a temple to present a dupatta and sweets to the Maharaja. Every year hundreds of such dupattas were received, which form this collection'.[7] In this manner the priests marked auspicious occasions such as festivals or birthdays of the royalty.

Sanganer and Bagru developed unique techniques and styles of design under the royal patronage of the Jaipur rulers. Dedicated workshops, which included the *rangkhana* (for dyeing) and *chapakhana* (for printing), developed fine examples of fabrics for royalty that are seen in the City Palace collection and other museums today.

ENDNOTES

1. Sir George Watt, *Indian Art at Delhi (the official catalogue of the Delhi exhibition 1902–1903)* (Calcutta: Superintendent of government printing, 1903), p. 247.
2. Chandramani Singh, *Textiles and Costumes from the Maharaja Sawai Mann Singh II Museum* (Jaipur: Maharaja Sawai Mann Singh II Museum Trust, 1979), p. 33.
3. Vandana Bhandari, *Costumes, Textiles and Jewellery of India – Traditions in Rajasthan* (New Delhi: Prakash Books, 2004).
4. Jaya Jaitley and Subrata Bhowmick, *Crafting Indian Scripts* (New Delhi: Daastkari Haat Samiti, 2012), p. 18.
5. In conversation with Shanti Kabra, New Delhi, March 2015.
6. In conversation with Brij Ballabh, Jaipur, August 2016.
7. Maharaja Sawai Man Singh II Museum and Chandramani Singh, *Textiles and Costumes from the Maharaja Sawai Mann Singh II Museum* (Jaipur: Maharaja Sawai Mann Singh II Museum Trust, 1979), p. 28.

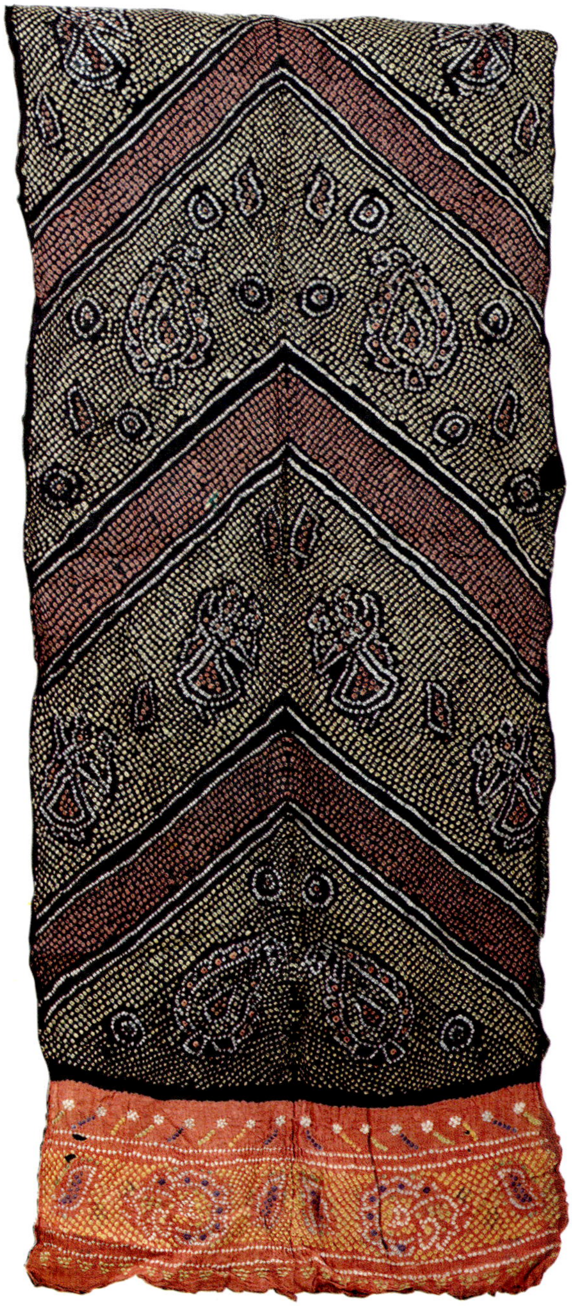

Bandhini

Odhni

Black cotton with red horizontal zigzag stripes between wider panels of yellow carrying motifs of dancing girls, paisley shapes, and a floral design. The latter two motifs along with a dancing peacock, on a red base, form the border which is edged on both sides with a line of white dots.

61 x 116 inches

MSMS II Museum, Jaipur

TC -537-73

NATURAL DYES

The art of dyeing and mordanting has been understood for 5000 years in the Indian subcontinent, as evidenced by a fragment excavated from the site at Mohenjo-Daro and until the 19th century all colouring substances for textiles were obtained from natural sources. 'The term "natural dye" refers to dyes obtained from plants, insects and mineral substances and used for dyeing textile materials'.[1] Dyeing with natural colours is the technique of colouring fabric and yarn by immersing it in a solution of colouring substance obtained from vegetable, animal, or mineral sources. B.C. Mohanty details the various natural dyes and processes used across India since the earliest times.

Jaipur has a long and continuing tradition of natural dyeing and the region is known for the skill with which colour is applied on fabric while creating design. The most popular colours used in the region were red, blue, black, and yellow; and these were applied using techniques like tie-dye and block printing.

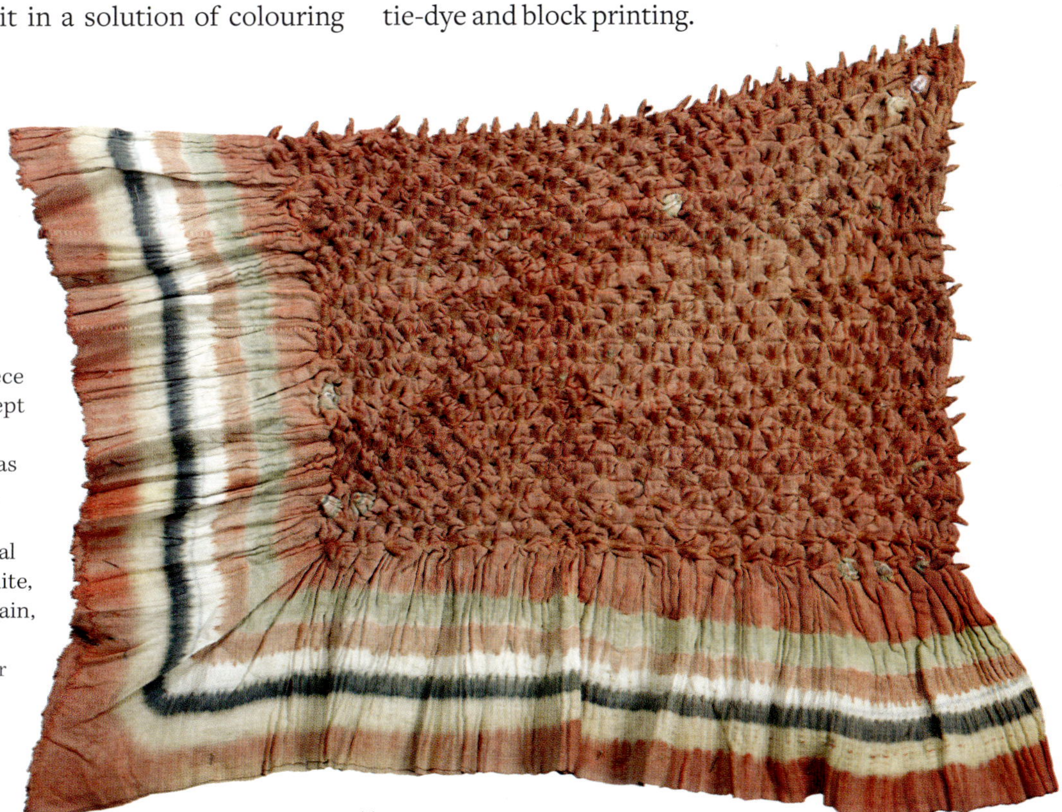

Bandhani
Odhni
This red cotton piece has been tie-dyed and kept in an unopened state in four folds. The ground has tiny raised mounds, and the edges are bordered with stripes in the natural colours of green, red, white, black, yellow, and red again, successively.
MSMS II Museum, Jaipur
Tc.42.74

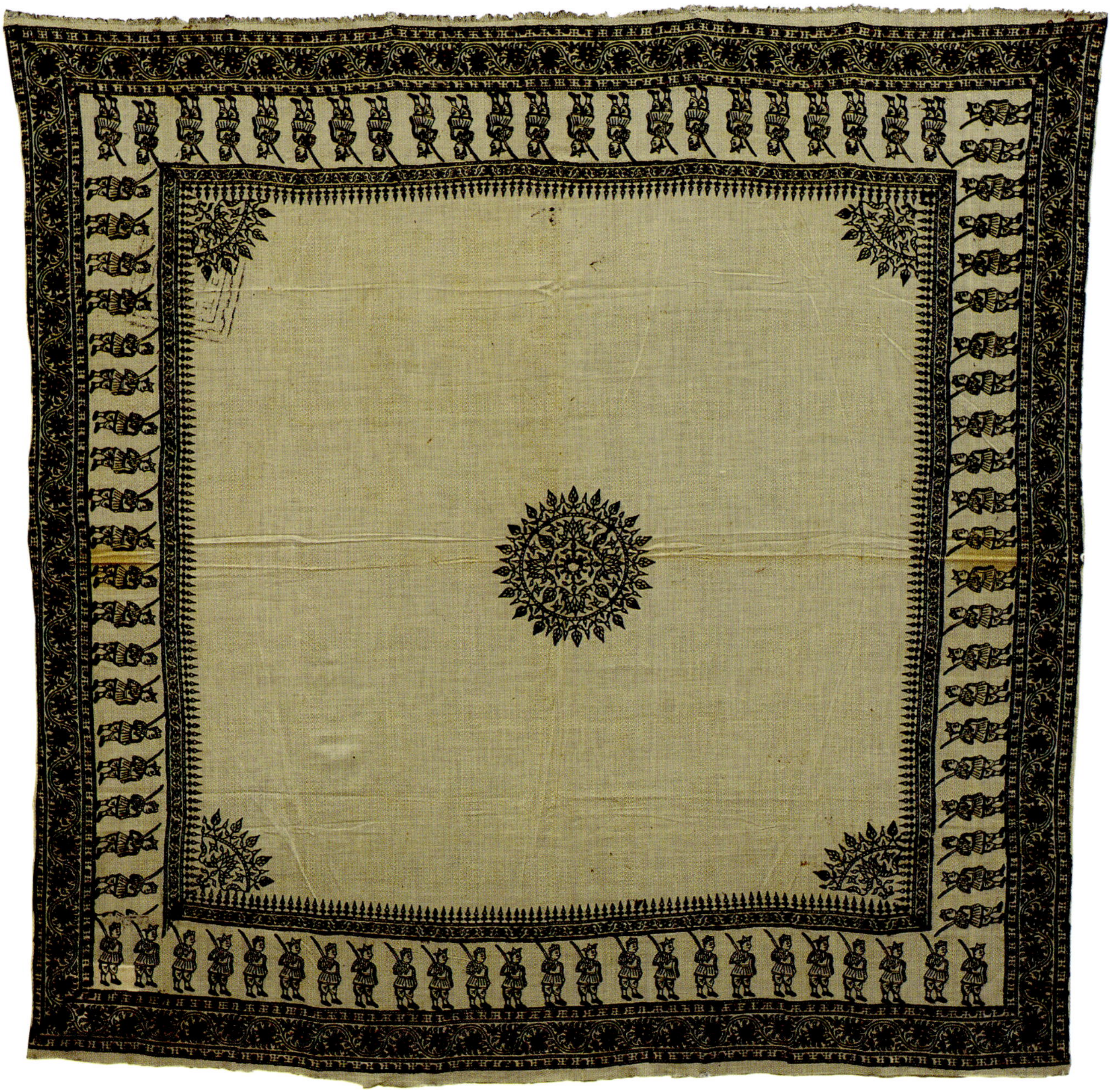

Block Print

Handkerchiefs

White cotton printed in black and grey, is edged with multiple scrolling borders, the central one with human figures, perhaps soldiers carrying arms. A floral motif adorns the centre, quarters of which are repeated at the four corners. An octroi stamp is visible.

35 x 35 in

MSMS II Museum, Jaipur

LA 239

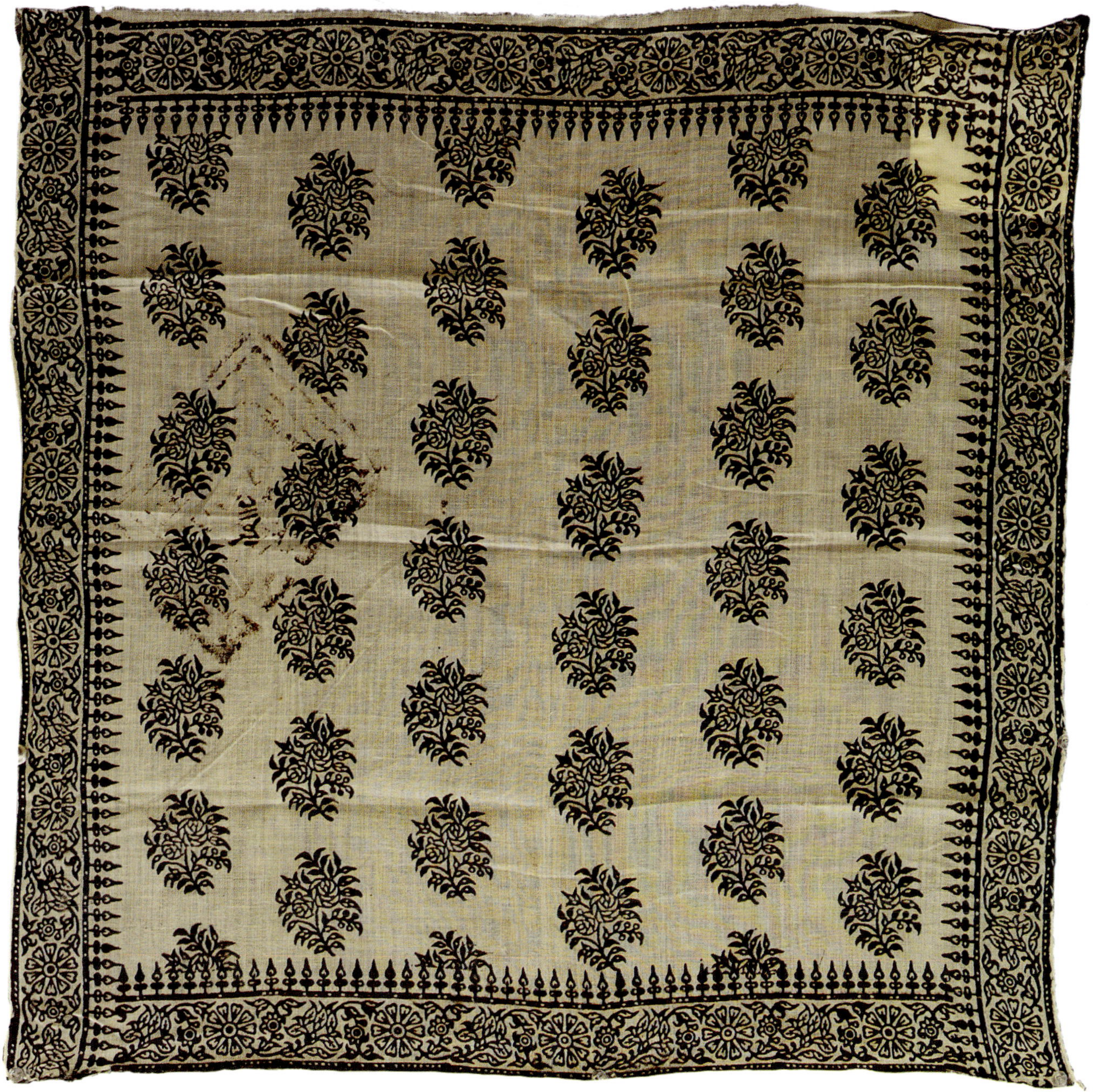

Block Print
Handkerchiefs
White muslin printed in black and grey is filled with rosette *butis* in a half-drop repeat pattern and edged with a floral scrolling border.
18 x 18 in
MSMS II Museum, Jaipur
LA 231

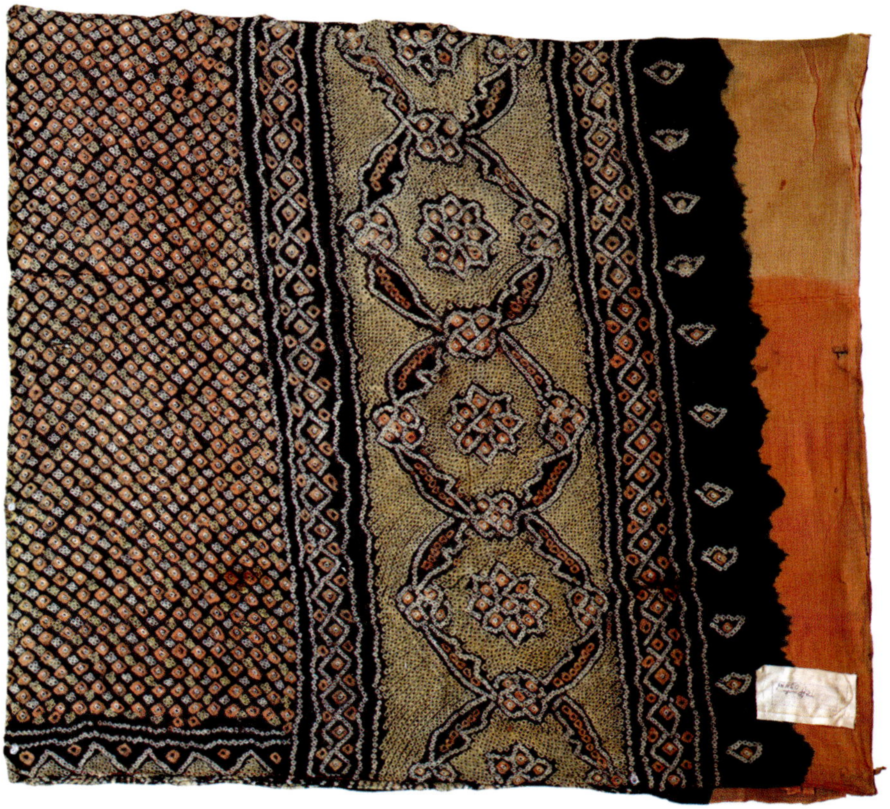

Bandhani
Odhna
Indigo cotton is filled with tiny *buti*s in red and white, the other colours used in the dotted designs being orange, yellow, and black. The sides are edged with a zigzag pattern, and the two ends have a wider and more elaborate border with a scrolling roundel, finishing with a row of small diamond-shaped *buti*s and a red strip.
336 x 151 cm
MSMS II Museum, Jaipur
Tc.P.2.

Small clusters of dyers, generally near water bodies, developed around the city of Jaipur and each of these specialized in the production of different types of textile techniques. The colours obtained were unique due to the quality of the minerals and other chemical substances in the water of these areas. Colours were and continue to be an important part of the Indian society as they celebrate seasons, festivals, ceremonies and even moods. They were also traditionally indicative of a person's status in society. The dyer communities—known as *rangrez* or *neelgar* in Rajasthan—understood the finer nuances of dyes and dyeing, and their understanding of colour is aptly described by Pupul Jayakar:

> A superlative knowledge of colour chemistry and of the rich resources of madder dyeing gave to India's coloured cloths a quality of growth and maturing, in which the colours ripened in the sun. The sun was a catalytic agent which constantly acted and reacted upon the minerals, vegetables and water, so that colour came to life in response to the

sun's rays; the fading too was like flowers that age in the sun, giving back their colour to the energy that gave it birth.[2]

Shades of red produced in India were famous across the world. The 'Indian red' was sourced from the roots of plants like madder, *Rubia tinctoria, Rubia majishta,* and roots of plants of the Morunda genus. The dye obtained from these is generically known as 'al'. The roots of *chay* or *Oldenlandia umbellate*, also yield red colour.

The chemical substance extracted from the roots of these plants is alizarin and this combines with alum to produce rich shades varying from pink to deep red colour. The process begins by dissolving alizarin in water and heating this solution. Fabric treated with alum is immersed in the dye bath. As the temperature is raised, a red colour develops in the areas treated with alum, which acts as the mordant.

Indigo or *neel* is the main source of blue colour and is commonly obtained from the leaves of the plant *Indigofera tinctoria*. A substantive dye, indigo has a good wash fastness and a poor rub fastness. The dye in its raw form is not soluble in water and thus is mixed with an alkaline substance to produce indigo white. This solution, which is a chemically reduced state of the dye, is stored in closed vats, mostly underground. Indigo vats are continuing vats, which are replenished with dye, lime, and jaggery from time to time. The fabric is immersed in this solution in a cold state. On exposing the fabric to air, the indigo is oxidized and produces a blue colour. Repetitive immersion in indigo and exposure to air gives deeper and richer shades of blue.

The colour black is traditionally produced by fermenting scraps of iron metal with jaggery. This is sieved and thickened with a gum solution

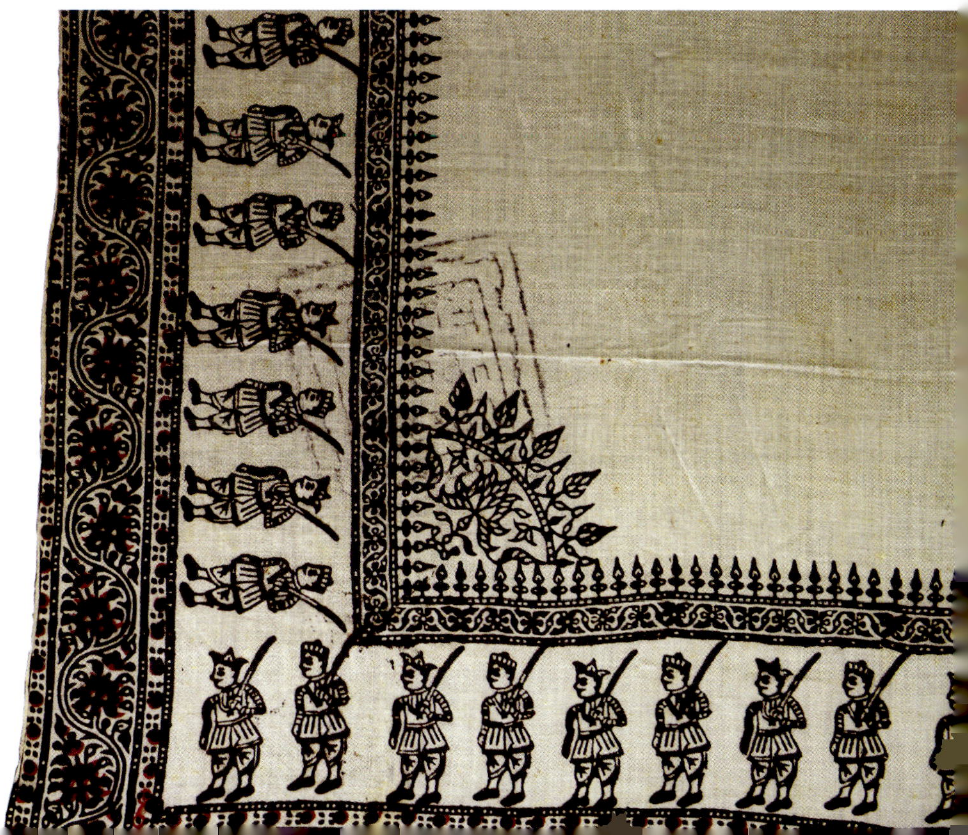

Block Print
Rumal
Closeup of a white cotton printed in black and grey, edged with multiple scrolling borders, the central one with human figures, perhaps soldiers carrying arms. Quarter of a floral motif adorns each corner of the kerchief. An octroi stamp is visible.
35 x 35 in
MSMS II Museum, Jaipur
LA 239

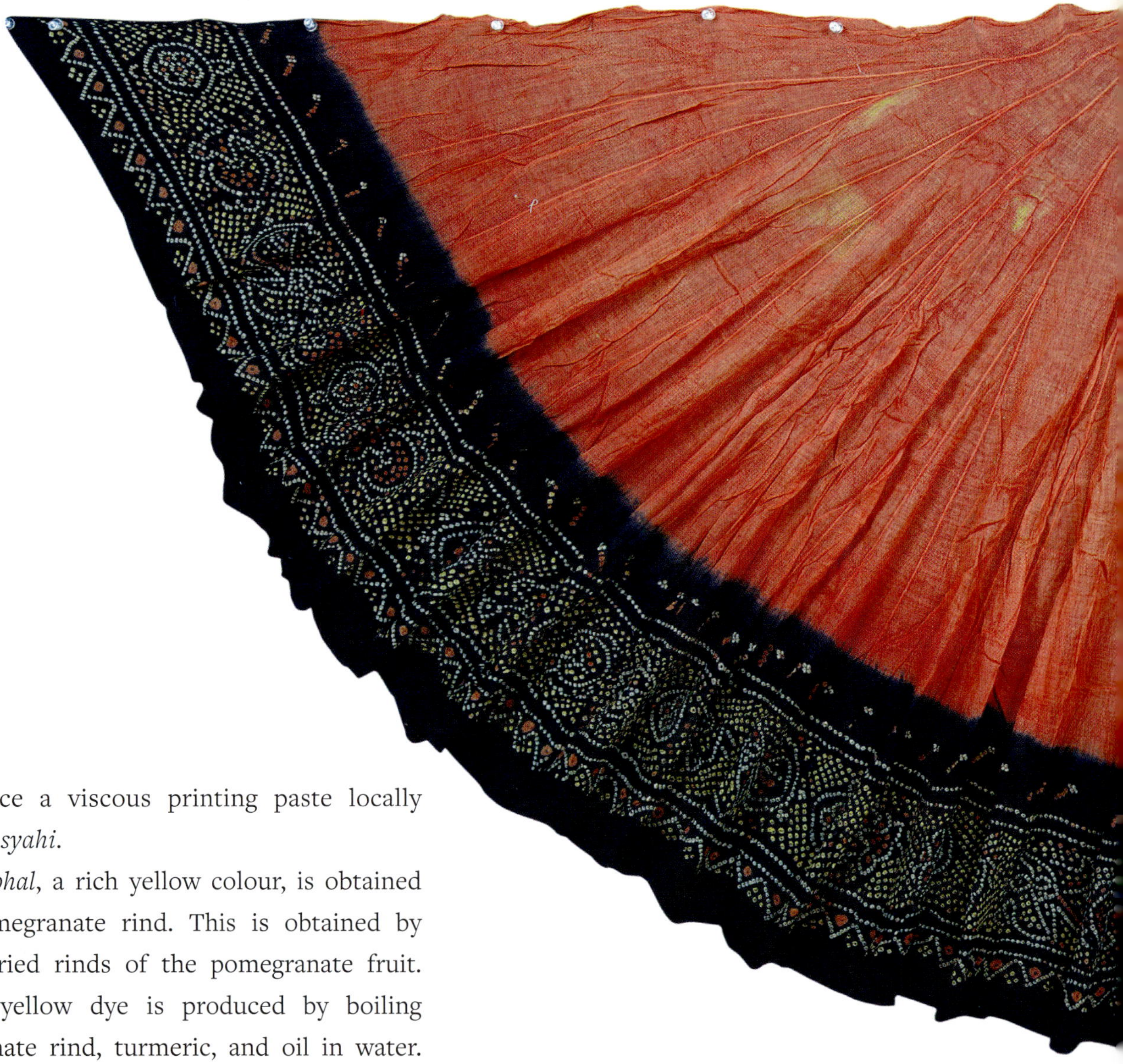

to produce a viscous printing paste locally known as *syahi*.

Nashphal, a rich yellow colour, is obtained from pomegranate rind. This is obtained by boiling dried rinds of the pomegranate fruit. Another yellow dye is produced by boiling pomegranate rind, turmeric, and oil in water. The application technique is called *potna*, which literally means 'to smear'. The solution colours the fabric to a rich yellow. Traditionally, the fugitive yellow colour also used to be obtained from the rhizome of turmeric plant and petals of safflower.

The colour green was obtained by a combination of indigo and pomegranate dye. Green was also made by overdyeing indigo with turmeric.

Bandhani
Ghaghra
Naturally dyed muslin, with a red base and black *bandhani* border dotted in various colours like red, white, and yellow with paisley motifs.
MSMS II Museum, Jaipur
Reserve collection

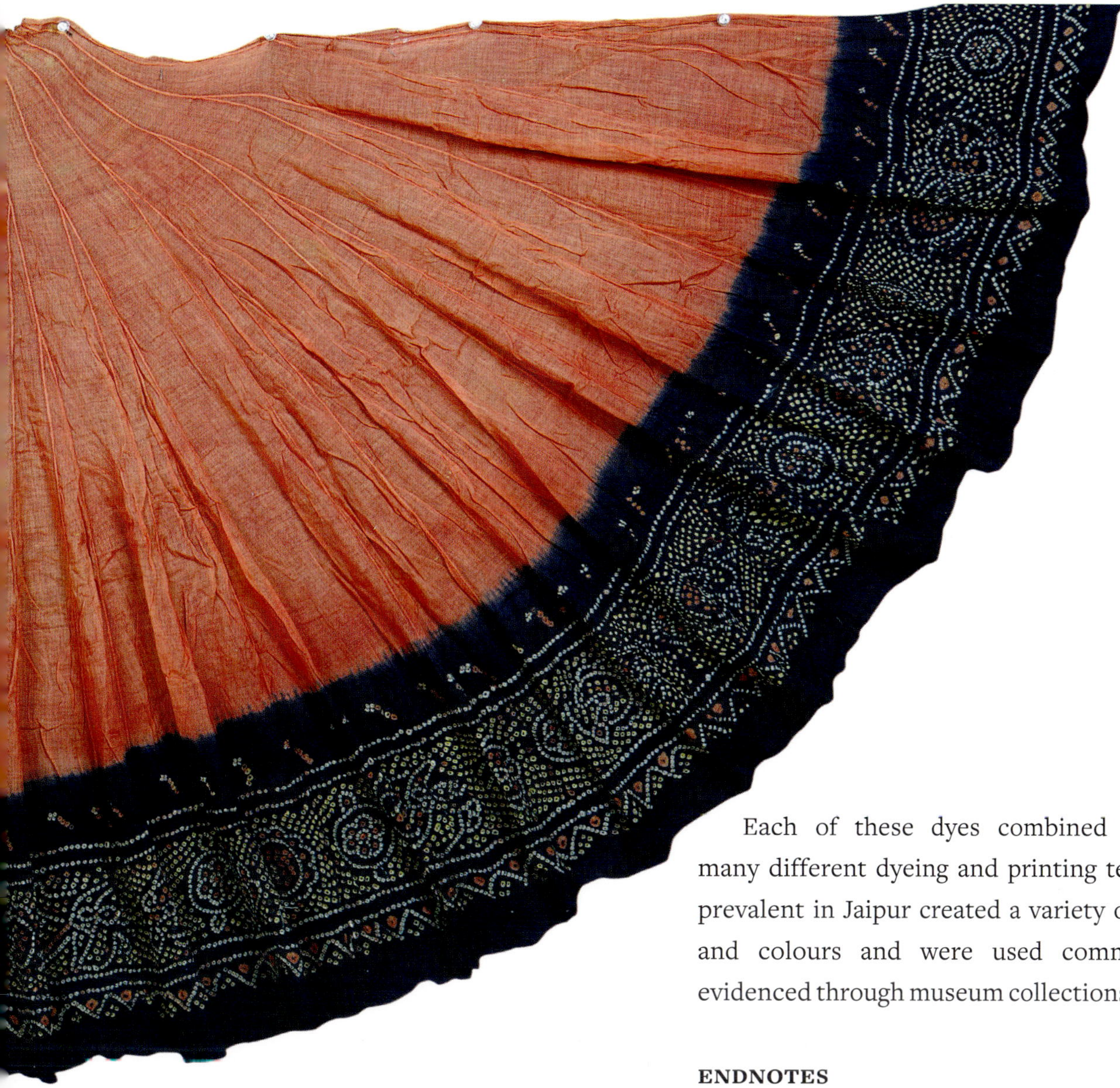

Each of these dyes combined with the many different dyeing and printing techniques prevalent in Jaipur created a variety of designs and colours and were used commonly, as evidenced through museum collections.

ENDNOTES

1. B.C. Mohanty, K.V. Chandramouli, and H.D. Naik, *Natural Dyeing processes of India* (Ahmedabad: The Calico Museum of Textiles and The Sarabhai Foundation Collections, 1987), p. 1.
2. Pupul Jayakar and John Irwin, *Textiles and Ornaments of India: a selection of designs*, ed. Monroe Wheeler (New York: The Museum of Modern Art New York, 1956), p. 20.

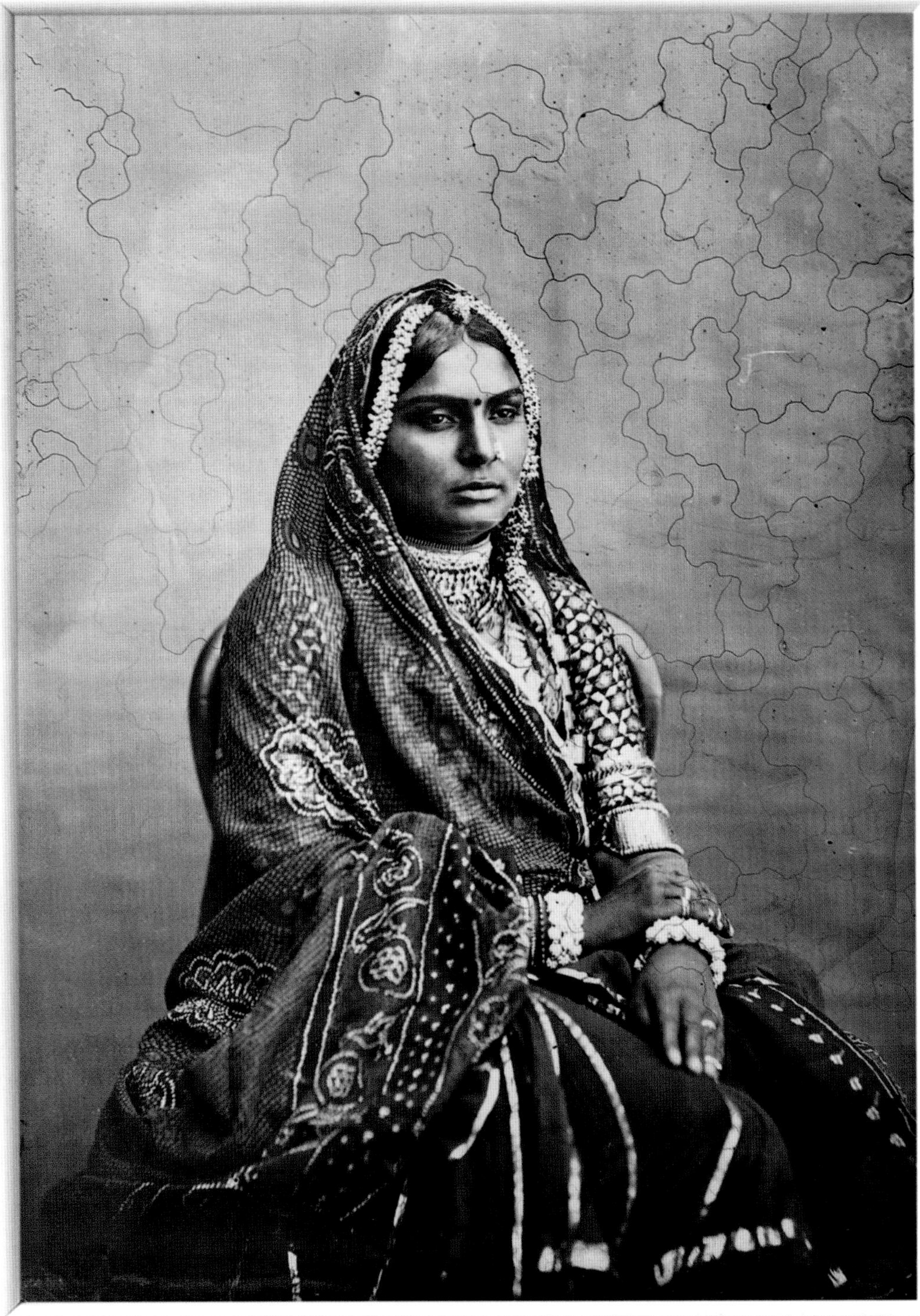

BANDHANI

Bandhani is the art of patterning textiles using the resist dyed technique of tie-dye. The term describes both the technique and the finished product and the words *bandhani* and *bandhej* are derived from the Sanskrit word 'bandha', meaning 'to tie'.

Central to a woman's life in Rajasthan, *bandhani* carries forward the long cultural heritage of tying folklore to the everyday lives of women. The tie-dyed *chunri* is symbolic and marks the various milestones in a woman's life—betrothal, marriage, the birth of a child, and even death. Women also wear different types of *bandhani* textiles to celebrate the many seasons and festivals through the year. The special status of these textiles is also reflected in their use as offerings to the local Rajasthani deities Bayasar and Mahayama, offered by mothers praying for the health of their children.

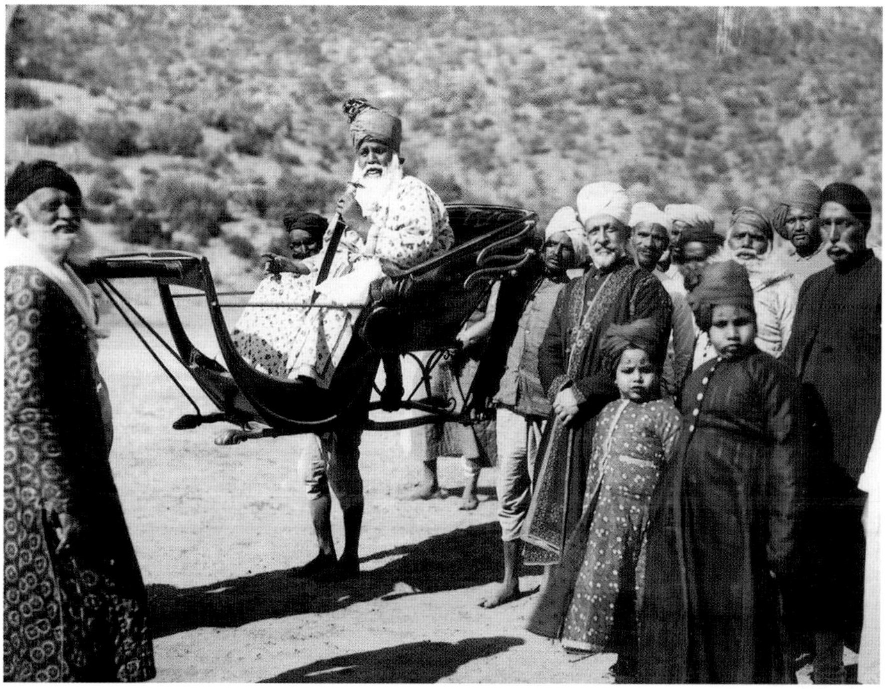

Maharaja Sawai Madho Singh II, c. 1900 with his sons, Ganga and Gopal, along with courtiers. The young boy is wearing a *bandhani achkan*. Children's garments were cut in a miniature form of those of the adults and remained stylistically similar.
Reserve collection

Facing page: Portrait of a woman in the traditional dress of Rajasthan. A fine tie-dyed *bandhani odhna* is draped over a *gota* embroidered *kanchli* and a skirt embellished with *gota* work.
MSMS II M 2012.04.0019-0011

The origins of *bandhani* date back to the 6th or 7th century CE with frescoes in the Ajanta caves providing the earliest visual references to these textiles in India. Early literary references are also found in the 7th century text *Harshcharita* penned by Banabatta, a poet in the court of King Harsha.

Bandhani is widespread and is found in different states of India like Madhya Pradesh, Tamil Nadu, Rajasthan, and Gujarat. The finest work is produced from the latter two. Rajasthani *bandhani* is produced primarily in and around the cities of Jaipur, Jodhpur, Bikaner, Nagaur, Churu, Sikar, and Bundi. Among them, Jaipur retains its reputation as a leading *bandhani* centre and the art has enjoyed the direct patronage of the royal houses since the earliest times.

The designs of *bandhani* come to life on different types of base fabrics, like fine muslin, and medium or heavier cottons. In the case of apparels, the silhouettes are kept in mind while executing the technique, a tradition extending from the times of *angarkha*s to modern tailored garments, like shirts, skirts, and trousers. A number of placement designs are seen on the garments in the museum collection. The fabric choices are dictated by the final use of the piece. Light mulmul or voile are preferred for *odhni*s, lighter cottons for *safa*s and *pagdi*s, and heavier cotton for skirts, pyjamas, etc. The work is also

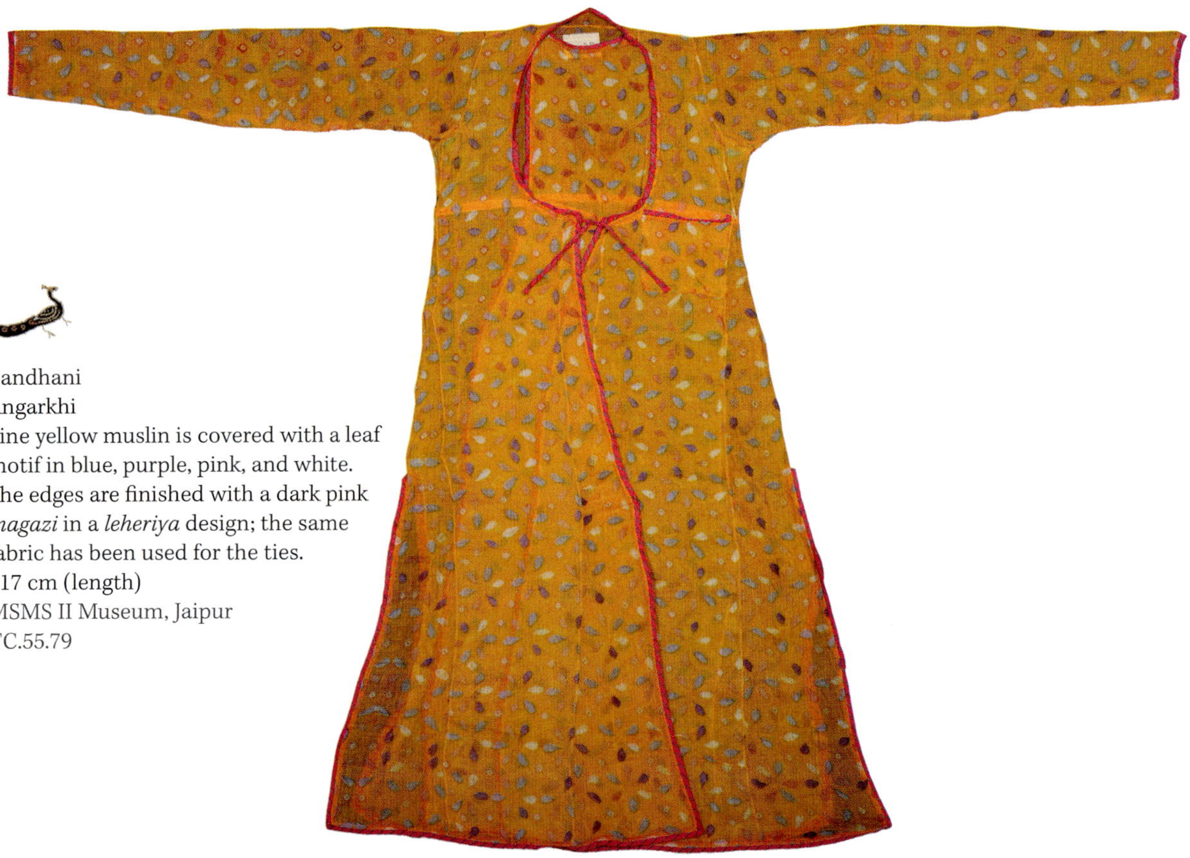

Bandhani
Angarkhi
Fine yellow muslin is covered with a leaf motif in blue, purple, pink, and white. The edges are finished with a dark pink *magazi* in a *leheriya* design; the same fabric has been used for the ties.
117 cm (length)
MSMS II Museum, Jaipur
TC.55.79

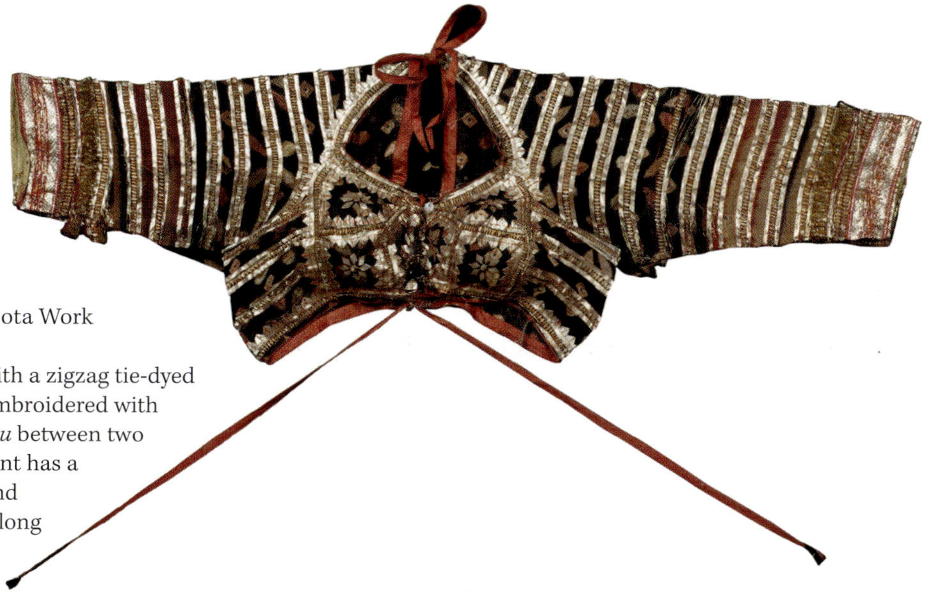

Bandhani and Gota Work
Kanchli

Black muslin, with a zigzag tie-dyed design in red and yellow, is embroidered with narrow vertical rows of *gokhru* between two rows of plain *gota*. The garment has a wide complex work of *gota* and *gokhru* all over, and a *kinari* along its inner edge.
MSMS II Museum, Jaipur

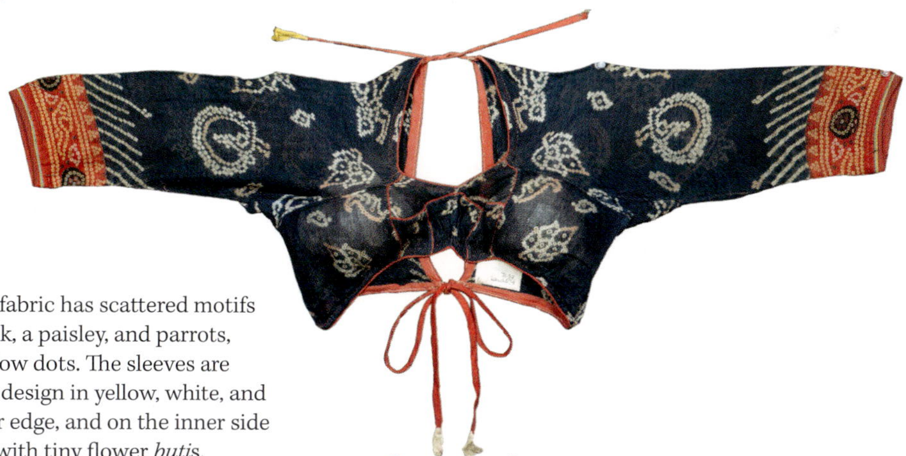

Bandhani
Kanchli

The indigo cotton fabric has scattered motifs of a paan leaf, a dancing peacock, a paisley, and parrots, all formed of fine white and yellow dots. The sleeves are bordered in red with a scrolling design in yellow, white, and indigo, a red *magazi* on its outer edge, and on the inner side a row of diagonal white stripes with tiny flower *buti*s.
MSMS II Museum, Jaipur
Tc.54.73

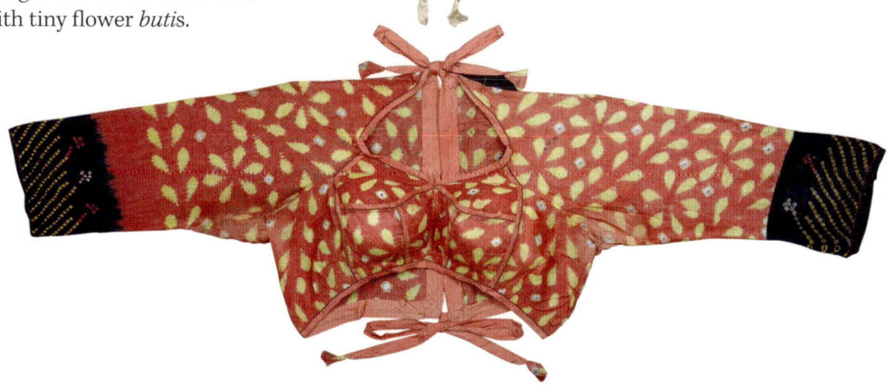

Bandhani
Kanchli

Orange cotton fabric with an all-over leaf design in yellow, with a lighter shade of orange used for the ties and a piping on the neck and bottom. The sleeves have been bordered with a black band, which has yellow diagonal stripes and alternating white and orange *buti*s on it.
MSMS II Museum, Jaipur
LA.257

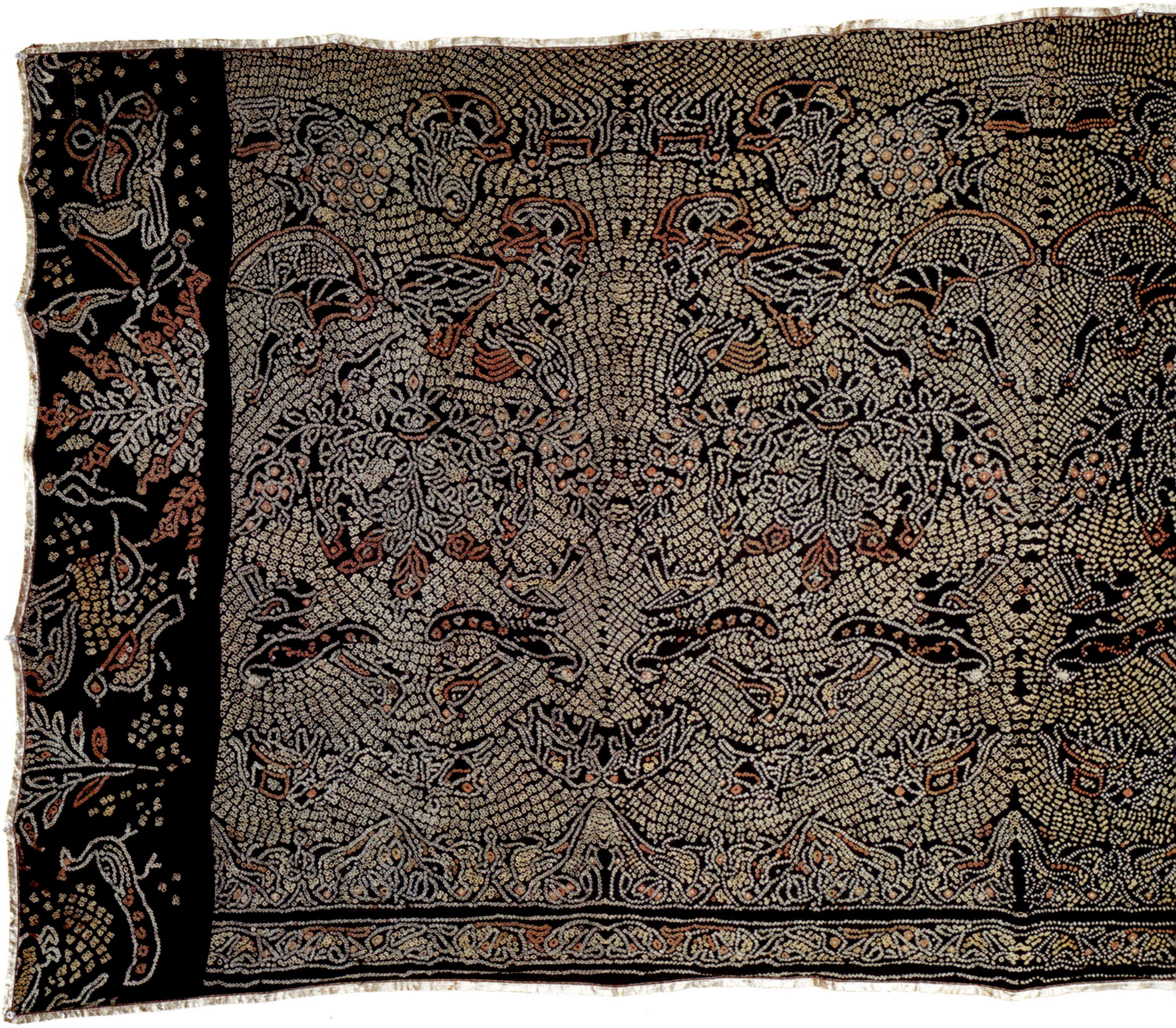

done on thin silks and diaphanous chiffons, particularly for saris.

Bandhani employs a vast number of craftspersons who work on the piece at different stages for the creation of this colourful textile. The process is initiated by washing the fabric to accentuate its softness and absorbency by removing the starch and impurities. In the next step, the textile is folded into two, four, or more layers for the tying process. The *karigar* (artisan) or the *rangrez* (dyer) marks the layout of the pattern on the material. Rough outlines are drawn on the fabric before tying the fabric using tiny, intricate ties. Over time, however, for refined and

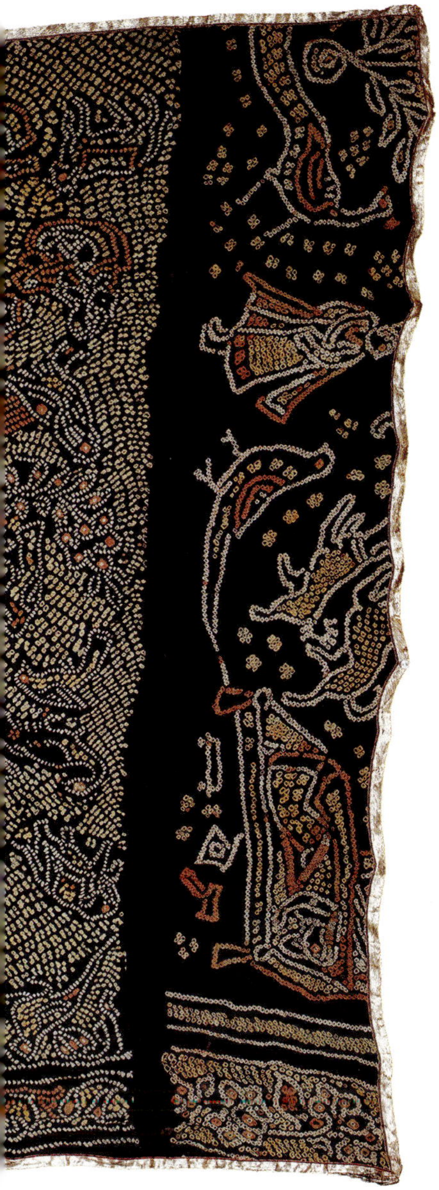

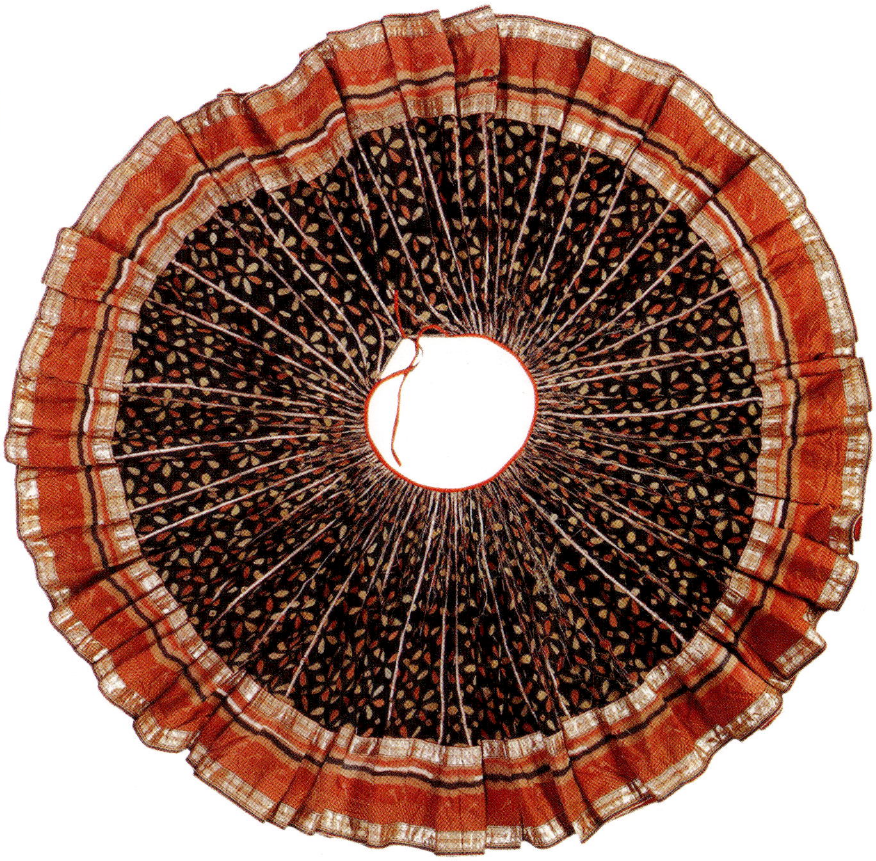

Bandhani
Diwali ghaghra
Black muslin base with red, beige, and white *butis*. The border—between two rows of broad *lappa/gota*—is in fine red *bandhej* with narrow stripes in red, black, and gota on the inside edge. The bottom end has pipings in black, blue, and red, finished with *ghungroos*.
MSMS II Museum, Jaipur
LA 1

Left: Bandhani
Odhna
The blue cotton is covered with an all-over pattern of dotted designs in white, yellow, and red. The two ends have motifs of a woman, a stool, peacock, sparrow, parrot, a camel, and a shrub. Dancing peacocks, elephants, birds, dancing women, and on one edge women on a bed, a tree, flowers, Krishna playing his flute, a sitting peacock, a man riding a horse, a cock, sparrow, parrot, a sitting camel, and women playing the dholak adorn the middle. The side borders are narrower and simpler, and their edges finished with silver *gota*.
MSMS II Museum, Jaipur
Tc.583.73

fine work, artisans have started using wooden blocks. These are dipped in fugitive dyes, like *neel* or *geru* (red ochre and water solution), to print the pattern on the cloth. The dye is kept in a printing pad into which, a cord is dipped which is then used to delineate the fields. Into these fields, the individual patterns are stamped with

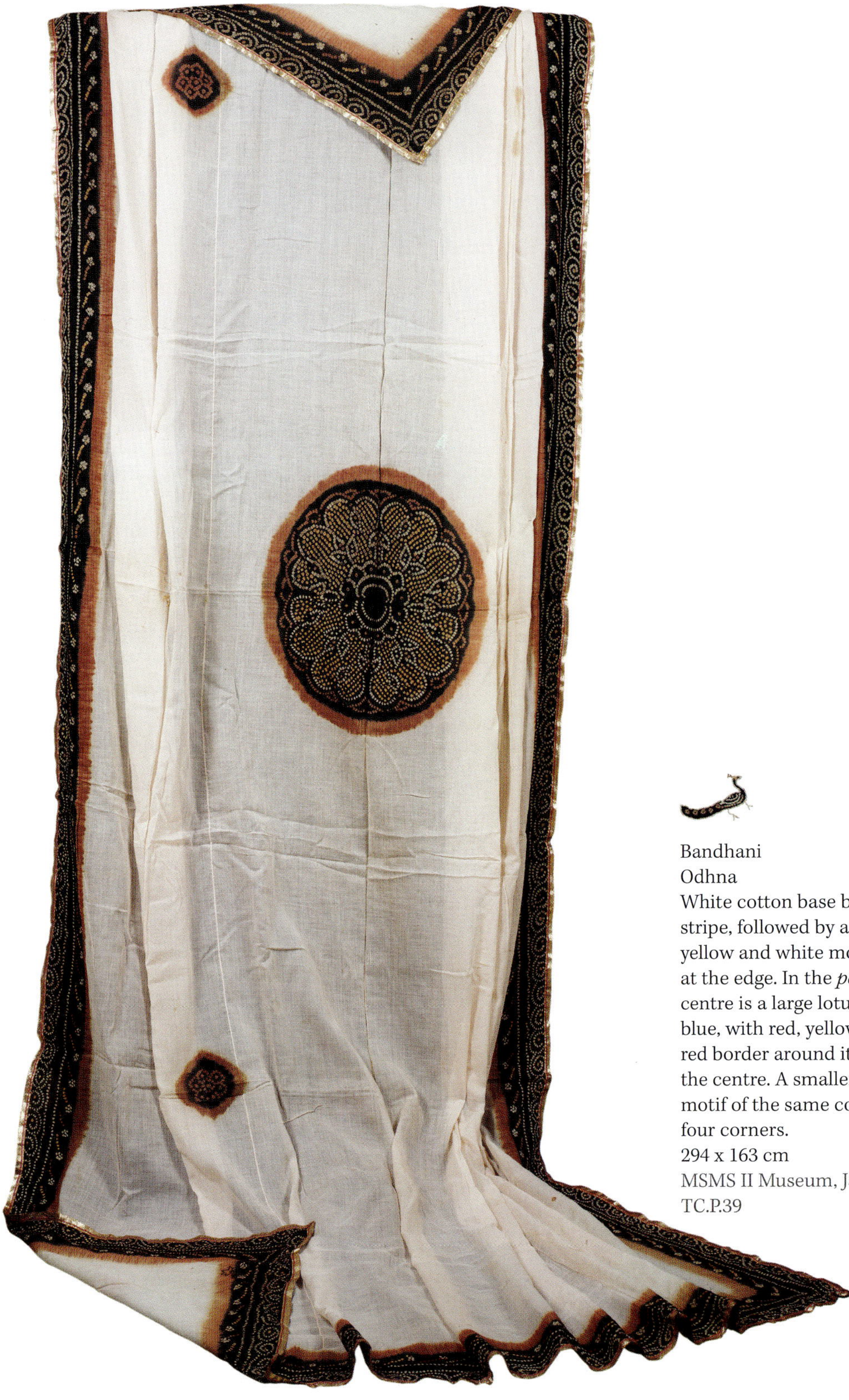

Bandhani
Odhna
White cotton base bordered by a red stripe, followed by a black one with yellow and white motifs, and then *gota* at the edge. In the *pomcha* style, at the centre is a large lotus flower in deep blue, with red, yellow, and white dots, a red border around it, and a *chanda* at its the centre. A smaller diamond-shaped motif of the same colour ornaments the four corners.
294 x 163 cm
MSMS II Museum, Jaipur
TC.P.39

woodblocks, which are dipped in the fugitive dye. The entire process of transferring the design is termed as *chapai* or *likhai*.

The process of tying the fabric requires immense skill and patience, and is done by women and young girls who are known as *bandhanaris*. The resist is usually formed by either the cloth itself or additional materials such as thread, mustard seeds, and rice to create varied designs. The cotton thread used for tying is loosely twisted and sometimes moistened or coated with wax to prevent the dye from penetrating into the tied areas. The tying method is led by the thumb and forefinger of the right hand and the thread is made to pass through a fine millet-stem bobbin, so that it runs smoothly and evenly. The folded material is lifted with the nail of the small finger, which is grown especially long and pointed, or with a brass nail called *nua* or *nolia* worn over the finger, while the left hand thumb presses the material together, causing it to bunch for tying. At the end, the tying thread is passed below in such a way that when pulled, it becomes tight. The thread, uncut, is led to the next point to be tied. Gradually the entire fabric is tied and readied for the next process of colouring.

The dyeing of the fabric is done mostly by men. The textile is soaked in cold water to ensure that the subsequent uptake of colour is even. The area that has been resisted retains the base colour of the fabric, while the un-resisted area absorbs the colour of the dye. Individual parts are dyed by hand at times (for example, with pink or orange directly around the tied portions of cloth. For this purpose, a piece of felt is tied around a wooden handle, with which the dye can be applied. In earlier times, a special effect was derived in soft and light fabrics, like *mulmul* and silk, by dyeing them in different colours on either side of the fabric (*dorukha*) leading to two different designs.

The dots, along with the light-coloured dyed spots, which are to be retained, are now likewise tied. This process, known as the *lipai* technique, is especially popular in the *bandhani* practised in Rajasthan. After the first dyeing, the fabric is rinsed, squeezed, and dried. It is tied further to resist areas that would add pattern to the fabric. The textile piece is then dyed in darker colours, like red, green, or black. The yellow and other light-coloured tied points are retained in the textile, while another set of points is tied securely to build upon the design. Gradually, multiple colours are introduced into the design with each new colour securing more dotted patterns.

The *pallu* or end piece is generally the pièce de resistance of the creation. It is dyed in a darker shade like black, while the field remains a bright red or green. To achieve this, the central field is wrapped in a resist foil and only the border is soaked in the dark dye solution. If the opposite is desired, that is, the field is to be dyed in a darker shade and the borders are to be left in the lighter colours, the end-pieces and selvedge borders are loosely stitched together with needle and thread, then wrapped in plastic and immersed in the dye bath. Bright red can be discharged with caustic soda and sodium hydrosulphite. The textile that has been dyed is washed by the local washermen and is, if necessary, starched.

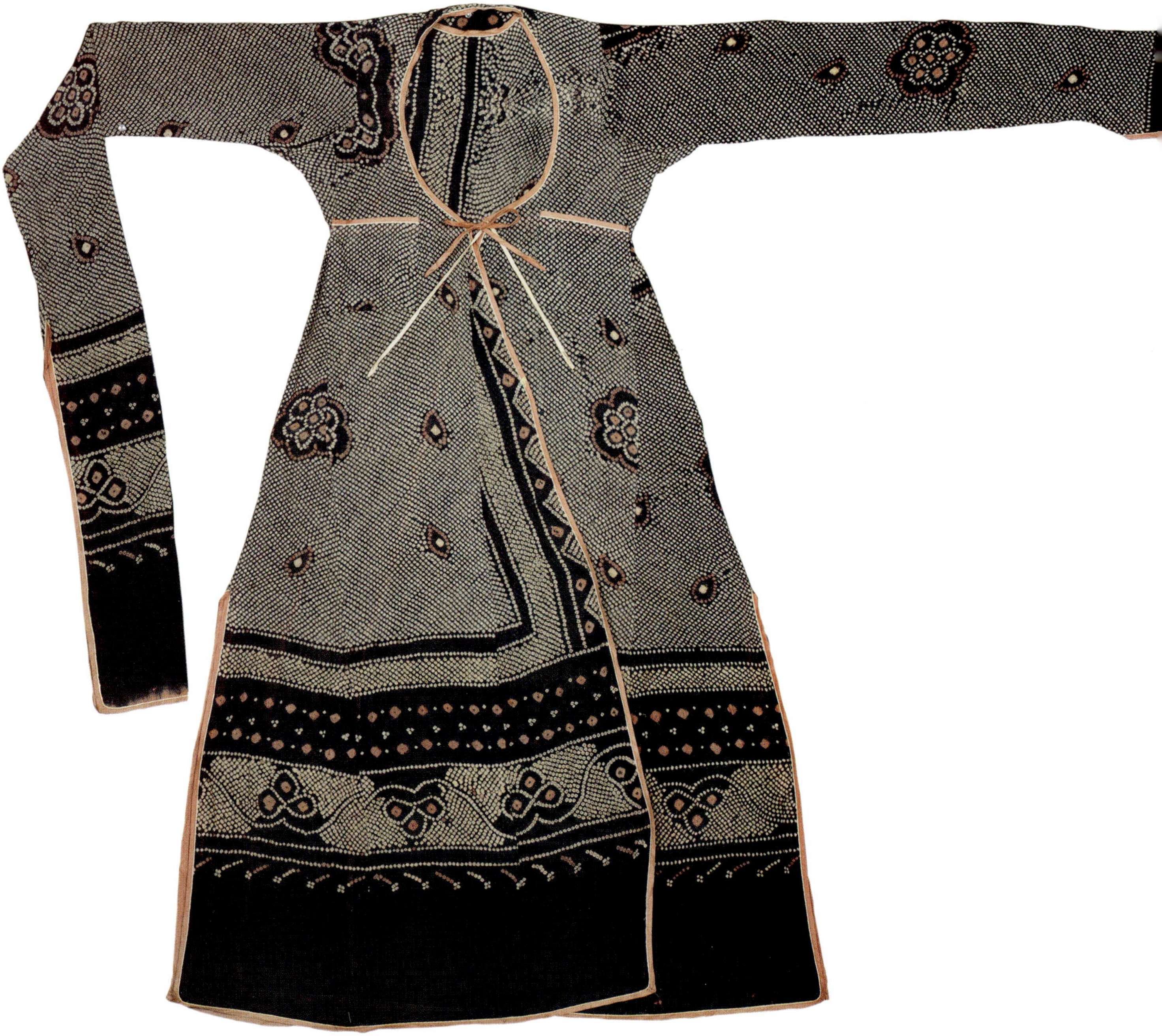

Bandhani
Angarkhi
Fine black muslin with an extremely delicate all-over striped design in white, scattered floral motifs in red and white, and small *buti*s in yellow and red. The design is specifically engineered for the shape of the garment. The bottom, and the extra long sleeves, are bordered with multiple panels of floral designs. A narrow border runs down the front opening, and a double *magazi* of red and yellow cotton pipes all the edges and the pocket openings, and forms the ties as well.
124 cm (length)
MSMS II Museum, Jaipur
Tc.437.73

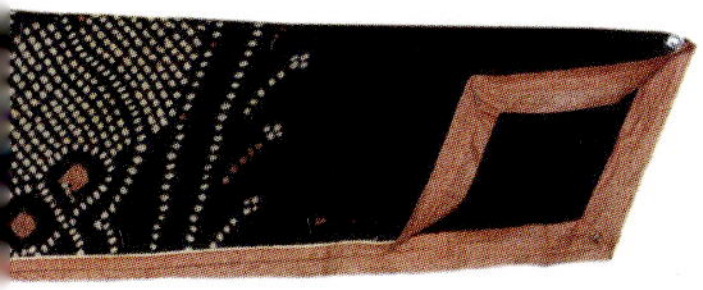

A distinctive feature of *bandhani* textile is retaining the ties of the four-fold until they are sold. They may be opened on one corner to show the fineness of the ties and colour scheme, but are otherwise kept intact with their dyeing threads until purchased. To open the *bandhani*, the material is pulled crosswise skilfully to release the ties in one swift motion.

The arid landscape of Rajasthan draws energy from the colours that its people wear. The more barren the landscape, the brighter are the colours worn. Using *pakka* (permanent) and *kaccha* (temporary) colours, an array of shades are created—some pure colour and others an indeterminate mixture. *Bandhani* mostly uses white, yellow, red, black, green, and deep red colour. A typical piece would have a yellow ground (*pomcha-piliya*; *pom* signifying lotus and *piliya* meaning yellow) with a stylized flower in the centre. The cloths made in a variety of colours include dove-grey and black, though more often brighter shades of yellow, pink, green, and red are seen.

Apart from the plethora of colours, *bandhani* has many patterns and designs. Amongst the basics, *danas* (dots meant to signify grains), *teen bundi* or *tritik* (three dots), and the *sangam*, involving a mix of three colours are very popular. Other designs include the *jaldar*, or the design of dense flowers and leaves, *ladoo* (a very close repetition of small dots), and *dabba-dabbo*, a design made in two parts in the shape of boxes. Motif usage is also very popular with peacocks, parrots, lions, tigers, geometric designs, and natural flora used in abundance.

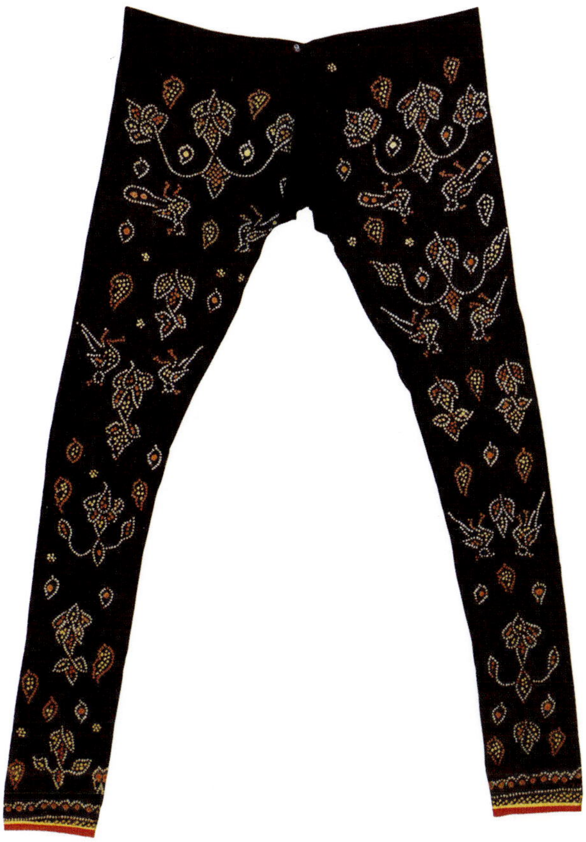

Bandhani
Pyjama
Cotton base with yellow, white, and dull red dots, portraying peacocks, flowers, and leaves. The bottom is edged with a floral *magazi* in yellow and dull red.
MSMS II Museum, Jaipur
TC.437.73

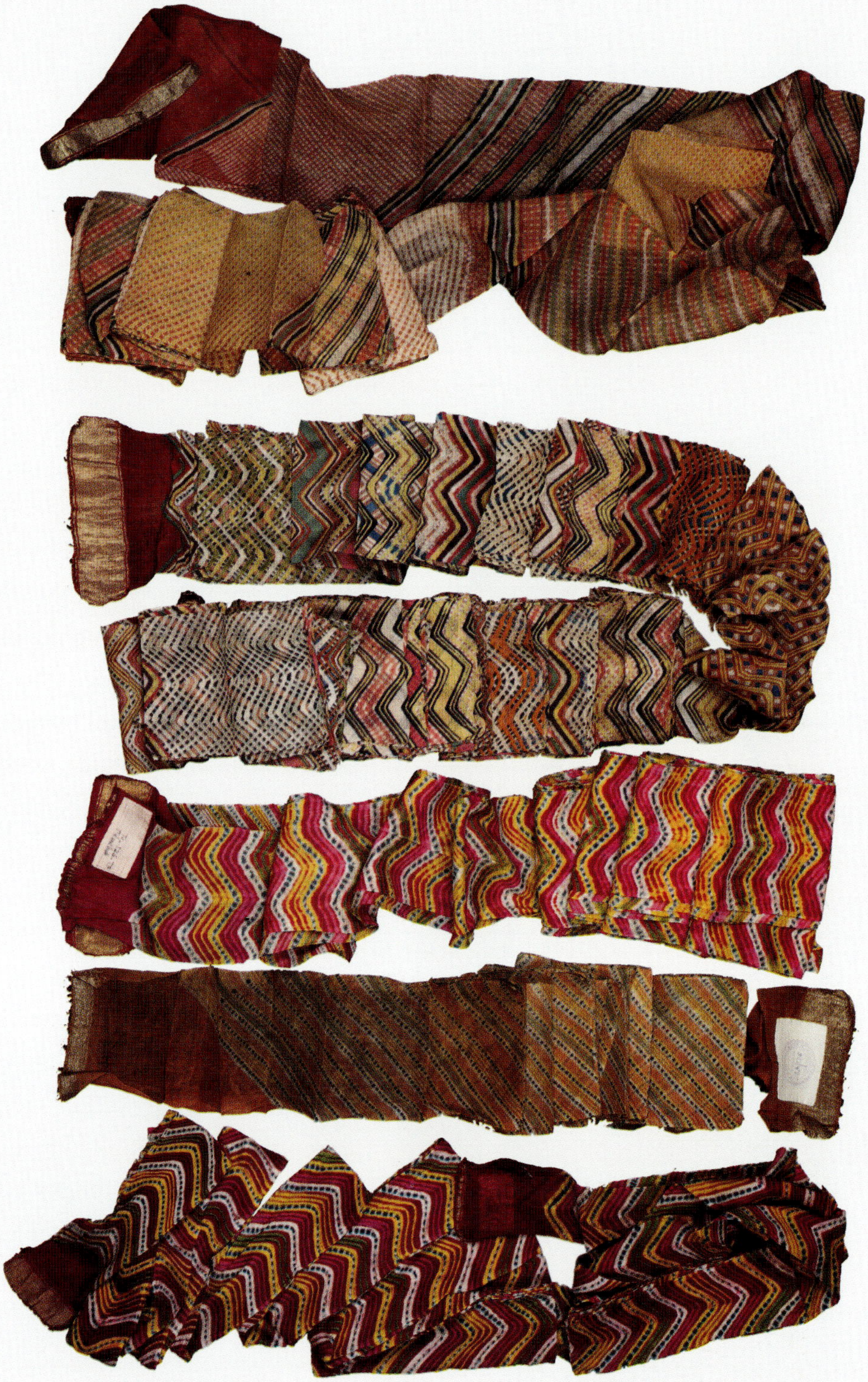

Leheriya
Turban pieces
Multi-coloured turbans; each is adorned with *leheriya* stripes and repeat patterns, and tie-dyed motifs alternately.
MSMS II Museum, Jaipur
Reserve collection

LEHERIYA

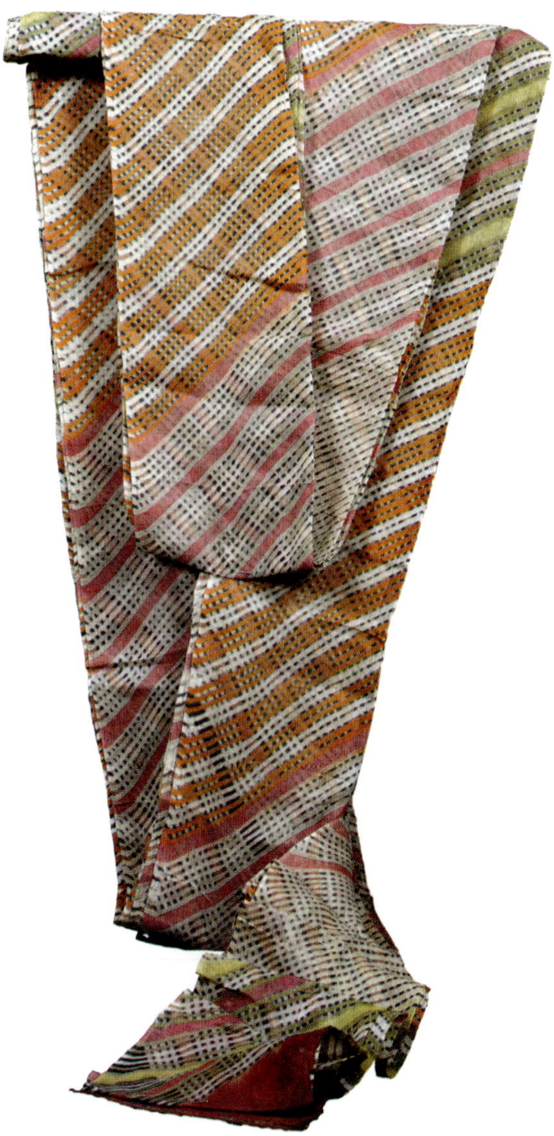

Leheriya meaning 'waves' is a pattern created by using the basic technique of tie-dye. The dyer creates diagonal lines or stripes to produce wave-like patterns, creating an effect of gentle movement on the fabric surface.

The process begins by holding the square or rectangular washed cloth diagonally from opposite corners. The cloth is rolled and wrapped around a wooden pole, usually while it is still wet, though it may also be in a semi-dry or dry state. The thread that ties up the cloth acts as a resist, yielding a pattern of diagonal stripes after dyeing. The resisted portion retains the base colour of the cloth and the un-resisted area acquires the colour of the dye. The varying thickness of the thread and the distance between threads allows the fabric to obtain stripes of different widths and thus be individually defined. The fabrics chosen are gossamer thin; the preferred ones

Leheriya
Turban
Cotton turban piece with *leheriya* designs of colours orange, pink, yellow, and green.
MSMS II Museum, Jaipur
Reserve collection

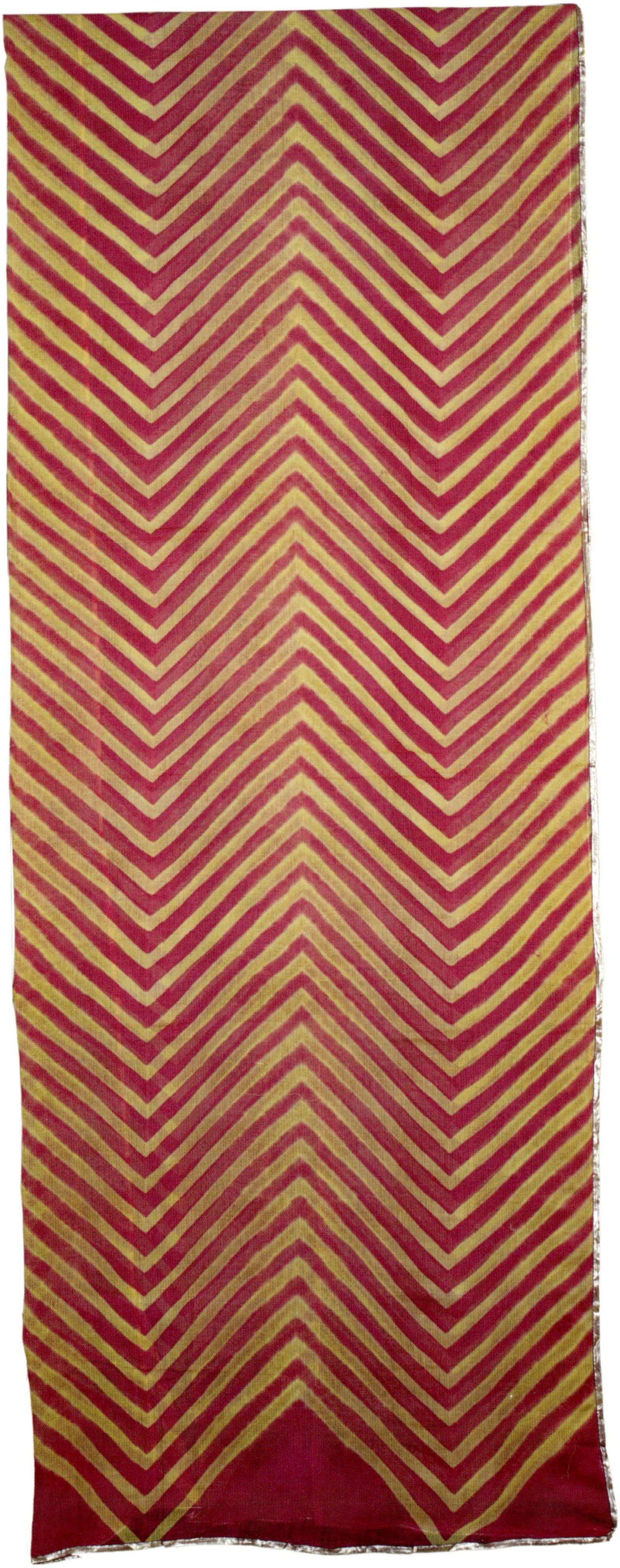

Leheriya and Gota Work
Turban
Fine muslin has a pink ground with yellow v-shaped striped *leheriya* in a repeat pattern. It is edged with silver *gota*.
MSMS II Museum, Jaipur
Reserve collection

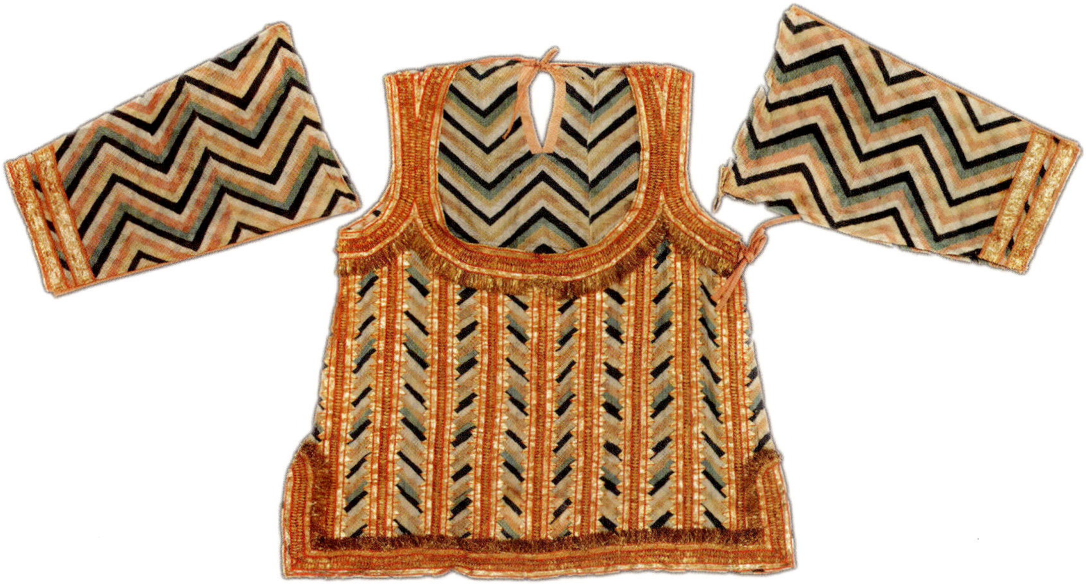

Leheriya and Gota Work
Matching set of kurti and ghaghra
Leheriya design in red, black, and yellow adorns the pieces. Embroidered in narrow vertical rows of *gokhru* and plain *gota*, the kurti constitutes a wide border on the neck, armholes, sleeve-ends, and bottom, with a *kinari* along its edge. The design of the kurti's sleeves is of special interest, as the garment can be worn either with or without them; cloth ties and looped buttons are provided for attaching them.
MSMS II Museum, Jaipur
TC.J.25b

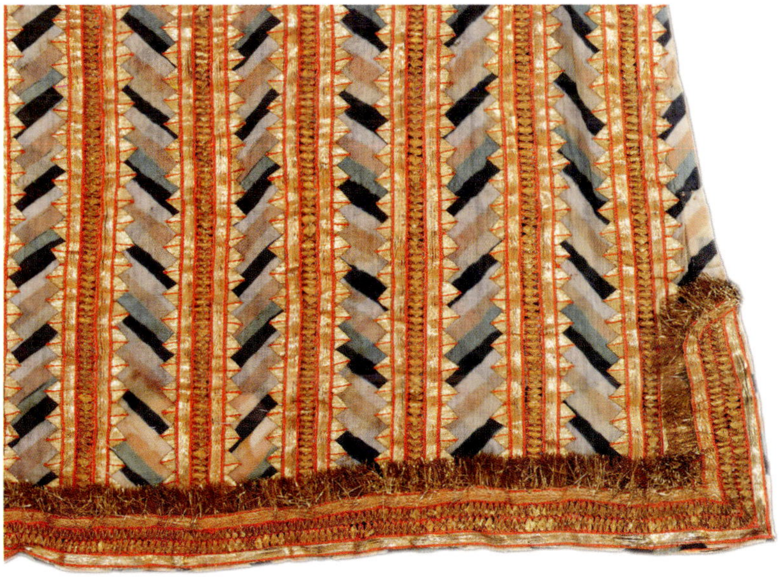

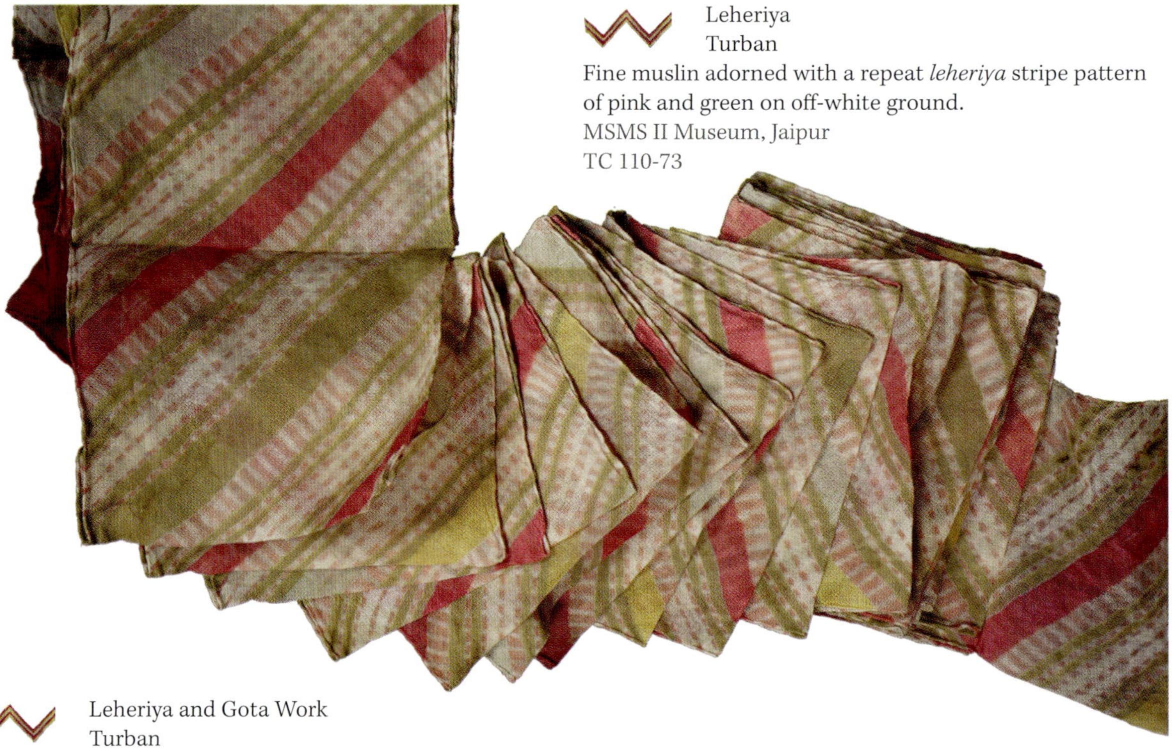

Leheriya
Turban
Fine muslin adorned with a repeat *leheriya* stripe pattern of pink and green on off-white ground.
MSMS II Museum, Jaipur
TC 110-73

Leheriya and Gota Work
Turban
Fine muslin with yellow ground and v-shaped pink *leheriya* stripes in a repeat pattern. The piece has been edged with silver *gota*.
MSMS II Museum, Jaipur
Reserve collection

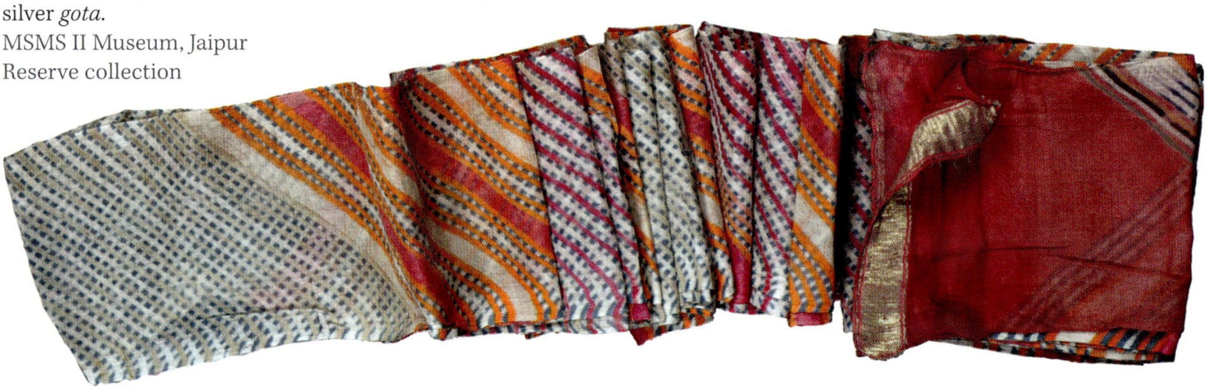

being cotton voile, fine silk, and chiffons. Thin fabrics allow even penetration of colour through the rolled cloth.

The skill of the dyer is expressed through his ability to create multi-coloured stripes after the first dyeing. The dyer accomplishes this by opening up some sections of the rolled fabric, leaving other sections still bound, and tying up fresh sections. Then the whole or part of the fabric is dyed. The steps generally followed in the dyeing are as follows: the fabric is rolled from the first corner, partly tied, and dipped

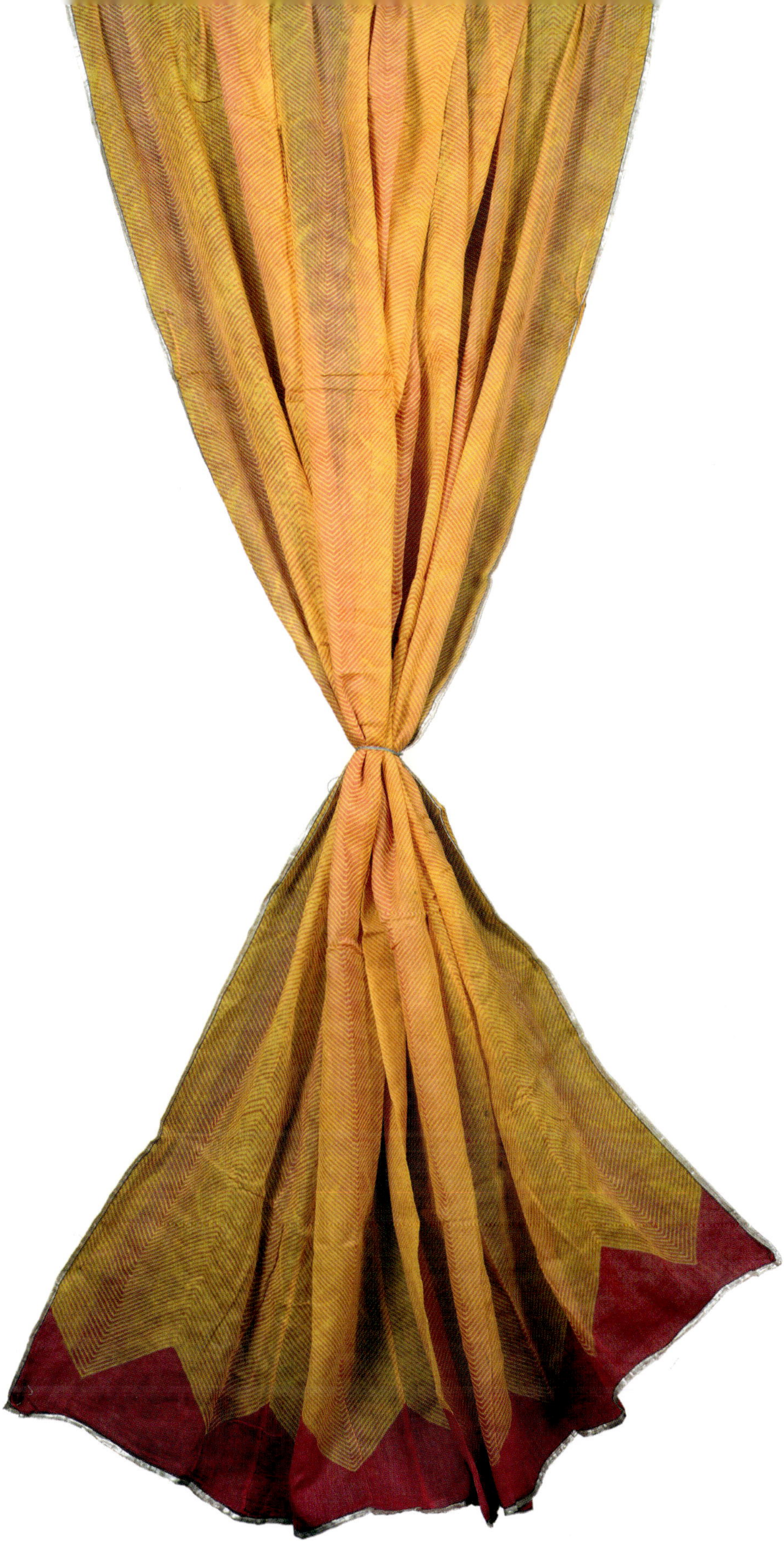

Leheriya and Gota Work
Turban
Fine muslin with yellow ground and v-shaped pink *leheriya* stripes in a repeat pattern. The piece has been edged with silver *gota*.
MSMS II Museum, Jaipur
Reserve collection

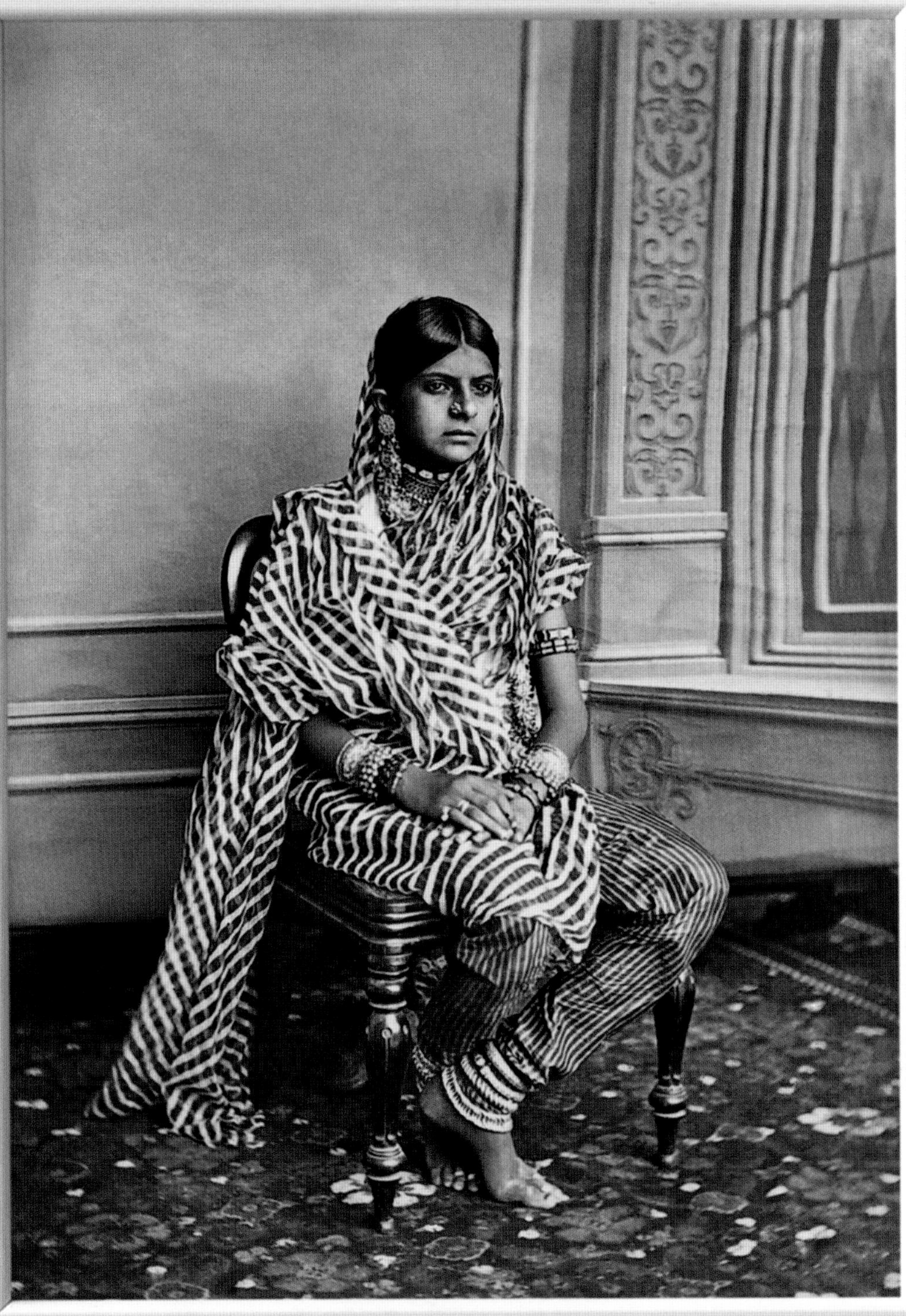

in the first solution; the resists are opened and then, the material is rolled up from the opposite corner, resisted by new ties, and is dyed in the second solution. Only those parts treated with both components appear dyed, thus producing interrupted diagonal lines. The tying is done for every new colour, which is to be added to the design, while some of the old ties may be opened to colour the earlier tied portions. Often, only individual parts between two ties are dipped in the dye, or the colour is applied by hand to these portions.

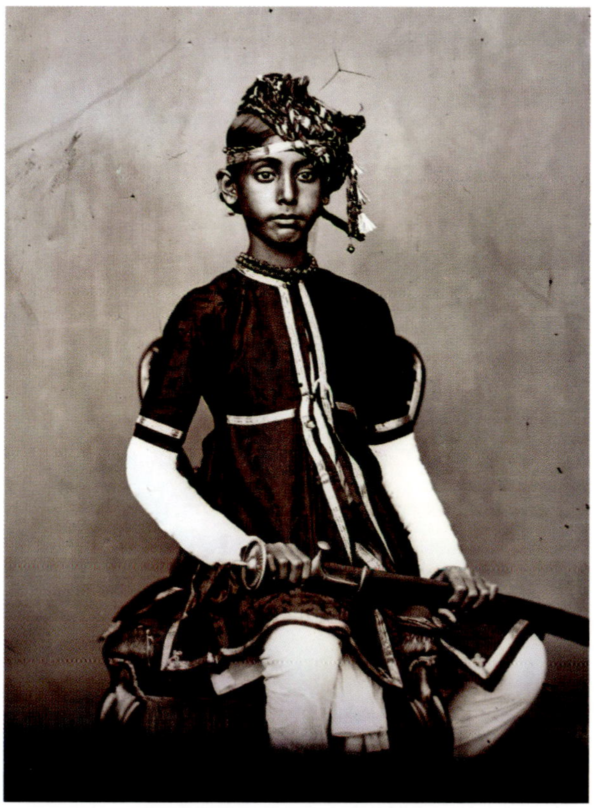

Portrait of a young boy wearing a short *angarkhi* with a churidar. His head is covered with a turban made of a twisted *leheriya* fabric.
MSMS II M 2012.04.0007-0004

Facing page: Woman draped in a *leheriya* dupatta and wearing a straight pyjama.
MSMS II M 2012.04.0004-0005

The alluring interplay of styles lends a stamp of identity to each creation. The intersection of diagonal stripes produces a chequered pattern called *mothra*. These stripes flow unidirectionally, intersecting at right angles, using a single colour. Unrolling the fabric, swiftly rolling it from the opposite corner, and repeating the process of tie-dyeing the cloth creates this effect.

Using this basic matrix, an extraordinary variety of linear designs are produced. A *panchranga* (five-coloured) design is the most auspicious, as the number '5' bears a special position in Hindu mythology. The *satranga* displays the seven colours of the rainbow. Other variations are *gandadar* (zigzag pattern), *indradhanush* (rainbow), *pratapshahi* (the powerful), *rajashahi* (royal), *samudralehar* (waves of the sea), and *salaidar* (fine striped pattern).

The tradition of the *leheriya* lives on as an unbroken continuum. The Marwari merchants' extended patronage to the technique through the 19th and 20th centuries and kept it alive in Jaipur, Jodhpur, and Udaipur. It was worn for the festivals of Gangaur and Teej, which mark the coming of spring and the advent of monsoon, respectively. Religious practices, festivals, and social norms lent sustenance to the craft.

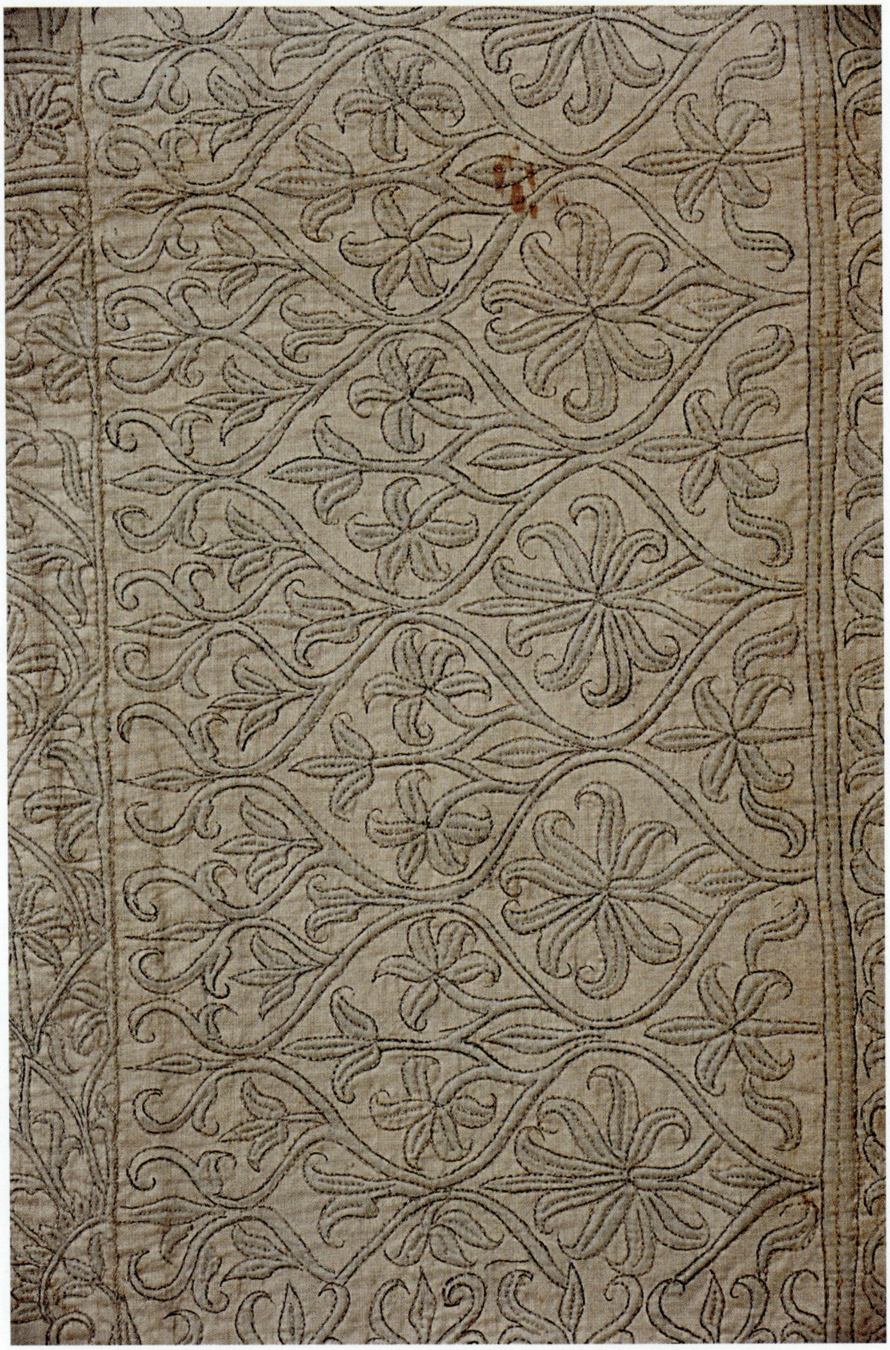

Machine Quilting
Quilt
Layers of white cotton fabric with a floral motif in an ogee layout and a border. Its style resembles a distinctive group of the embroidered Satgaon Quilts crafted in Bengal.
MSMS II Museum, Jaipur
Reserve collection

QUILTING

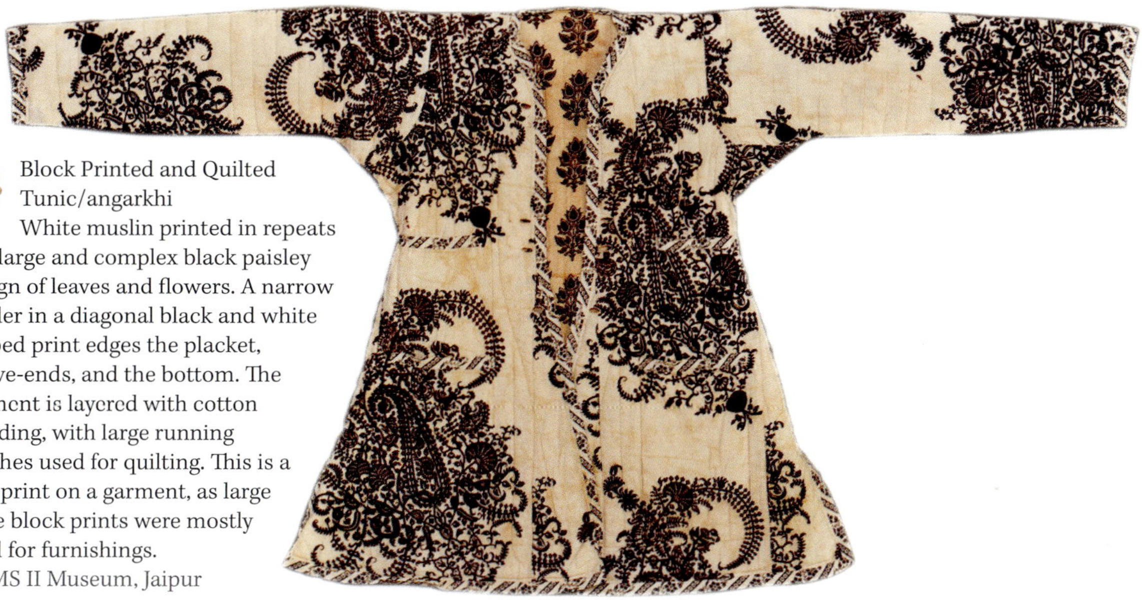

Block Printed and Quilted Tunic/angarkhi
White muslin printed in repeats of a large and complex black paisley design of leaves and flowers. A narrow border in a diagonal black and white striped print edges the placket, sleeve-ends, and the bottom. The garment is layered with cotton wadding, with large running stitches used for quilting. This is a rare print on a garment, as large scale block prints were mostly used for furnishings.
MSMS II Museum, Jaipur
LA-198

The people of India have practised the art of quilting through the centuries, creating objects that blend utility with beauty. Quilts form an intrinsic facet in the journey of textiles in the country, from rural settings to palaces and to the markets of Europe. As Patrick Finn has observed, 'Over millennia, Indian quilters incorporated ideas from around the globe and influenced those outside India. The advent of the Mughals and Portuguese saw the infusion of many new possibilities. The British introduced continental elements, and in the twentieth century, quilting emerged as a commercial business and focus of revitalisation projects.'[1]

The recycling of worn cloth, for functional and domestic purposes—largely for staying warm—was an integral part of the nation's enduring belief in sustainable lifestyles. Meant as reinforcement to the base fabric, the characteristic and refined embroidery is replete with symbolism, creativity, and finesse. This art form showcases the virtue of how embroidery changes an old and used fabric into a work of excellence.

In addition, this practice was embraced to express the religious symbolism of asceticism, as re-using fabrics also had underlying implications of renunciation and low value given to worldly riches and pleasures. Traditional quilting is perhaps a prime example of not only recycling, but also upcycling—a highly relevant added value to the production of quilts in India.

The history and origin of quilts is largely undocumented, and the fragility of the woven fabric used ensured that few examples have been preserved. However, their prevalence in early historic times is evidenced in the literature and sculpture of that era. In a pre-7th century depiction, we find a tunic quilted in a vertical design, and a 1st century BCE Kushana period sculpture of the Buddha draped in a *kantha* robe. 'The *dagala*, a quilted upper garment, is frequently mentioned in the poetry of Surdas and there are references to the *dhuniya* [carders] community by the 17th century.'[2] Importantly, the extant practice of this craft provides an understanding of the process.

The traditional process of making a quilt is simple, involving a few layers of old cotton cloth—saris, dhotis, sheets—laid on top of each other, and sometimes interspersed with cotton wool or feathers to form a padding. This is assembled according to the dimensions

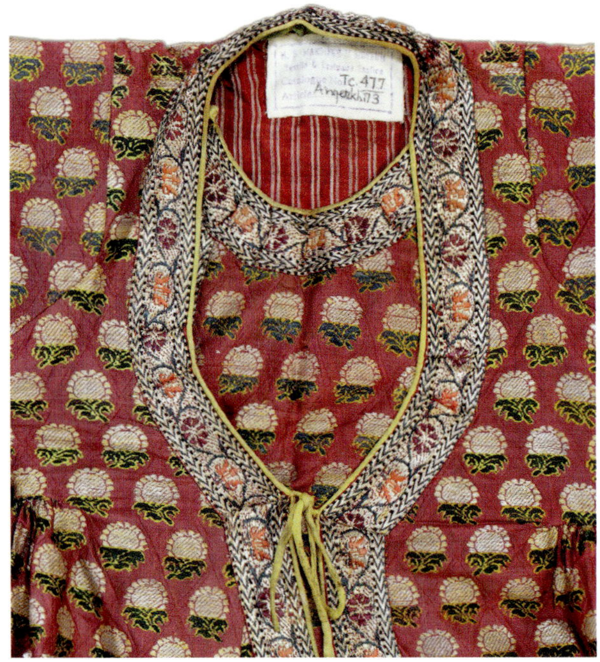

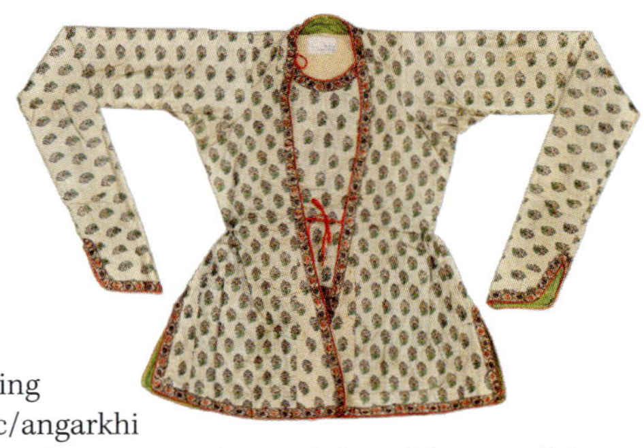

Quilting
Tunic/angarkhi
White silk woven with metal thread, has small *butis* in gold and green, with pink highlights. The sleeve ends are slit with a lacing in a green coloured fabric. A red and black zari border with a red piping is found along all the edges, and there are small red ties in the front. The garment is lined with off-white muslin, and is machine-quilted in an all-over diamond pattern.
MSMS II Museum, Jaipur
477.73

Top: Quilted
Child's angarkhi
The pink woven silk in a brocade technique has an all-over design of small sunflower-like *butis* in white and green. A scrolling floral border on the neck as well as on the placket is edged with a yellow *magazi*, which also forms the ties. The garment is lined with red and white striped cotton fabric, and is machine-quilted in an all-over diamond pattern.
71 cm (length)
MSMS II Museum, Jaipur
632.75

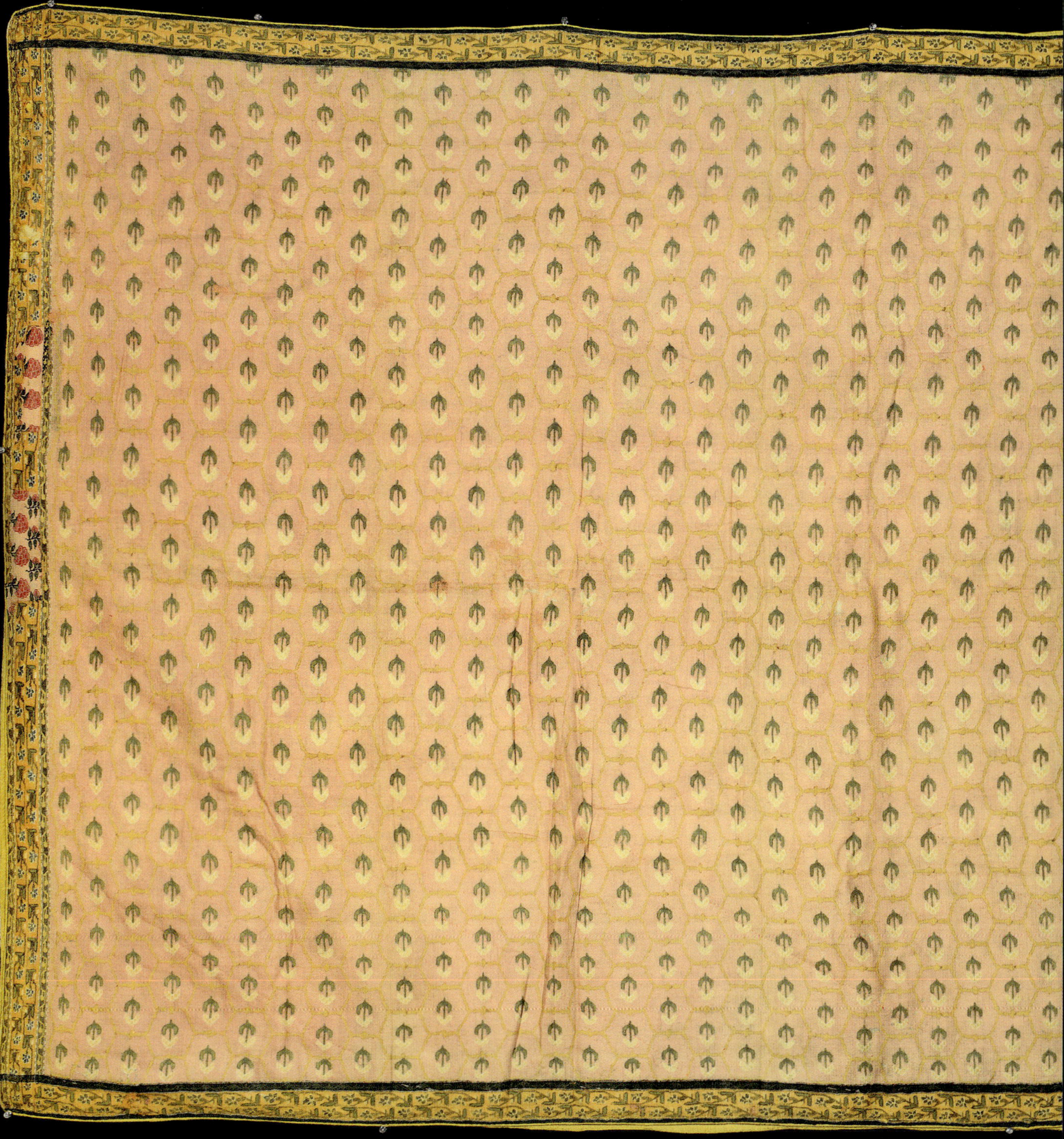

Quilting
Quilt
Peach cotton quilt covered with a small flower *buti* in white and green, printed in a yellow honeycomb lattice pattern. It is bordered with a floral scrolling design of yellow and dark green.
95 x 47 cm
MSMS II Museum, Jaipur
TC/970/76

of the fabrics at hand—the largest lengths for the back, shorter pieces for the padding, and the most preserved pieces of cloth are stitched together for the top. The layers are joined with a running stitch by hand (nowadays with a machine), manipulated to create different shapes and motifs displaying ornamented surfaces that are unique to different parts of India.

The usage of a quilted piece was determined by its thickness and size. Regular items included clothes, diapers, applications for protection against injury, bedcovers or mattresses, bags, and trappings for animals. Curtains, floor spreads, and blinds were also quilted to either preserve the heat or to keep it out, depending on the season.

Quilts are fabricated using local resources and skill sets in multiple ways—patchwork, appliqué, whole cloth, or combinations of these—to create varying effects. The choice of material, construction, and design depended on the region and culture, Gujarat hosting the maximum number of quilting styles, with Rajasthan close behind. Each region has a distinctive character and the products are known by different names therein—*kantha* in Bengal, *sujani* in Bihar, *ralli* and *godra* in Gujarat, *ralli* and *gudri* in Rajasthan, *koudi* in Karnataka, *kontha*s in Orissa, *ledras* in Jharkhand, *kanduri* in UP, *gudharis* in Maharashtra, *tatiyasthan gudri* and *kanduri* in Uttar Pradesh, *gudri*s that are appliquéd and embroidered in Orissa, and more. According to Finn, there are over 70 words describing quilts made across India.

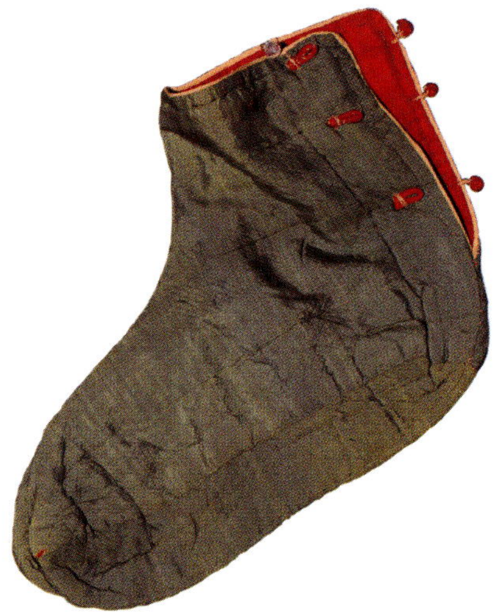

Quilting
Socks
Green silk sock lined with red and quilted with a running stitch. The cuff and back are edged with a fine yellow piping, and the back is open—with three red buttons and loops for closing.
MSMS II Museum, Jaipur
TC.673.75

Jaipur and Uttar Pradesh are especially known for producing *razai* or quilt. The continuing large scale production of these leads us to believe that Jaipur was a big quilting centre from the earliest times. It is recorded that trading in quilts was carried on till the 18th century. The lightweight Jaipur *razai* uses block printed muslin as a stitched cover. This is filled with delicate desi cotton wool and carded with a fluffing bow or a machine to make the cotton soft and billowy. This singular carding process has been honed over generations. At the end, the quilting, done by men and boys, follows a simple, straight, running stitch with a thick cotton thread.

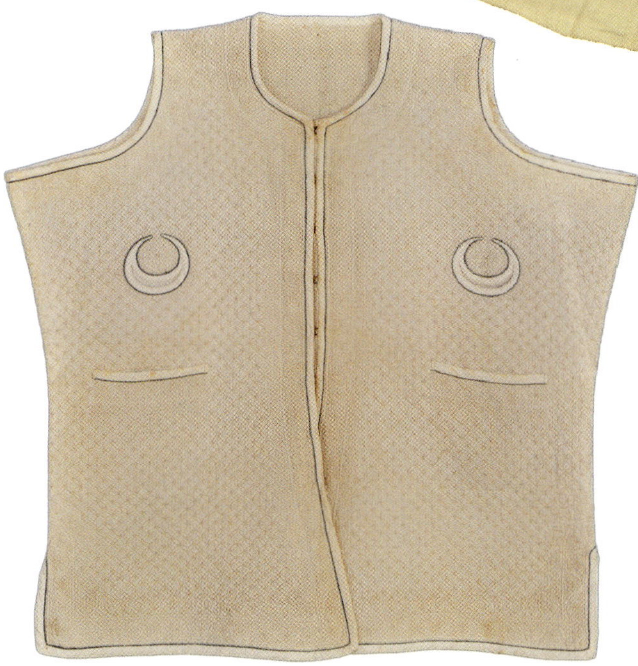

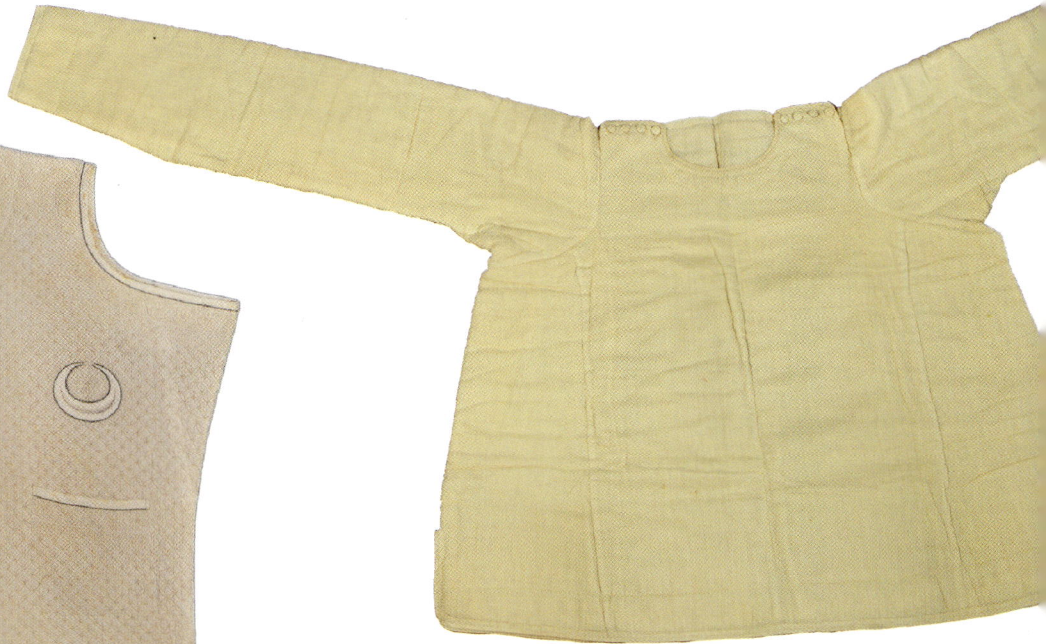

Left: Quilting
Waistcoat
White cotton machine-quilted in a self-coloured all-over floral design. A white crescent is appliqued above the pockets on both sides of the chest, and all the edges are piped with white fabric. A reflection of Satgaon Quilts can be seen in the piece.
MSMS II Museum, Jaipur
TC/G3

Right: Quilting
Sadri
Cream muslin quilted garment for a child.
(sleeve length-23"; length-20"; chest-40"; bottom-24")
MSMS II Museum, Jaipur
TC/C-51

Whether the fine machine quilted pieces in the City Palace Museum collection were made in Jaipur is not clear, but those padded with cotton wool were most likely from there, as the procedure used resembles that of *razai* making exercised in the city today.

Although very few quilts have survived from the past, there is a diverse representation available at the museum. The items include cotton, silk, brocade, and Kashmir embroidery with *mashru*, which have been documented in detail. A number of clothing pieces in the museum are quilted both by hand and by machine, with varying degrees of thickness and fineness in their workmanship.

ENDNOTES

1. Jasleen Dhamija, preface to *Quilts of India—Timeless Textiles*, by Patrick J. Finn (New Delhi: Niyogi Books, 2014).
2. Krystyna Hellstrom, Jaipur Quilts (New Delhi: Niyogi Books, 2012), p. 39.

Varak
Odhni
Fine light orange/yellow muslin printed with silver floral *chand-tare butis* in an all-over arrangement. Edged with a border and silver *gota*, the two ends have a row of large floral *butas*.
MSMS II Museum, Jaipur
TC B 92

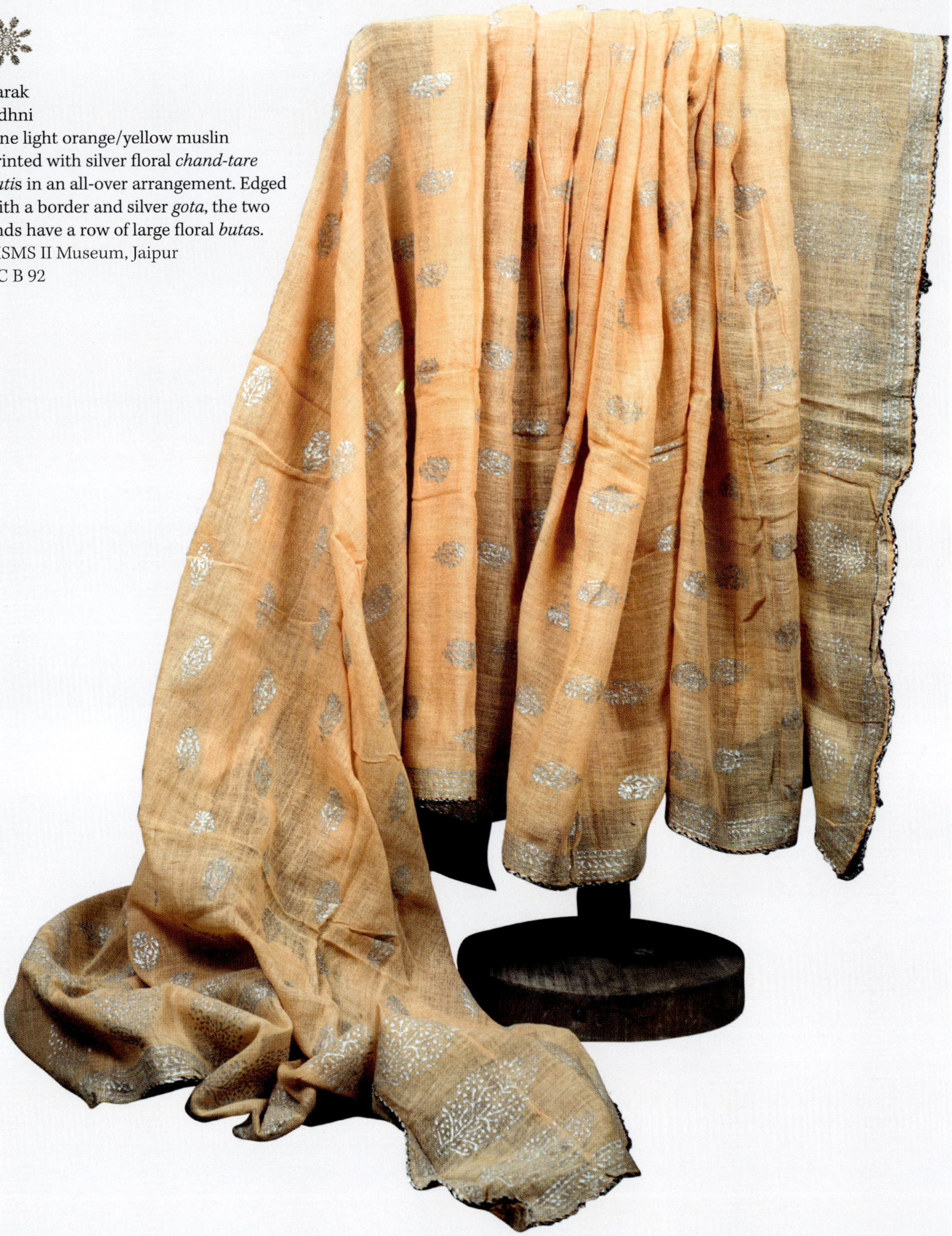

VARAK & KHADI

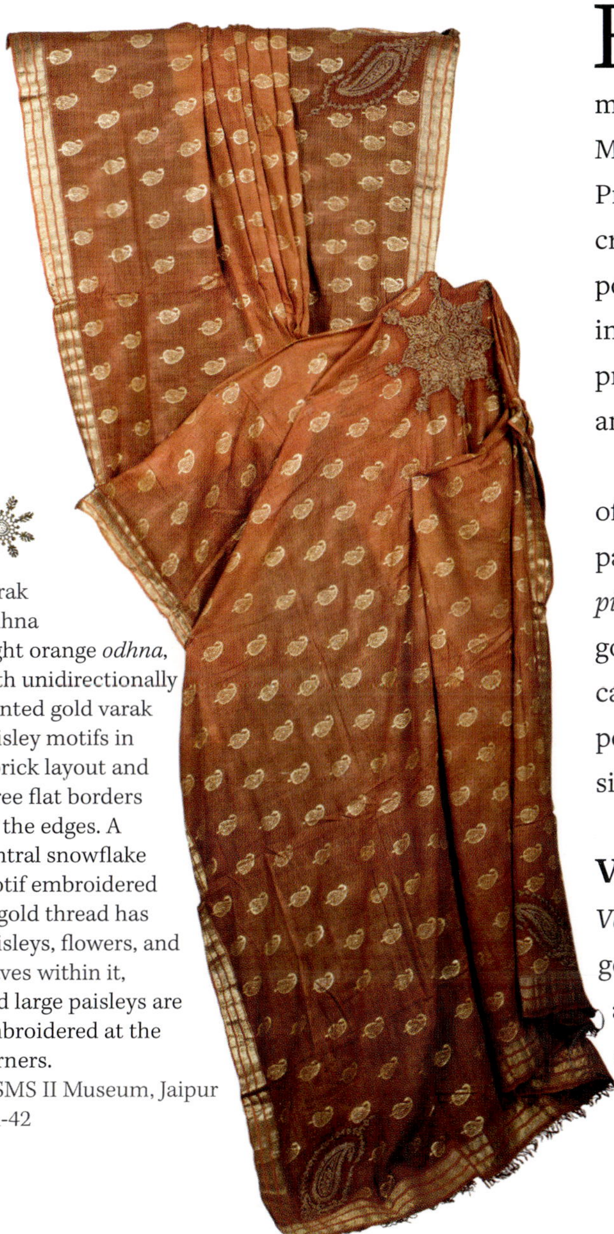

Varak
Odhna
Light orange *odhna*, with unidirectionally printed gold varak paisley motifs in a brick layout and three flat borders on the edges. A central snowflake motif embroidered in gold thread has paisleys, flowers, and leaves within it, and large paisleys are embroidered at the corners.
MSMS II Museum, Jaipur
LA-42

Evidence, as early as the 5th century BCE, points to block printing in India using metallic substances. Rulers in Rajasthan, Gujarat, Madhya Pradesh, Delhi, Uttar Pradesh, Himachal Pradesh, and Andhra Pradesh patronized the craft for many centuries henceforth. Records point to its vibrant presence 80 years ago even in the village of Samba in Jammu. In Rajasthan printing with *varak* was known as *sunehri* (gold) and *rupehri* (silver) printing.

The hallmark of this craft is the stamp of royalty. Royal clothing, flags, bedspreads, palanquins, tents, curtains, pillow covers, and *pichhwais* bore gold printing. The printing of gold and silver on textiles fall into two broad categories: *khadi* or printing using a metallic powder, and *varak* or the application of gold or silver leaf.

Varak

Varak is an exceedingly thin metal foil made of gold or silver. It is used on textile surfaces to set agleam particular parts of the design. Gold and silver *varaks* are often applied as garnish on festive foods, made in the Ayurvedic tradition, because of their healing properties; used for

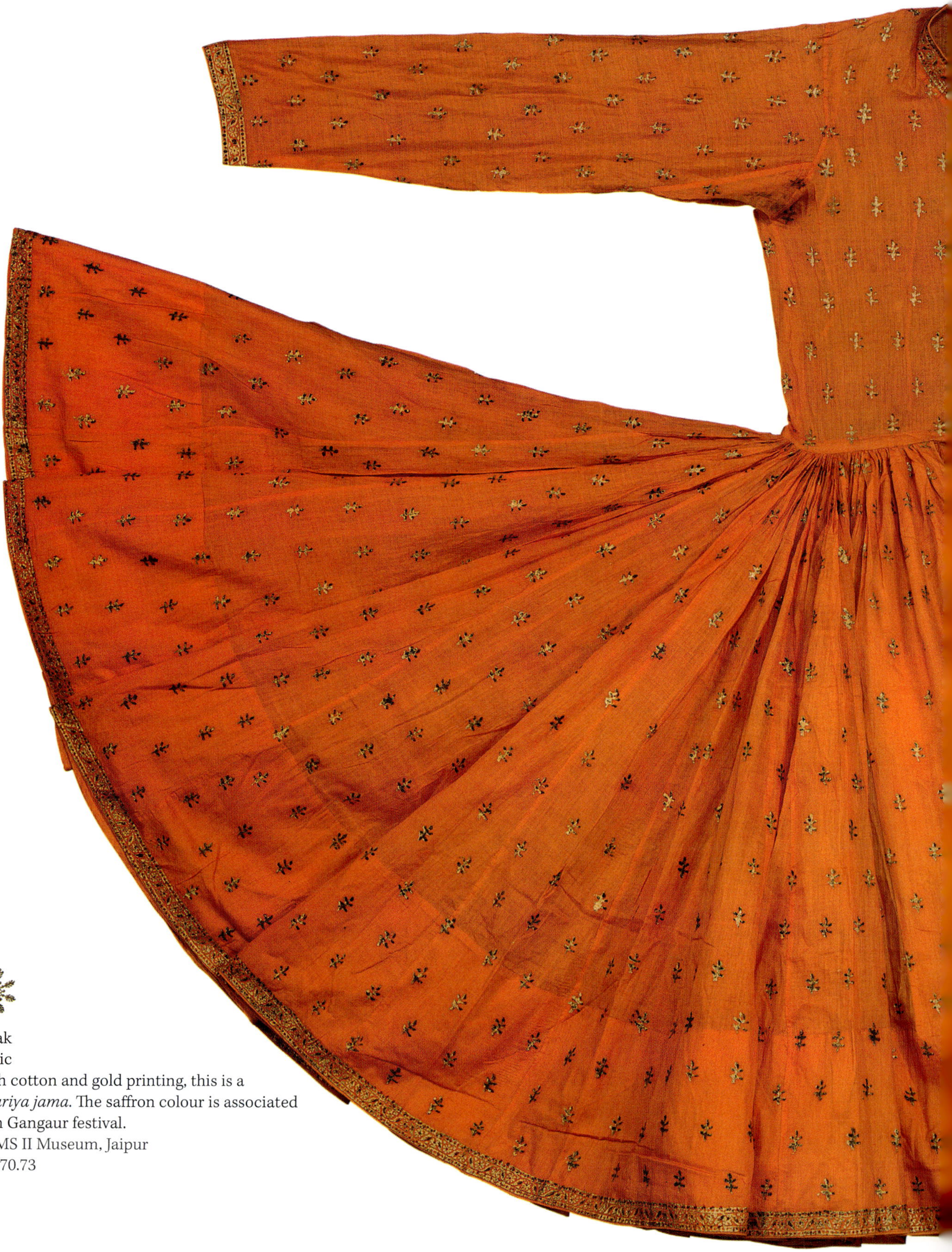

Varak
Tunic
With cotton and gold printing, this is a *kesariya jama*. The saffron colour is associated with Gangaur festival.
MSMS II Museum, Jaipur
Tc.470.73

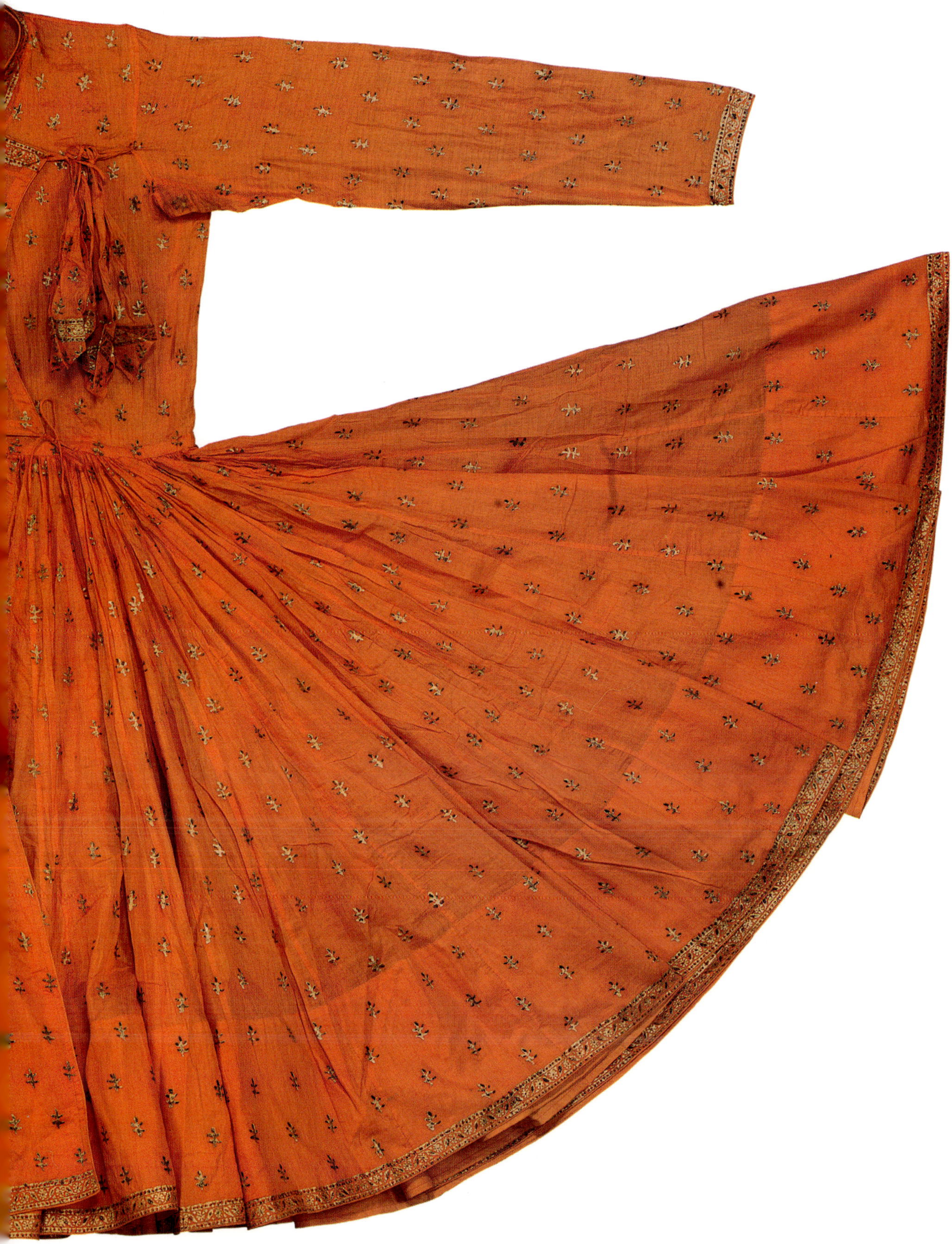

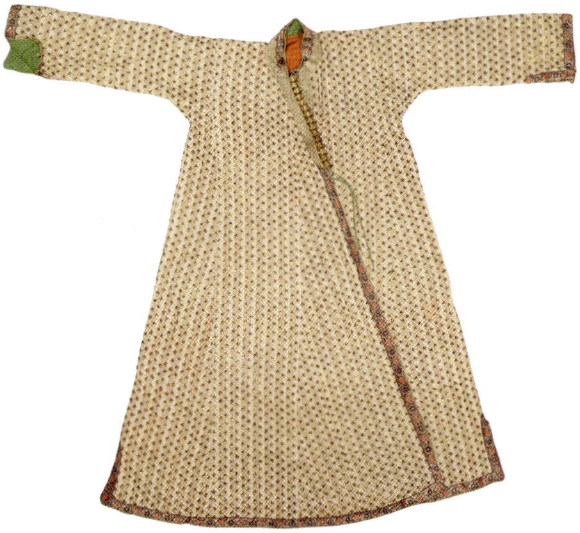

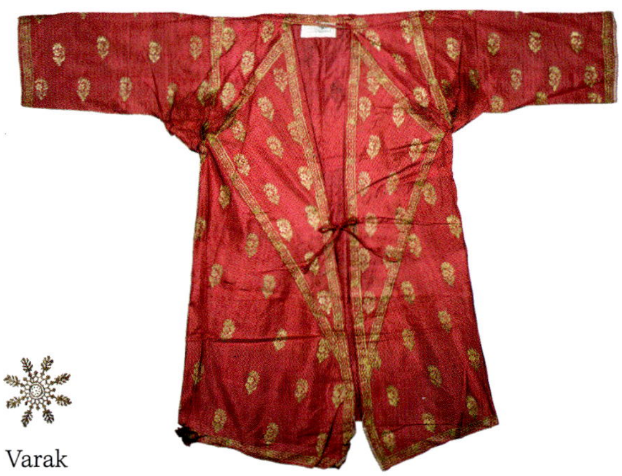

Varak
Jacket
Deep pink cotton jacket with an all-over gold floral motif, and a gold border at the sleeve-ends, armhole seams, neck, bottom, and front opening. The border also outlines the shape of a large lapel on both sides of the opening, which is secured with a red tie.
MSMS II Museum, Jaipur
TC 434-73

Top: Varak and Quilting
Angarakhi
With a cream and beige striped base, this tunic has an all-over print of small *buti*s in gold and black running along the stripes in an all-over print. The neck, sleeve ends, the front opening, and the bottom have a woven border in beige, black, and red. There are ornamental zari *ghundi*s and green ties in the centre of the chest. The garment is stitched in panels, and quilted with fine cotton wadding and linings in green and dull red.
MSMS II Museum, Jaipur
TC-481-72

enameling on metal; and it is also common to see *varak* on religious idols in Hindu, Buddhist, and Jain temples, as it is considered auspicious to offer *varak* as ornaments at the temples.

Today, Jaipur, Sanganer, Jodhpur, and Sawai Madhopur in Rajasthan keep alive the tradition of *varak* production. Surat, Lucknow, Varanasi, Hyderabad, and Delhi are smaller centres for this craft. Though many households in these places still actively practise the craft, it no longer remains their main occupation due to the spiralling costs of the raw materials.

An inseparable part of printing, the wooden block—or *chhapa*—is synonymous with varak printing. Each of these blocks varies in shape. Designing the wooden block requires consummate skill. The artisan needs to be adept both in the selection of the wood, and in the making of the mould and its handle. The newly made wooden block is always kept immersed in oil for longevity as well as protection against moths and termites. These blocks vary in shape and in the motifs imprinted on them. Each of them possesses a wooden handle on the top to allow the artisan a firm grip during the transfer of the motif impression onto the cloth.

Earlier, the handle of the block as well as the carved design would be made using a single piece of wood, but today, handles are nailed separately on to the carved block. The blocks have minute perforations for multiple reasons: for the air to escape, to minimize the formation of air bubbles, and to prevent the obstruction of printing paste while printing. Wooden blocks used for *varak* printing are carved only in positive relief. In some

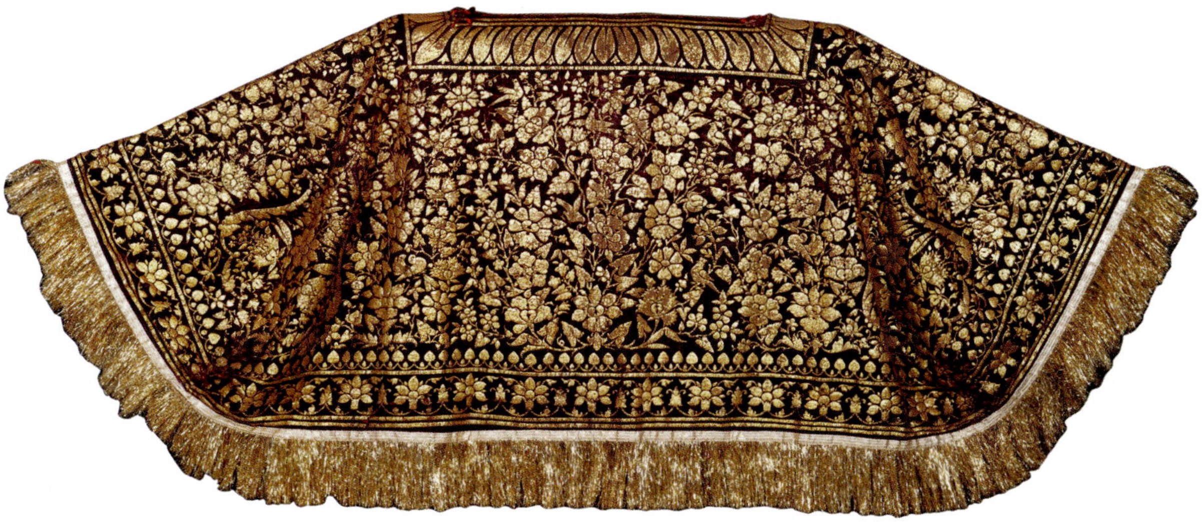

Varak
Mahadol cover
Aubergine velvet doli cover, with a red cotton lining, an all-over thick and raised gold print—a garden of flowers/*buti*s and birds—with a leaf designed centre, and a floral border edged with white tape, finished with a gold *kinari*.
MSMS II Museum, Jaipur
TC 887.75

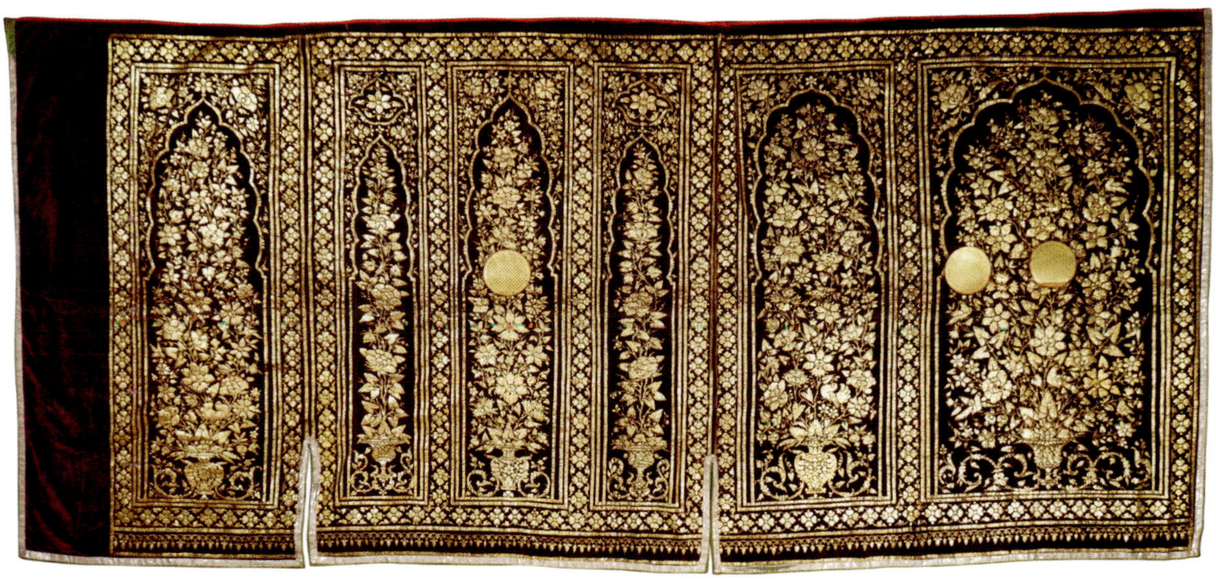

Varak
Cover piece
Aubergine velvet piece with raised gold printing of intricate and ornate tree-of-life motifs, within arched panels of irregular sizes separated by a scrolling border. The sides are framed by the same border and finished with a silver *gota*. Three circular *jali*s have been provided for air circulation and to see outside.
MSMS II Museum, Jaipur
TC-484-75

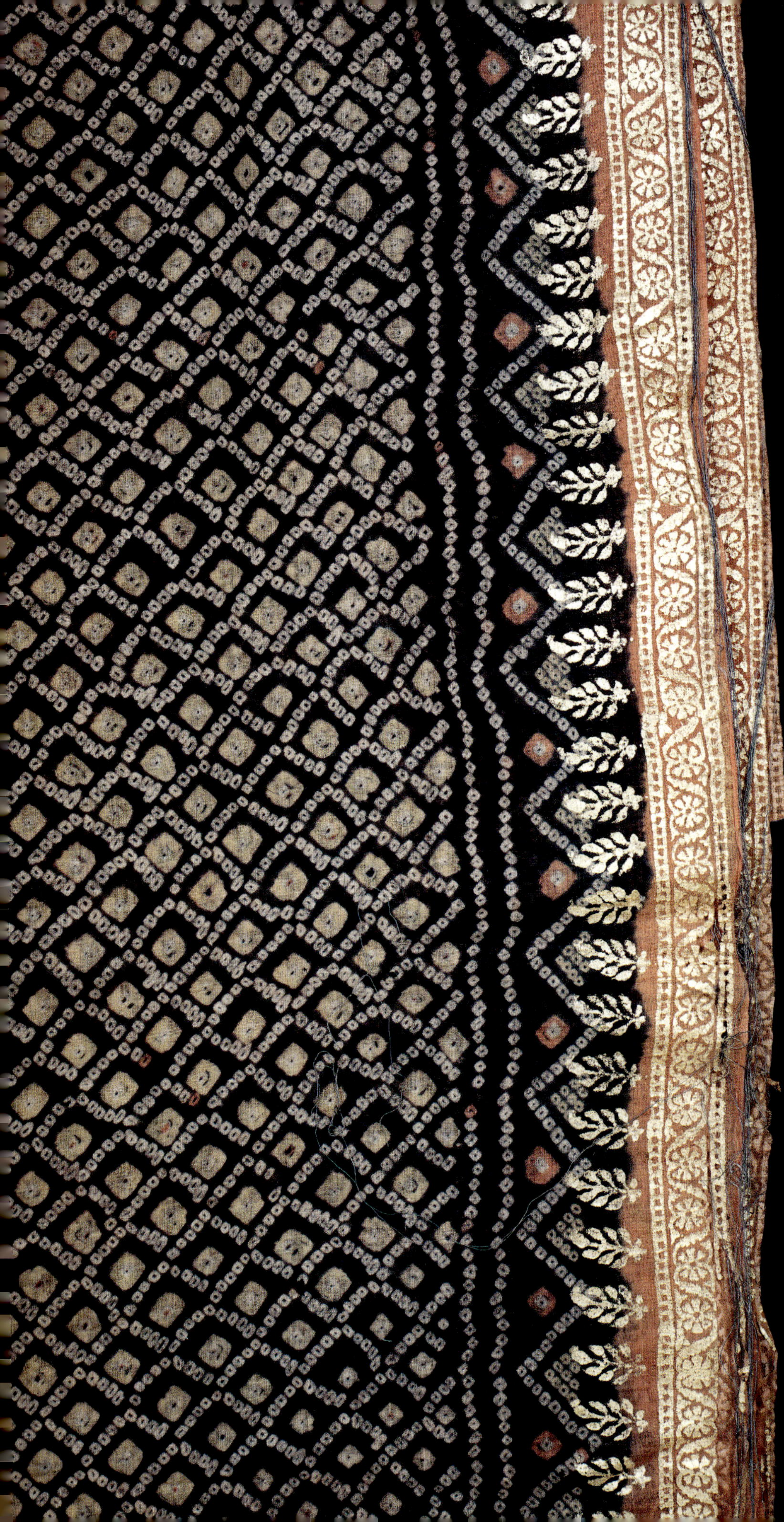

Varak and Bandhani
Odhna
Black cotton base with an all-over design of a tie-dyed diamond-shaped motif in yellow, red, and white. Its border, edged in orange, is over-printed with gold *varak* in a floral bel and small *butas* of a leaf shape.
MSMS II Museum, Jaipur
TC P 57

cases, they are armed with iron spikes to emboss the design. Metal stencils are made using a brass sheet, which is cut according to the required shape. The design is traced on paper and then glued to the brass sheet. Small holes are drilled in the design and the motif is finely cut out, using a wire saw.

The art of making *varak* is a very specialized process and involves interleaving leather membranes dusted with finely powdered soapstone, with gold or silver pieces in between. These layers are then stacked in small bundles bound on all four sides with a *cheep* or *chimti* (wooden clip), and placed in a thick leather case known as a *pharma*. The pouch is pounded with an iron hammer on a fixed stone slab for anywhere between three to eight hours, or until the metal substance inside is flattened to a fine gold or silver leaf.

The weather conditions, such as humidity and temperature, affect the quality, especially of gold *varak,* as it is more malleable and susceptible to developing cracks if the air is too dry.

The fragile finished leaves are stored in a flat position (so as not to crush or crumple them) between fine kite or butter paper, and preserved in a dry and cool place.

When printing with gold/silver leaf *varak*, the fabric is spread on a *pattiya*, a low, padded wooden printing table. Wooden blocks are preferred, because they offer a wide workspace, where a sufficient quantity of *varak* can be spread to impart lustre.

Varak washes away when the cloth is laundered. It was traditionally used only for embellishing wedding garments. Recent attempts to circumvent this have been achieved by increasing the amount of adhesive used. The adhesive paste uses *safeda*, a fine white powder and a resin, or *saresh*. Both are heated to their melting point, and then mixed and strained in order to remove any particles and impurities to make a uniform, viscous paste. The readymade paste, which has a longer shelf-life, is also available commercially. The paste is spread thin on a printing pad (a piece of blanket) in a tray. The block is pressed gently on the paste, and then stamped onto the fabric to imprint the design on its surface.

The *varak* is then applied onto this sticky surface, with a small pad in the shape of a little pouch of muslin, which is filled with cotton wool, onto which it adheres. After the complete design has been covered with it, a soft hand brush removes all the residual *varak*. Finally, the cloth is burnished with a rolling pin attached with an agate stone or *moro*, which imparts a glazed effect.

Varak printing has often been accompanied by coloured printing, giving an impression of *jadau* or *meenakari*. At other times, it has also acted as an enhancing technique used with other typically Rajasthani tie-dye textile styles, such as *leheriya*s and *bandhani*s. And in exceptional cases, it has been used to highlight printed photographs of maharajas and historic figures as is seen in the example of the *rumal*s or kerchiefs, from Udaipur.

Varak motifs are an amalgamation of Indian and Persian designs and include *keri-ki-bel* (paisley creeper), *mehrab* (arched niche), *keri-buti*

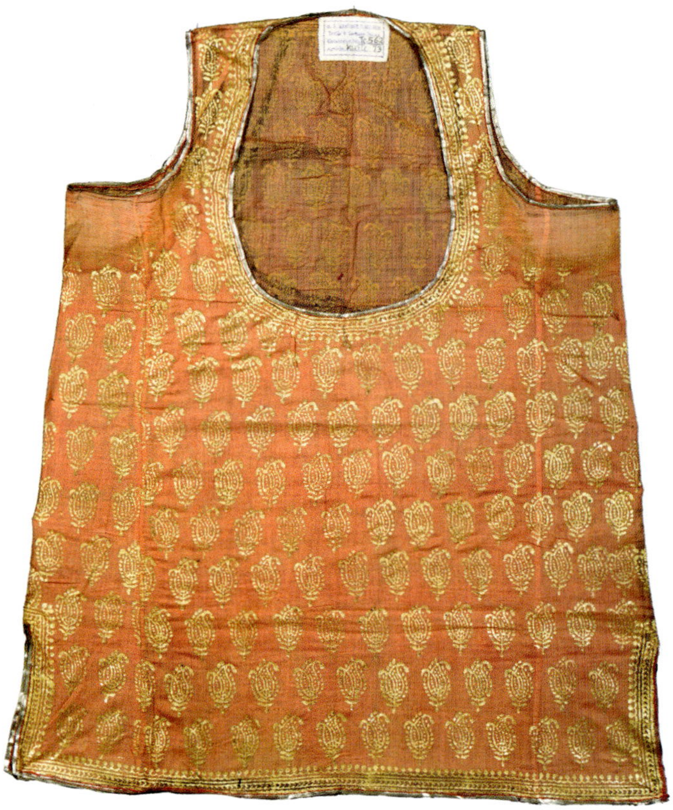

Varak and Gota
Kurti
Light orange kurti with gold printing of a paisley *buti* in an all-over pattern, and edged on the neck and bottom with *chaumasia gota* on the outside.
MSMS II Museum, Jaipur
TC 562.73

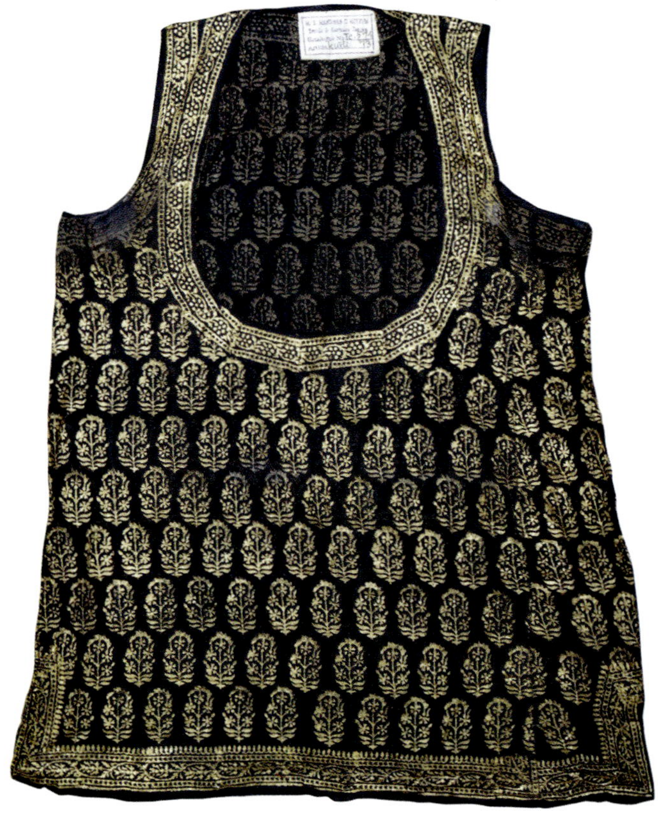

Varak
Kurti
Blue cotton muslin with floral *buta* printed in gold foil, an all-over brick layout, and a floral scrolling border on the neck, armhole, hem, and side slits.
MSMS II Museum, Jaipur
TC 574.73

(paisley), *phul-ki-bel* (floral creepers), *jawar bhat* (jowar pattern), *badam buti* (almond design), as well as figures of deities, such as Radha-Krishna along with *gopis*.

Some other motifs include *putli* (puppet), calf, *gamla* (vase), *suraj* (sun), *chakri* (circular design), *ghevar* (local sweet), *mogre-ka-phul* (white flower), *jhad* (bush), *mor* (peacock), *buta* (large floral pattern), and *kamal-ki-bel* (lotus creeper). Some other designs are created by using dots, a special effect that emanates from the use of wooden blocks with nails: for example, the *jalebi* (a sweetmeat), *kairi* (paisley), and *kenkda* (crab).

Khadi

Khadi, or *chamki* work, as it is popularly called, uses metal in a granular and powdered form to

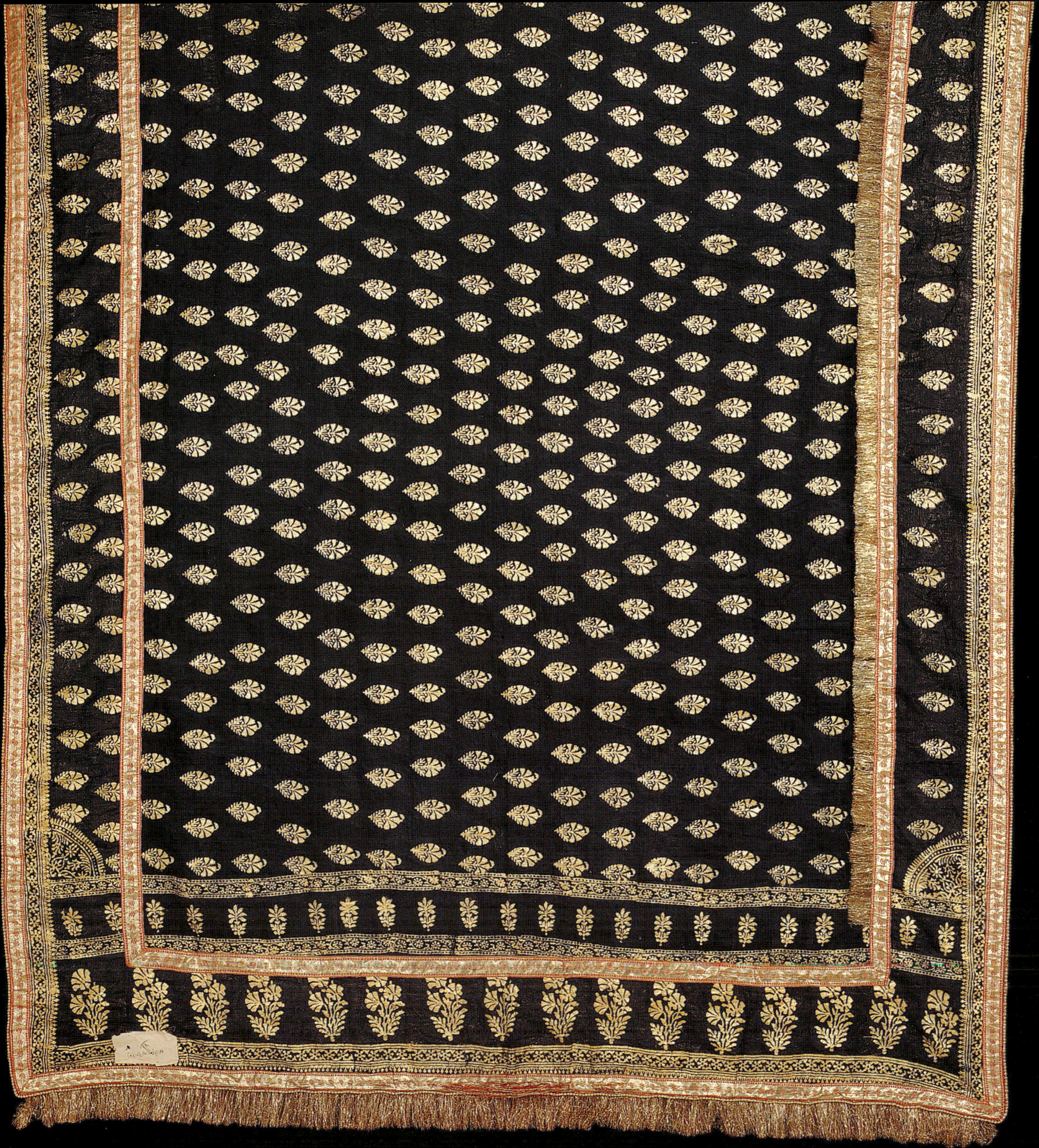

Varak
Odhna
Black fabric with a small floral motif in gold, in an all-over brick pattern. It is bordered by two separated rows of zari on a red tape, and a narrow gold tape along the inside of the outer one. The two ends are finished with a gold *kinari*, and between the two zari, red borders is a panel of large floral *butas*. After this panel, there is another row of a smaller flower *buti* between two rows of a thin zari border. There is a quarter-circle *khaja* motif near the corners.
MSMS II Museum, Jaipur
LA 44

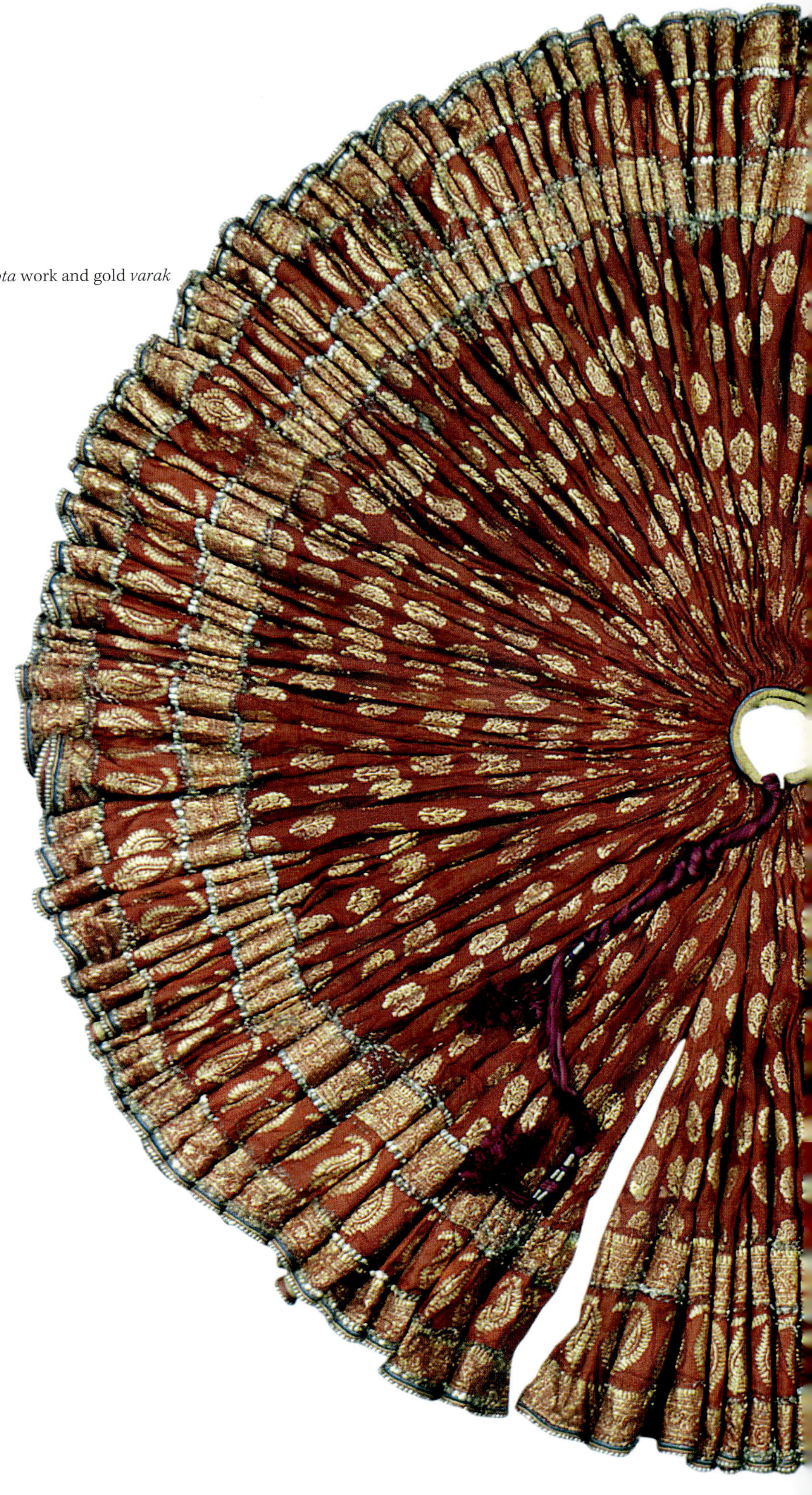

Varak and Gota Work
Ghaghra
Red coloured muslin with *gota* work and gold *varak* embellishing the garment.
MSMS II Museum, Jaipur
Tc 464.73

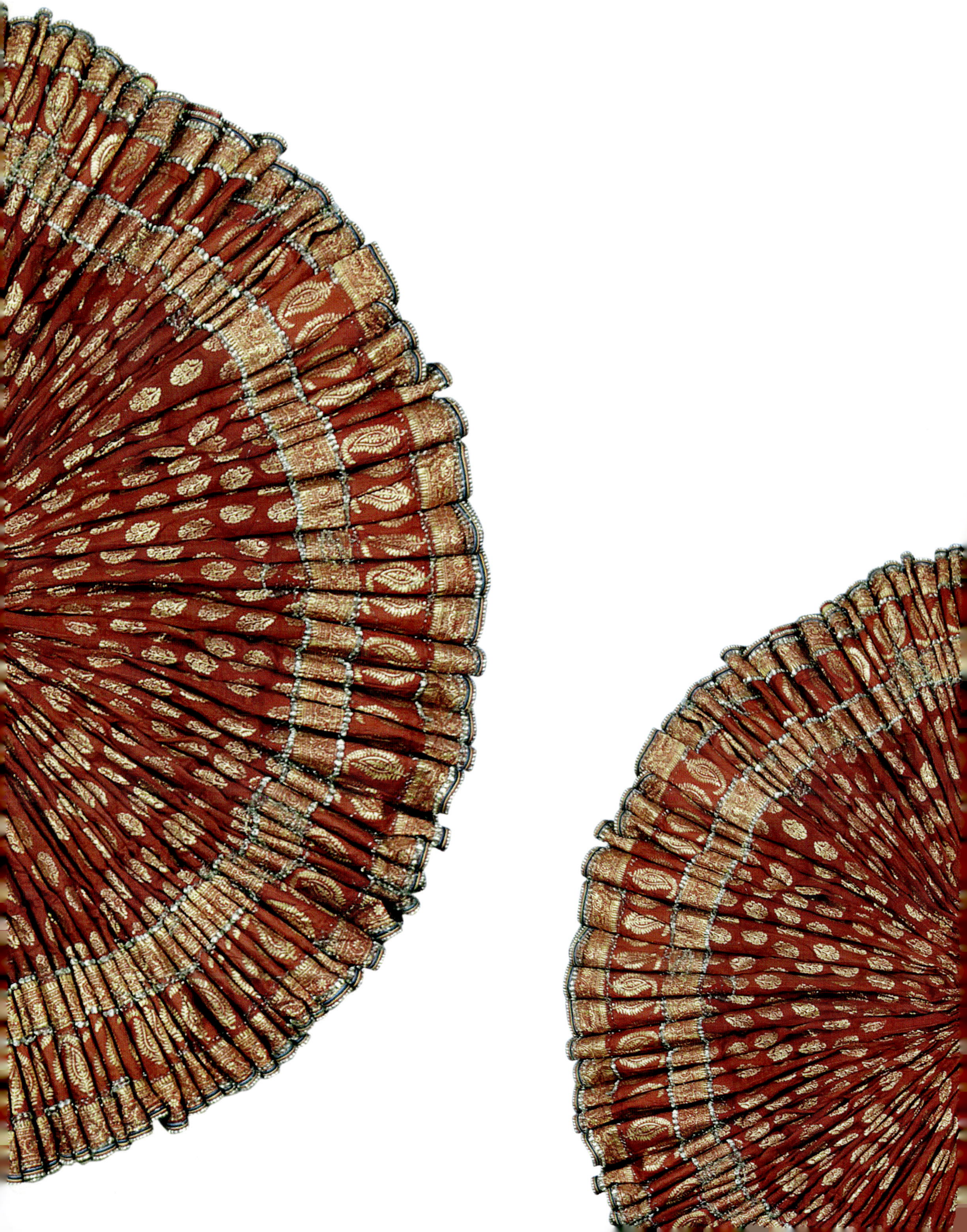

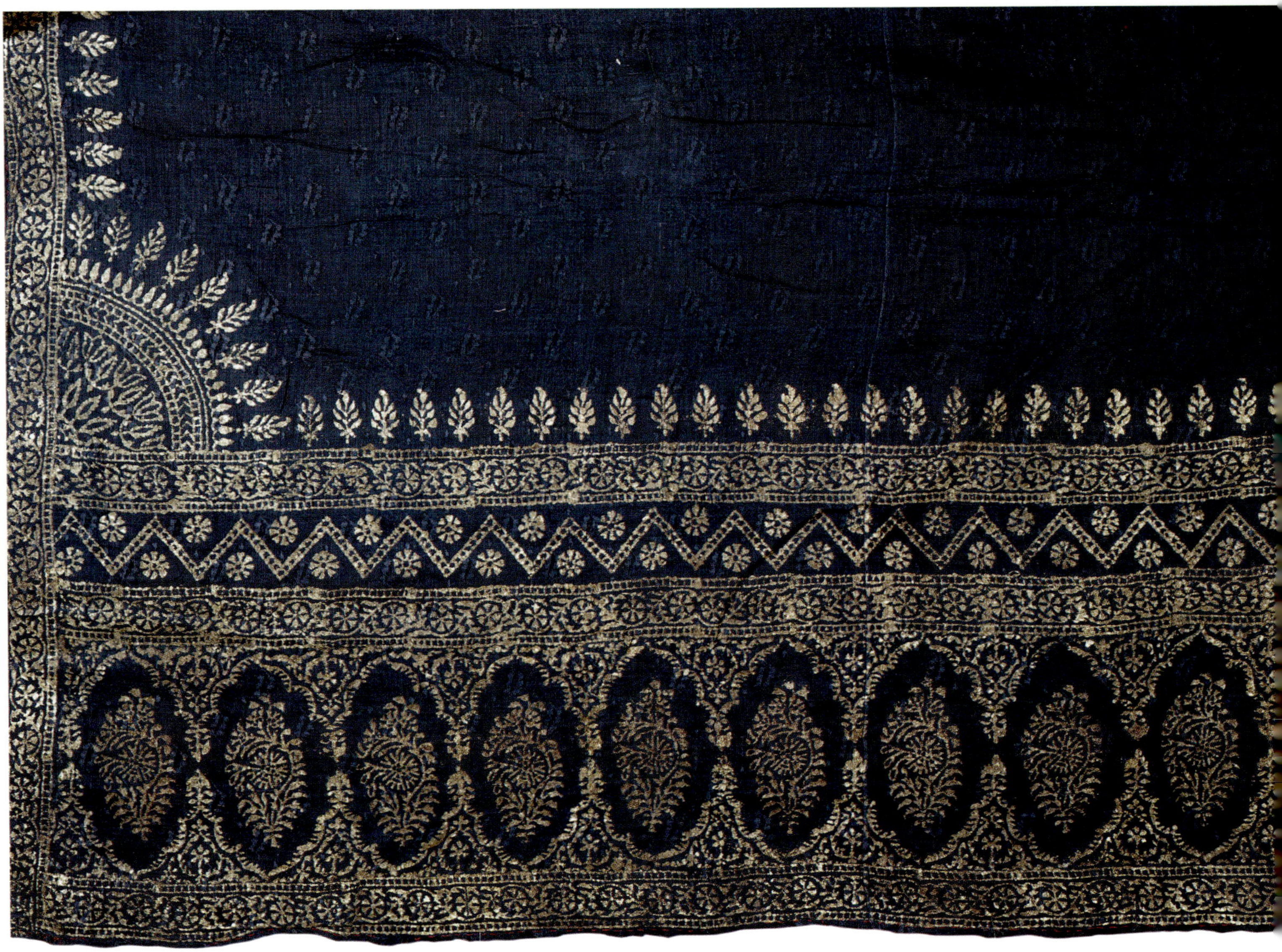

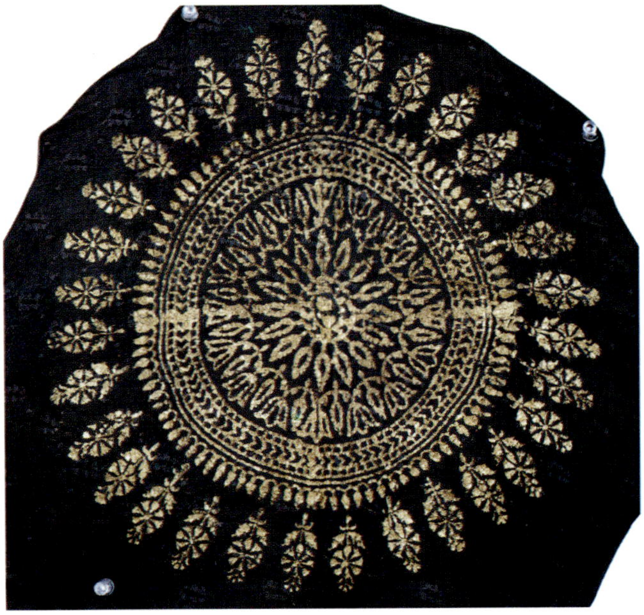

Varak
Odhni
Dark blue cotton with a self-design weave and gold printing of a large circular *khaja* motif in the centre with a radiating multi-floral design.
MSMS II Museum, Jaipur
TC 13 198

add shine and brilliance to the fabric. Flakes of crushed mica or cheaper metal powders have replaced the use of pure gold or silver dust for printing. There is also evidence to show that metallic dust was earlier mixed with the printing paste, *rogan*, and directly applied to the cloth with a wooden block or a stencil (*sancha* and *datta*). *Rogan* is a synthetic adhesive, which when used in isolation, creates a white design on the cloth surface.

Motifs are transferred to the cloth by applying an adhesive on the textile surface, either with a brush, a block, or through a stencil. Two types of blocks, wooden and metallic, were used for tinsel printing.

Wooden block printing remains the oldest, simplest, and the most artistic of all methods; and for tinsel, commonly blocks carved in relief are used. A special engraved brass block called *sancha*, one end of which has a design or motif perforated on it like a stencil, is also used. The *sancha* is paired with a matching carved wooden *datta*, which fits its contours exactly. The two blocks are used together to stamp designs on the cloth.

The *sancha* comes in a variety of shapes; it can be round, oblong, square, or rectangular. It is filled with *rogan*, a thick viscous paste, which the craftsman either prepares himself or purchases as a premix. The *rogan* is often mixed with *chak mitti* (white powder) and kerosene oil. This mixture is heated briefly before it is poured into the *sancha*. The wooden *datta* is then inserted into the *sancha*, and with a syringe-like precision, the paste is pressed out through its perforated end and stamped onto the evenly spread cloth. The stamping action is swift but firm enough to allow the paste to form a thin adhesive film on the fabric. Gold or silver powder is sprinkled on it, before the paste dries. This sticks to the printed design and remains fairly permanent. The excess powder is brushed off, collected, and reused. The procedure is repeated till the entire cloth is printed and it is then hung out on a string to be dried in a shaded place, out of direct sunlight.

The designs are mostly drawn from nature, but the outlines of the motifs appear as broken lines, and more so, when there are curved lines. Common motifs include: *phul* (flower), *buti* (small floral design), *buta* (large floral design), *chandani* (scattered pattern), *mor* (peacock), *mogra* (flower), *keri* (paisley), *surajmukhi* (sunflower), *chakri* (circular design), *do kali ka phul* (two buds), *teen kali ka phul* (three buds), and *khaja* (central design like a sieve).

Single motifs are strewn around the surface of the textile to create sparkling effects. The base fabric is usually red in colour and does not require any pre-treatment as the fixing of the *khadi* is done on the adhesive paste printed on the surface of the fabric.

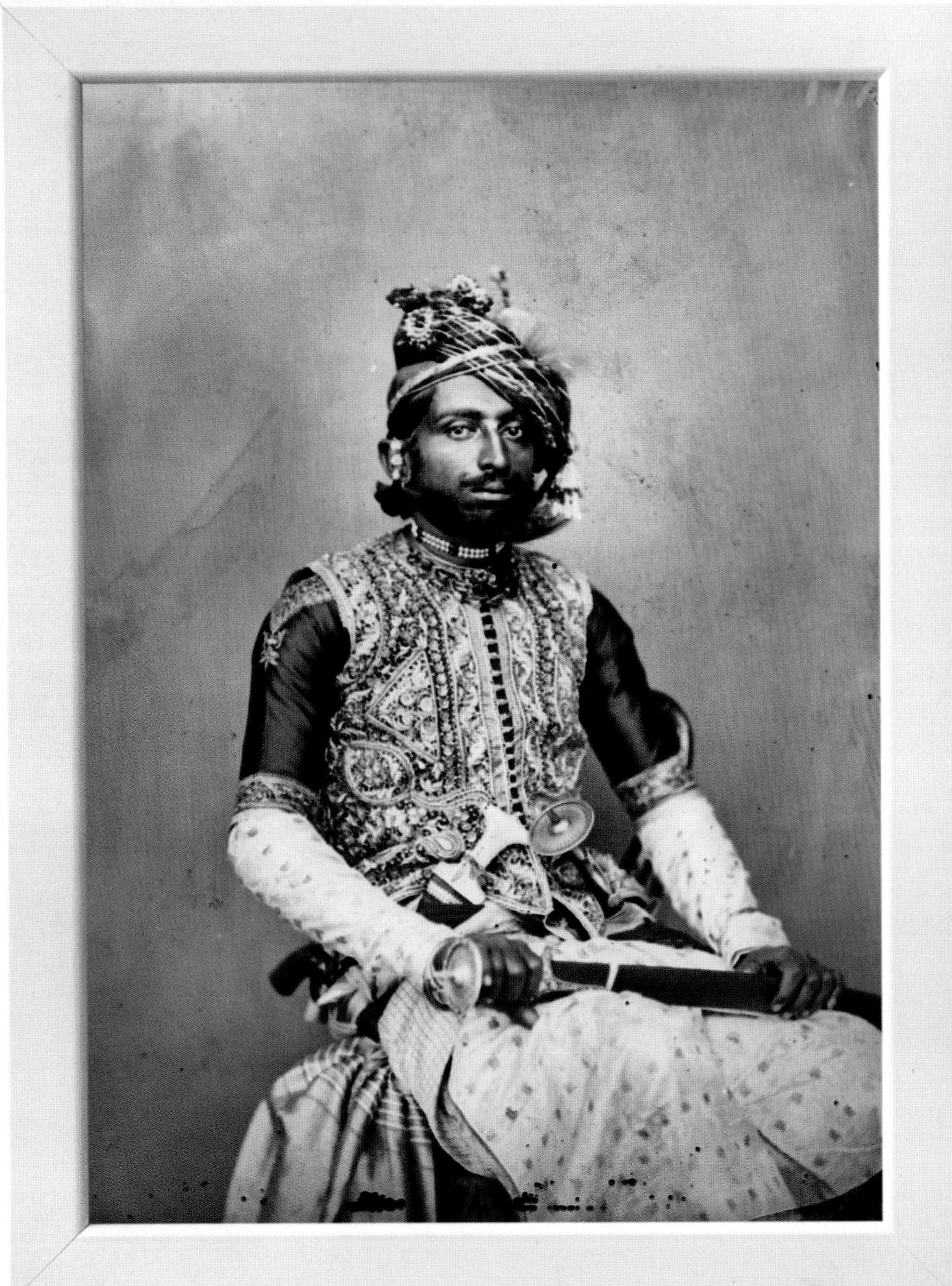

ZARDOZI

Originating from the Persian words 'zar' (gold) and 'dozi' (embroidery), *zardozi* makes use of pure gold and silver wires to fashion a hugely distinctive and illuminative style of embroidery. A contemporary *zardoz* (embroiderer) brings alive a vibrant royal tradition with roots in Mughal culture, which spread through the courts of Rajasthan. It involves adroit use of unalloyed and luminous gold and silver wires, as well as exquisite beads and stones of different sizes and shapes to fill in the patterns outlined by the zari. The outcome is nothing short of spectacular.

Today, the term 'zardozi' is used rather loosely and to refer to all metal-worked surface embroideries. Traditionally, the contours of the traced design are filled using metallic wires. Stylistically, *zardozi* juxtaposes geometrical shapes and *butas* (floral designs), or patterns like the *jaal* (lattice), *bel* (creeper), *chudi* (circular designs), and paisley in a fashion uniquely its own. Flowers, for instance, are often framed within triangles and circles. Borders of garments may sport motifs such as peacocks, parrots, or

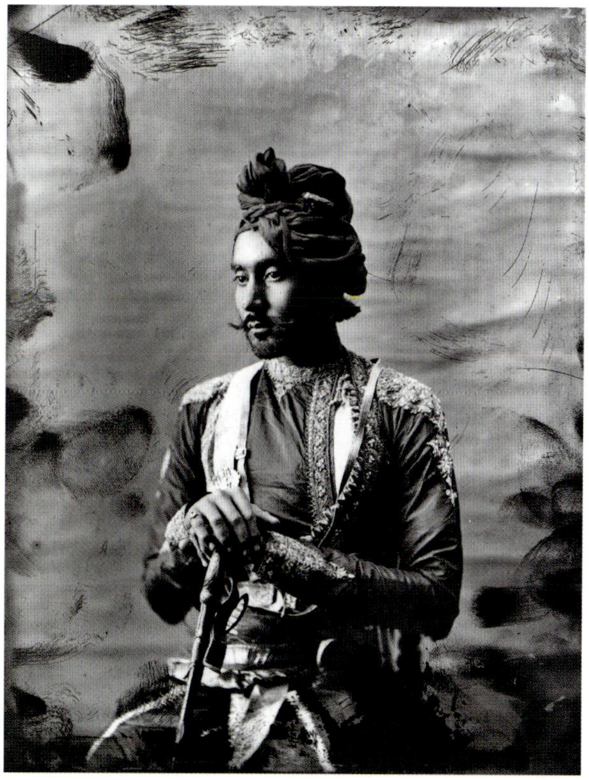

Portrait of a man in an *angarkha* with *zardozi* embroidery.
MSMS II M 2012.04.0012-0011

Facing page: The man is wearing a *zardozi* vest over his upper garment. *Zardozi* work can also be spotted on his sleeves.
MSMS II M 2012.04.0009-0012

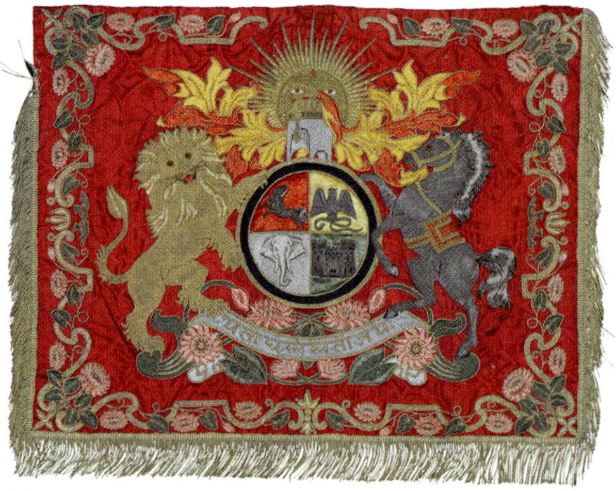

Zardozi
Wall hanging
Red silk with a multi-coloured crest, with a circular design in the centre flanked by a lion on one side and a horse on the other, and a sun above it. It has a scrolling floral border, and gold tassels along the edges.
MSMS II Museum, Jaipur
Reserve collection

mangoes, embroidered with several nuanced variations. Some of the heavier pieces have motifs of animals such as elephants, horses, and tigers. Delicate *jali* or netting is sometimes used over fabrics to beautify it further.

Over the years, two well-defined styles developed in metal embroidery. The *karchobi* (derived from 'karchob', which refers to the framework used to enclose and hold the fabric) is the first offshoot, where the fabric is stretched tightly on a wooden frame and then embroidered with gold or silver wires. This style is recognizable by the density of stiches it demands and by the fact that it uses heavy base materials, like velvet or satin. This style is predominantly used on coats, tent coverings, furnishings, and canopies. The other variation

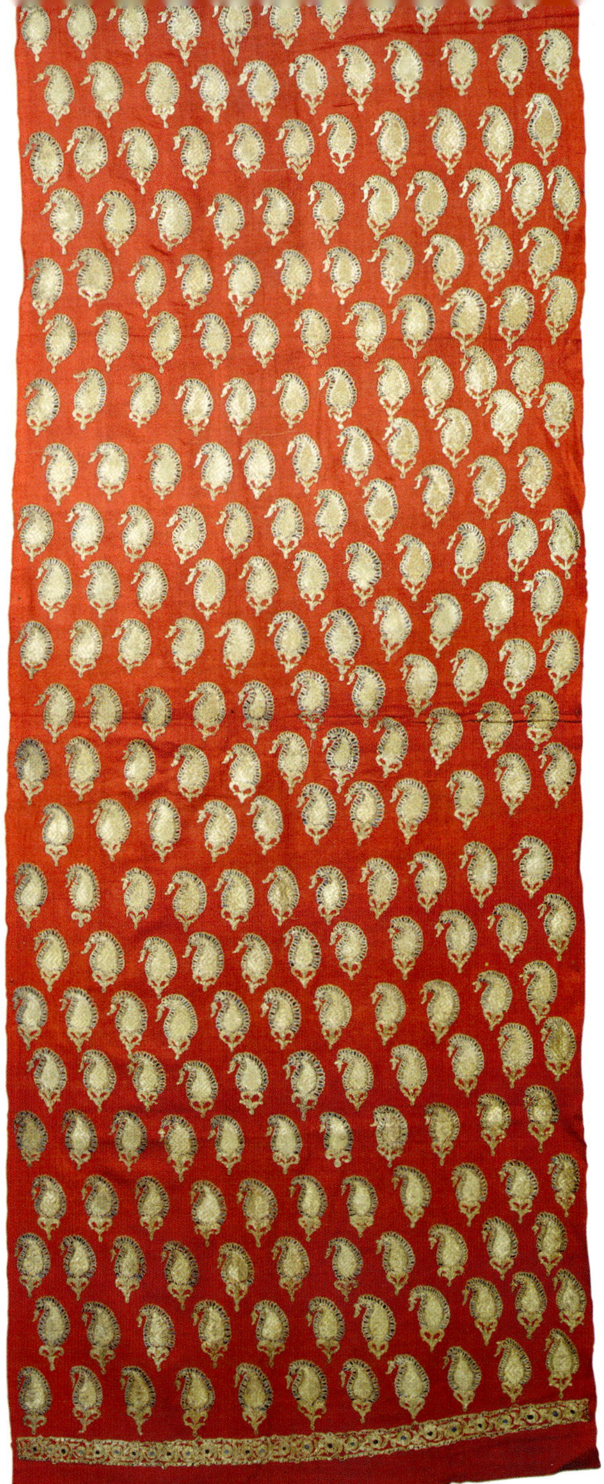

Zardozi
Red woollen fabric, embroidered with golden *kalabattu* (provide meaning) and blue and black silk threads. It has an all-over pattern of paisley motifs and a border of a scrolling bel of circular and leaf designs.
584 x 57 cm
MSMS II Museum, Jaipur
TC 77.73

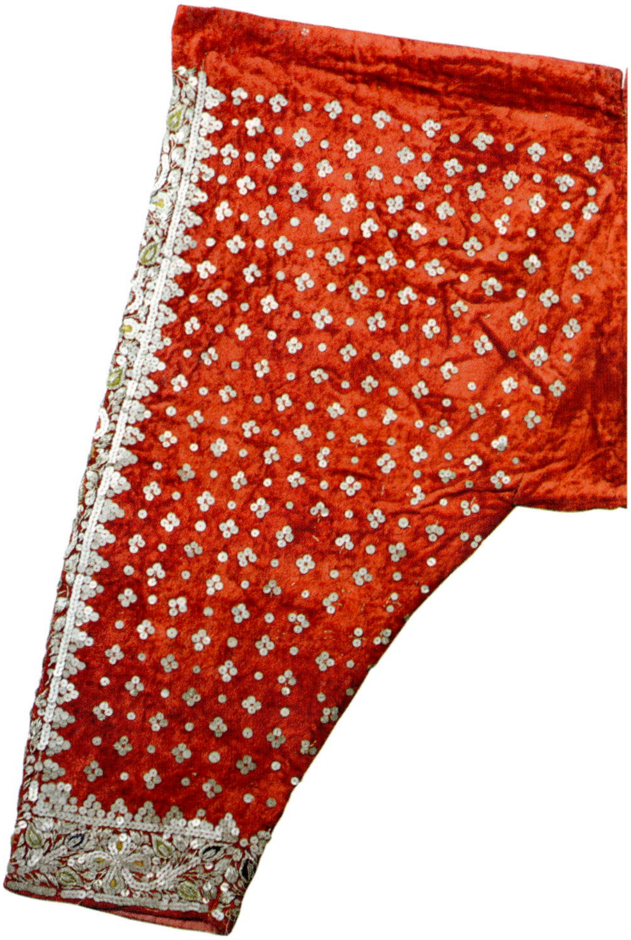

Left: Zardozi
Pyjama
Red velvet with all-over *buti*s, embroidered with *salma-sitara.* The bottom and sides are bordered with a floral bel of yellow and blue thread and silver sequins.
MSMS II Museum, Jaipur
TC-89.79

Below: Zardozi and Quilting
Coat
Velvet coat with *zardozi* embroidery along the neck, placket, and sleeve ends. There is quilting on the inside, which is lined with red silk.
(sleeve length-22"; chest-28"; length-24")
MSMS II Museum, Jaipur
TE/111

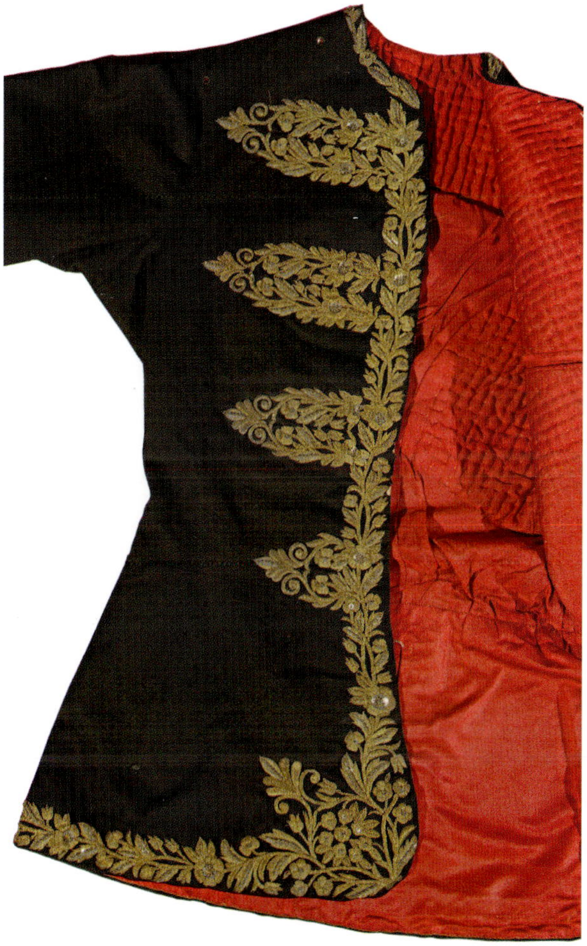

is called *kamdani*, where very refined and ethereal designs are created on fine silk or muslin. Embroiders use it extensively in their bridal wear creations, and on gossamer scarves and veils.

The wires that hold within them the essence of the art of *zardozi* are wound imaginatively and differently in each of the creations, thus creating an entirely new look each time. The *badla*, for instance, is a flattened wire which, when wrapped around silk or cotton threads, takes on the nomenclature of the *kasab*. These threads turn flexible with the wrapping and can be shaped into

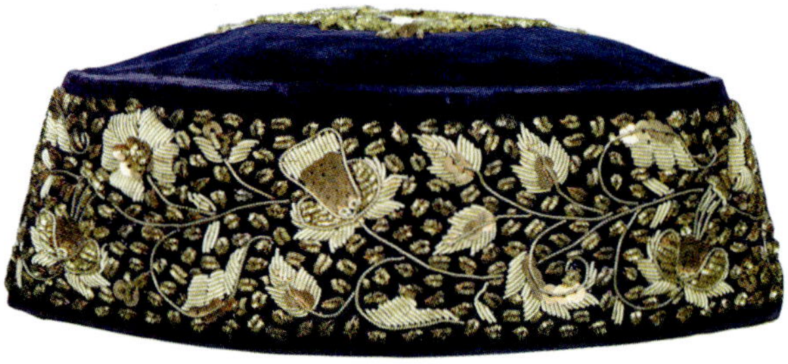

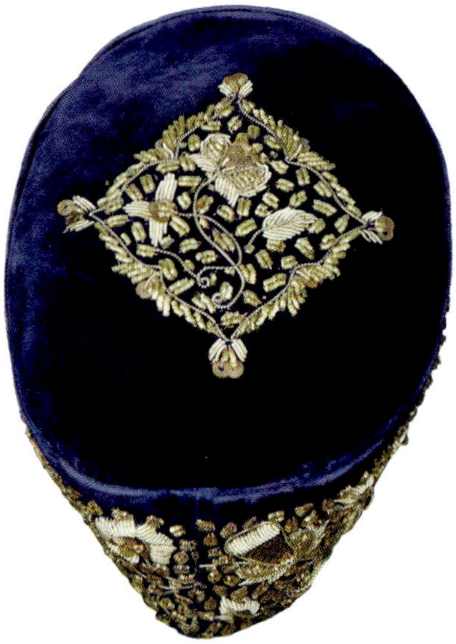

Zardozi
Cap
Purple velvet with gold *zardozi* embroidery. The top circular portion has floral motifs within a square shape, and the base is covered with a wide border in a floral design.
MSMS II Museum, Jaipur
TC 605-73

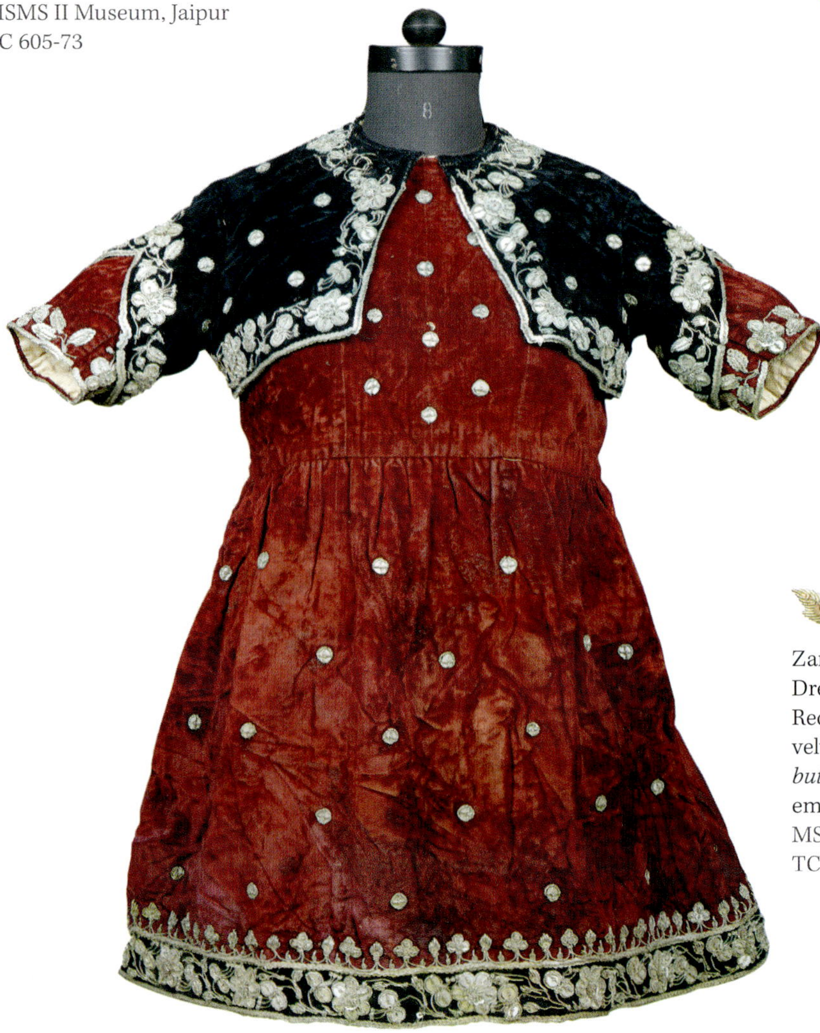

Zardozi
Dress with a small jacket
Red velvet dress with a dark blue velvet jacket; both have small round *butis* and floral scrolling borders embroidered in silver *zardozi*.
MSMS II Museum, Jaipur
TC-22-79

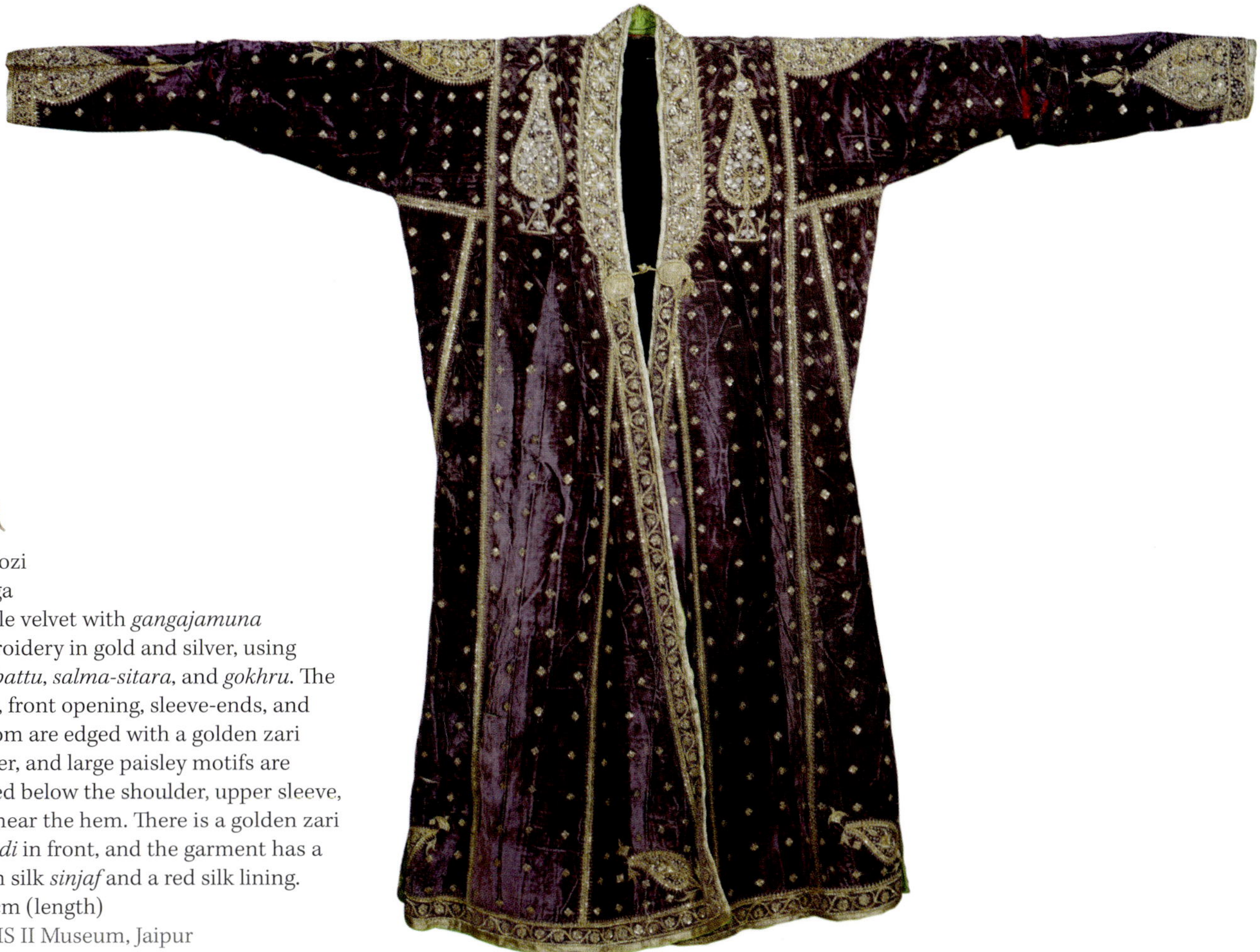

Zardozi
Choga
Purple velvet with *gangajamuna* embroidery in gold and silver, using *kalabattu*, *salma-sitara*, and *gokhru*. The neck, front opening, sleeve-ends, and bottom are edged with a golden zari border, and large paisley motifs are placed below the shoulder, upper sleeve, and near the hem. There is a golden zari *ghundi* in front, and the garment has a green silk *sinjaf* and a red silk lining.
138 cm (length)
MSMS II Museum, Jaipur
TC-854.75

varying thicknesses. Two main colours are used here—*sunheri* (golden) and *rupheri* (silver).

Metal wires are shaped by hand or machine to embellish and enhance the patterns; *salma*, *kora*, *chikna*, *dabka*, *katori*, *kinari*, *kangni*, *chalak*, and *sitara* are some variations. *Salma* refers to zigzag coiled wires used in fashioning the embroidery; it is generally interspersed with *sitaras*, round or star-shaped metal discs. In contrast, *kora* is a mellow, flexible coiled wire that allows for curved designs. It is often used to fill motifs; the wire is cut into small pieces and stitched onto the fabric by passing a threaded needle through it. Different variations exist—*safed kora* (silver coloured), *sada kora* (single gold polish), and *chikna sunheri kora* (a double polish of gold resulting in high lustre and fineness). *Dabka* and *nakshi* are tightly wound, thin shiny wires stitched onto the fabric surface; the *nakshi* is thicker than the *dabka*, and less flexible. It is hence used more for straight outlines.

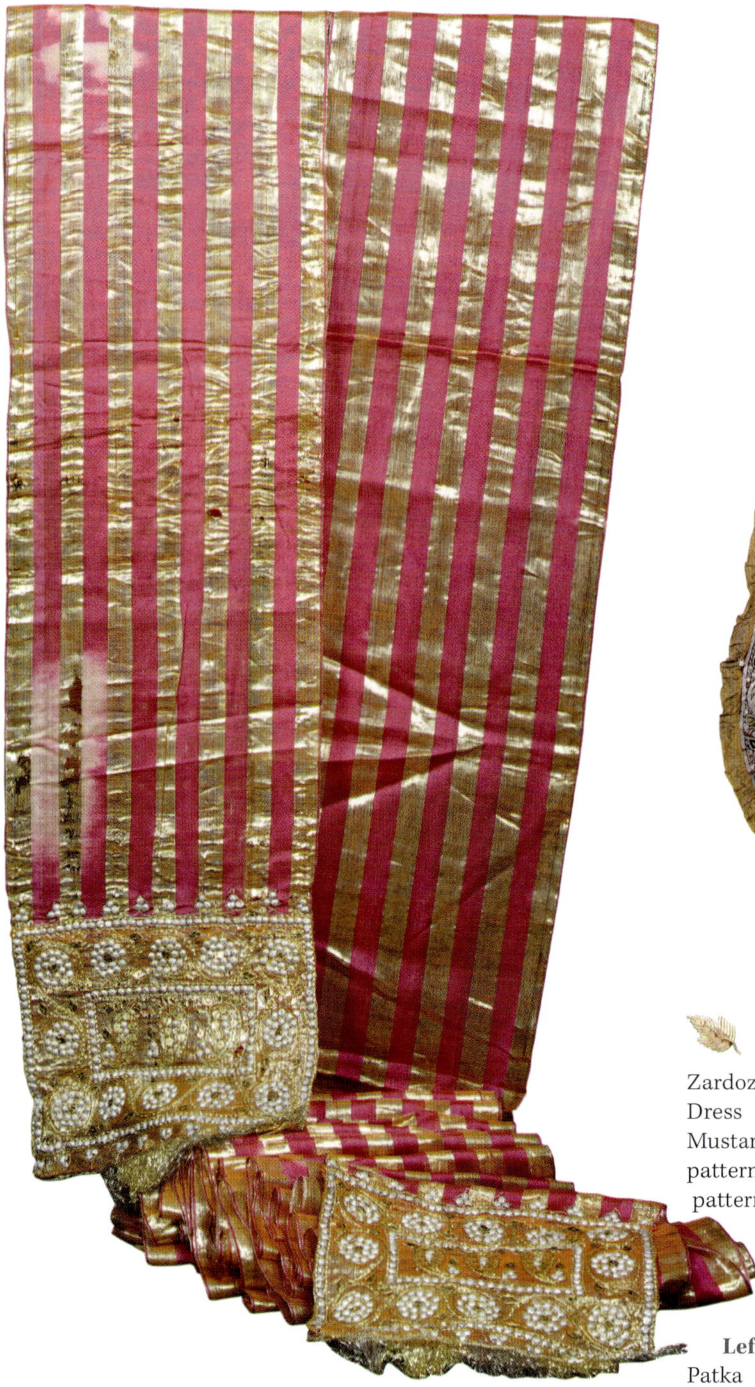

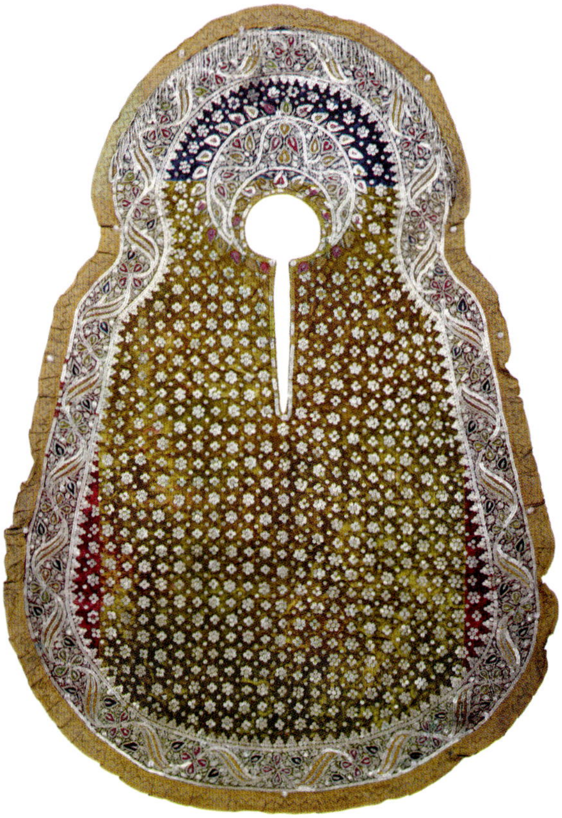

Zardozi and Sequin Embroidery
Dress
Mustard and deep blue velvet garment has an allover pattern of small sequined flowers and a floral and leaf patterned border. The neck area has *zardozi* and sequin embroidery.
MSMS II Museum, Jaipur
TC 4-79

Left: Zardozi
Patka
Deep pink tissue with gold zari stripes, the two ends are of gold tissue embroidered with circular motifs, using inverted round sequins as well as flat sequins in white and gold.
MSMS II Museum, Jaipur
TC.473.75

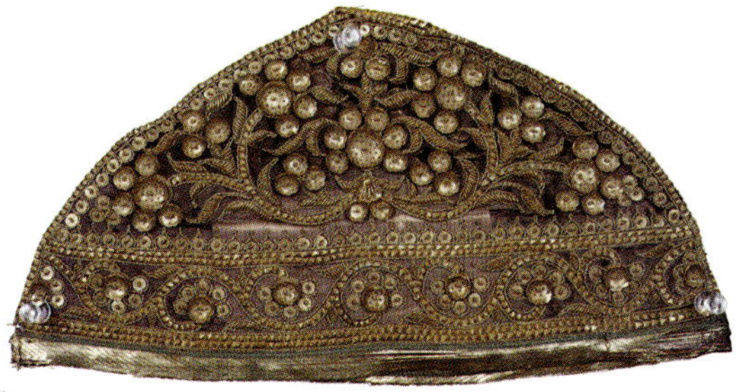

Zardozi
Topi
Embroidered with sequins and *dori*, the cap is entirely covered with a delicate floral motif. It has a wide border with a scrolling floral bel design, and a narrower panel running across the centre of the cap.
MSMS II Museum, Jaipur
TC.N.7

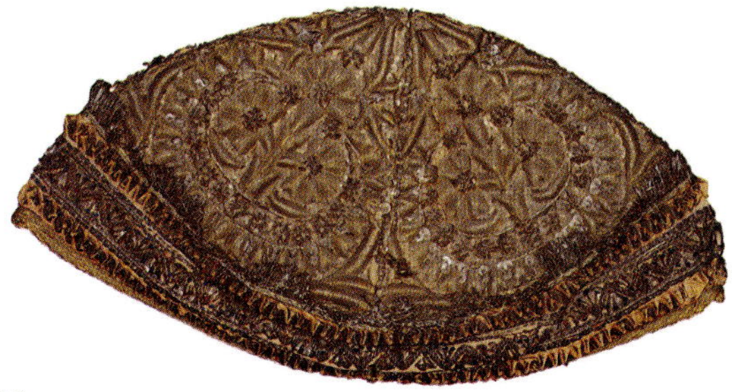

Zardozi and Karchob
Topi
Cream coloured base material decorated with *zardozi* and *karchob* work sequins in a floral pattern of multiple roundels, and bordered with a zigzag design in gold with red and blue dots.
MSMS II Museum, Jaipur
TC/F 57

In another beautiful variation, flat metal pieces with a hole in the centre in the form of a *chakri*, circular in shape, are used. The look that emerges is singularly different. In a similar vein, *sitaras* or *tikkis*, flat round discs made of metal, and now sometimes of plastic, have become an intrinsic part of the design. Inverted bowl-shaped metal pieces are at other times used with a hole in the centre and are known as *katori*. To add glitter and glitz, objects made of glass or plastic, for example, the *nalki*, *tili*, and *moti*, are stitched on to the surface.

Another facet of *zardozi* emerges through the stylistic use of the *dori*. As *dori* has thread-like properties, it is used to fashion loops and outlines of intriguingly different natures. *Kangni* is used popularly as an outline for all embroideries done on the *karchob*. As the wire is stiff, it can be fastened to the fabric by twisting with another *kangni*, or with a *dabka* or *kora*. A wire twisted thus, to fill outlines, is referred to as a *marori*. A *kacchi marori* is a single-ply *kora*, twisted with a *nakshi* and a *pakki marori* is a twisted thread plied with a *kora* or *nakshi*. The *kangni* may also be plied with a thread to make a *marori*. *Chaupel* is an interesting variation, though seldom seen these days. It is a flattened wire in gold, fashioned as a ladder while embroidering, and is available both in single and double gold polish.

Today, the tradition of *zardozi* has been given a new lease of life. It has been creatively adapted to modern clothing and furnishings and survives in many new avatars.

Vasli and Dhok

Heavy ornamentation using raised metal embroidery is seen in the royal palace collections. Textile products such as tents, floor coverings, and cushions were made using the technique of *vasli* and *dhok*. Couching of zari thread or metal wire was done on the *karchob* to create rich textiles covered with gold and silver. Raised

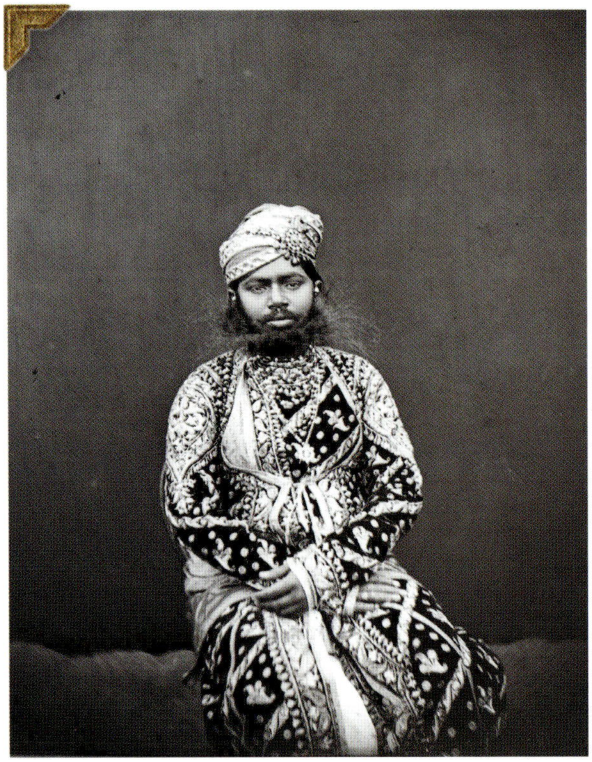
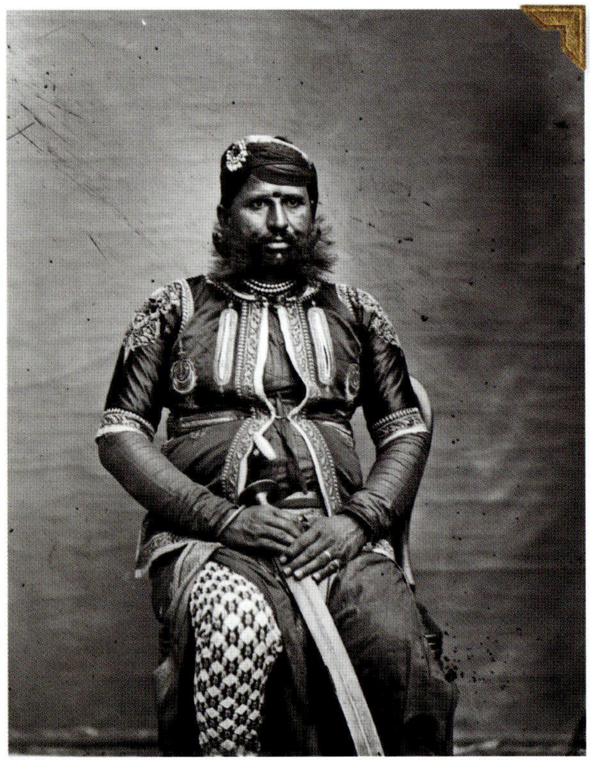
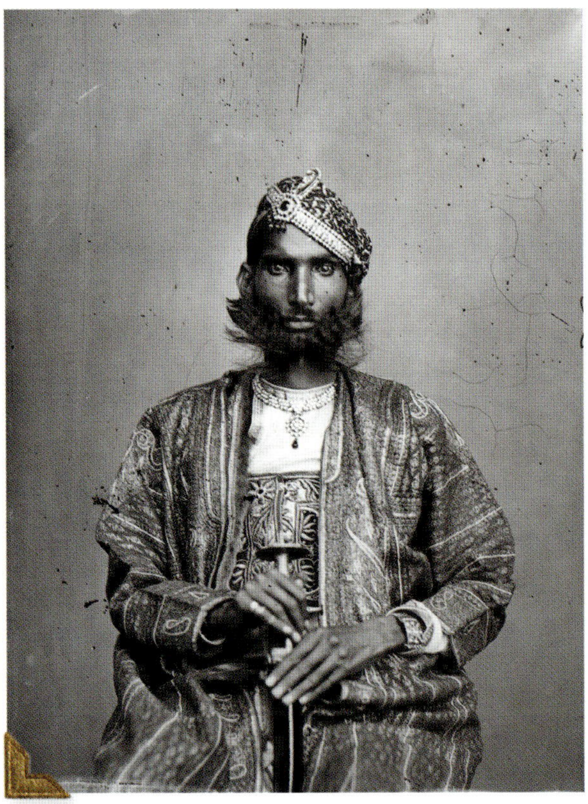
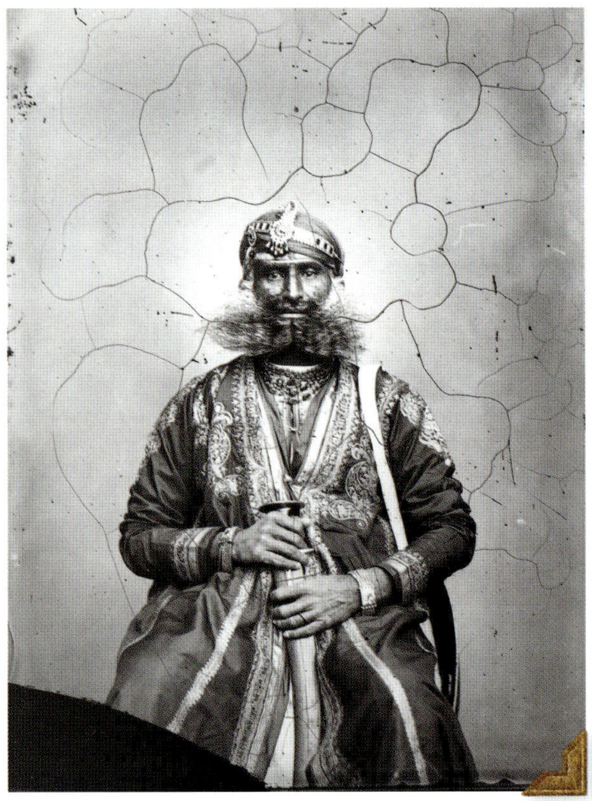

surfaces were created using cotton or wool wads, pasteboard, and other materials on large and often ornate fabrics like velvet. The fabric is stretched on a *karchob*. Patterns or designs are made with filling material, which is stitched to the base with a needle and thread. These raised motifs are covered using metal wire or thread using a satin stitch to create these richly embroidered textiles which were used by royalty.

This type of embroidery is now seen on wedding dresses, but traditionally this was done only for furnishing items, for the royalty.

Facing page: Portraits of men in traditional attire displaying various styles of clothing of the royal courtiers.
MSMS II M 2012.04.0021-0016
MSMS II M 2012.04.0009-0019
MSMS II M 2012.04.0025-0026
MSMS II M 2012.04.0039-0017

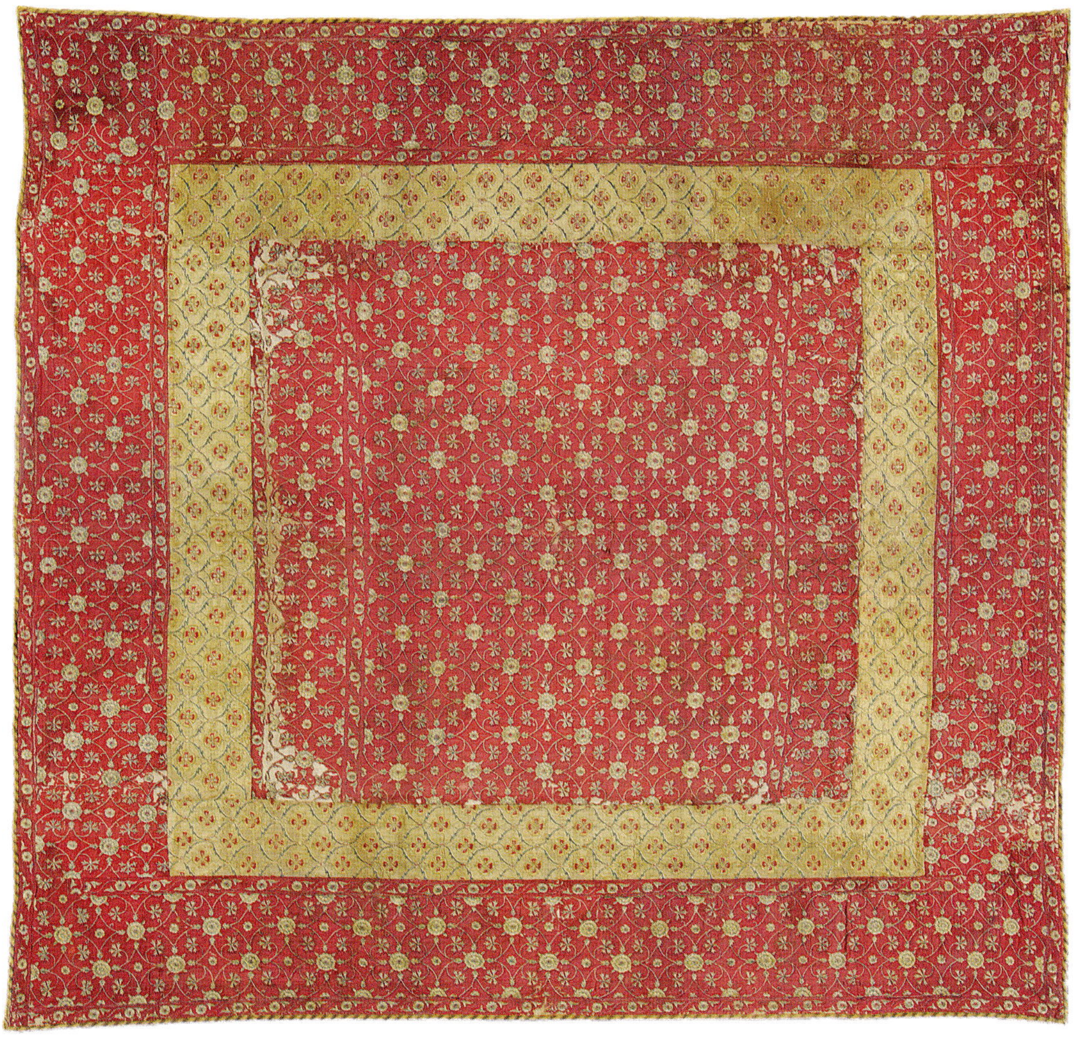

Vasli
Floor Spreading
Red velvet floor spreading embroidered in *vasli* style with metal thread on a *karchob*, and embellished with a floral bel and a delicate inner border with a large cartouche at its corners. It has a striped *mashru magazi*, and is backed with a red cotton lining.
MSMS II Museum, Jaipur
LA-27

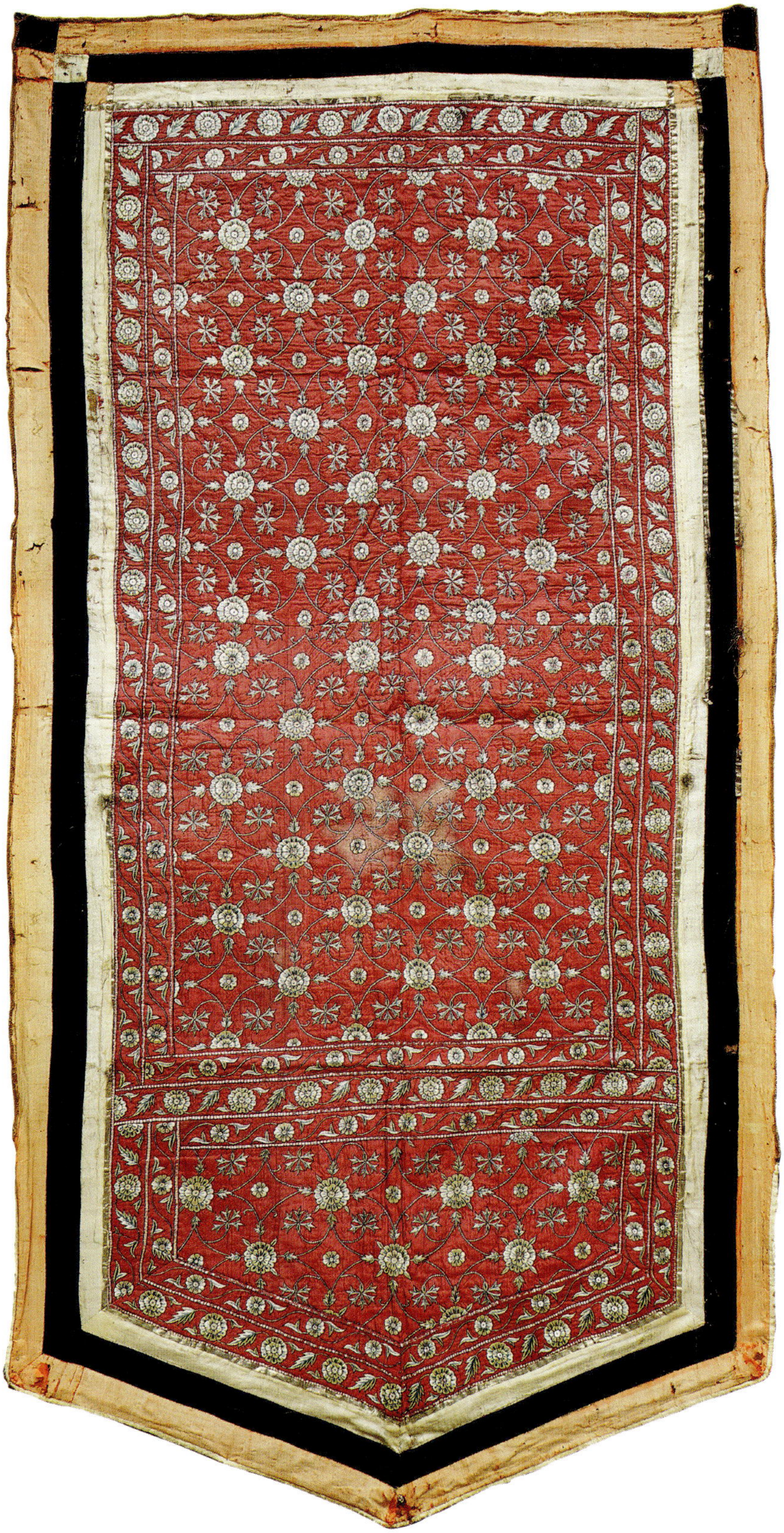

Embroidery in Vasli and Silk

Parda / Curtain

Red silk is embroidered with an all-over roundel motif in a brick layout. It is framed by two rows of different delicate scrolling designs, followed by a stitched border in three rows—zari, then a black fabric, and at the edge, a yellow one.

MSMS II Museum, Jaipur

LA 27

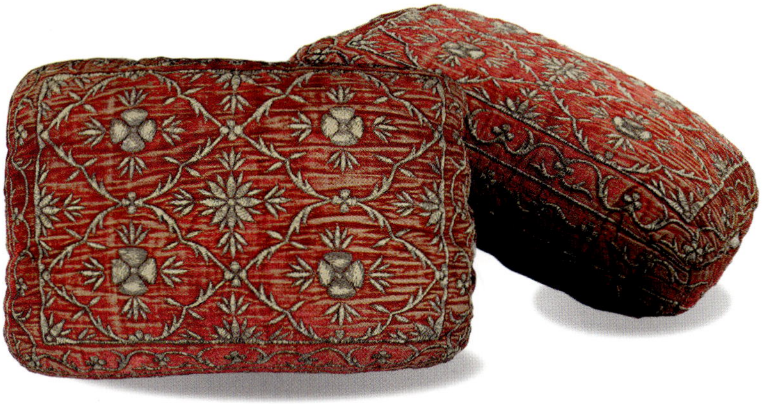

Vasli Embroidery
Takia / Pillow

Red velvet, with *karchobi* work in a *badrum* design, embroidered in golden zari with floral motifs arranged in a lattice pattern.
22 x 15 in
MSMS II Museum, Jaipur
TC/F 35

Vasli Embroidery
Bichhayat

Dull orange velvet, with a plain ground. The brown border has a scrolling ornamental pattern and its corners have been embellished with a distinctive round floral motif. Edged with a gold and silver fringe, on the inner side of the border is a floral cartouche at each corner.
MSMS II Museum, Jaipur,
TC 931.75

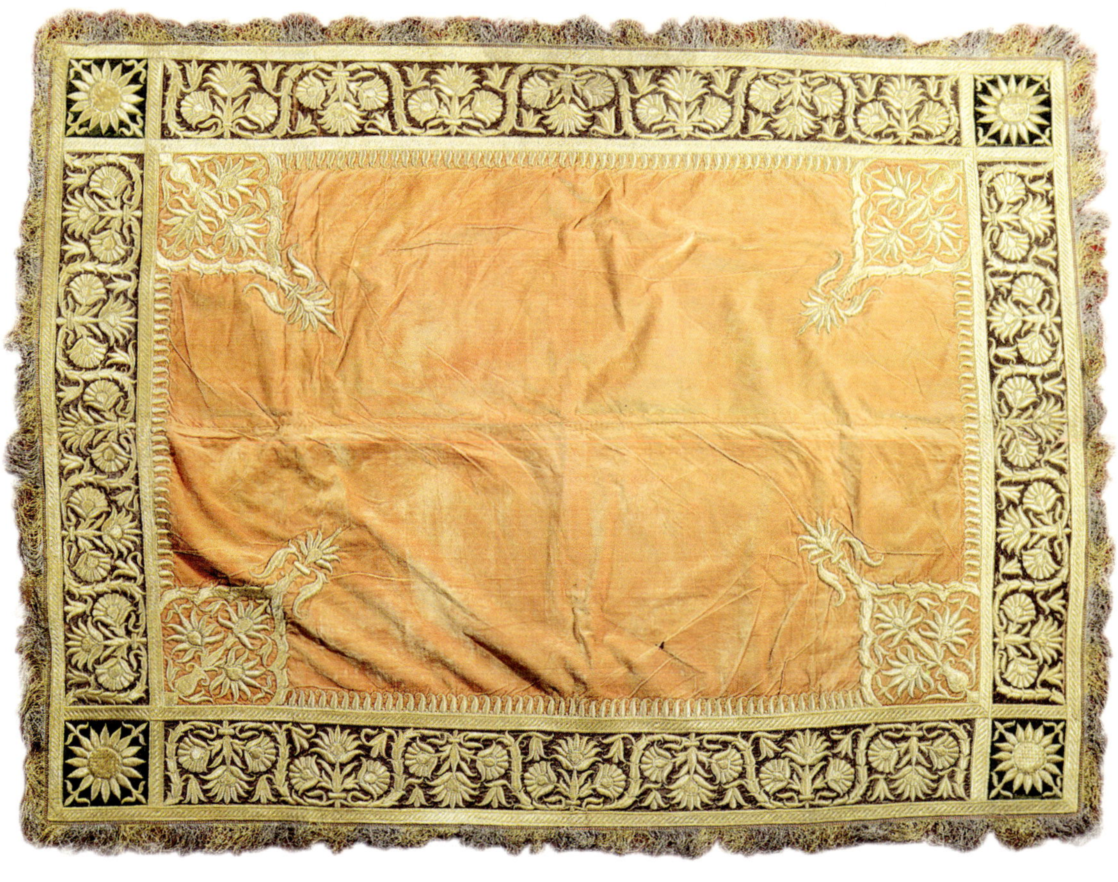

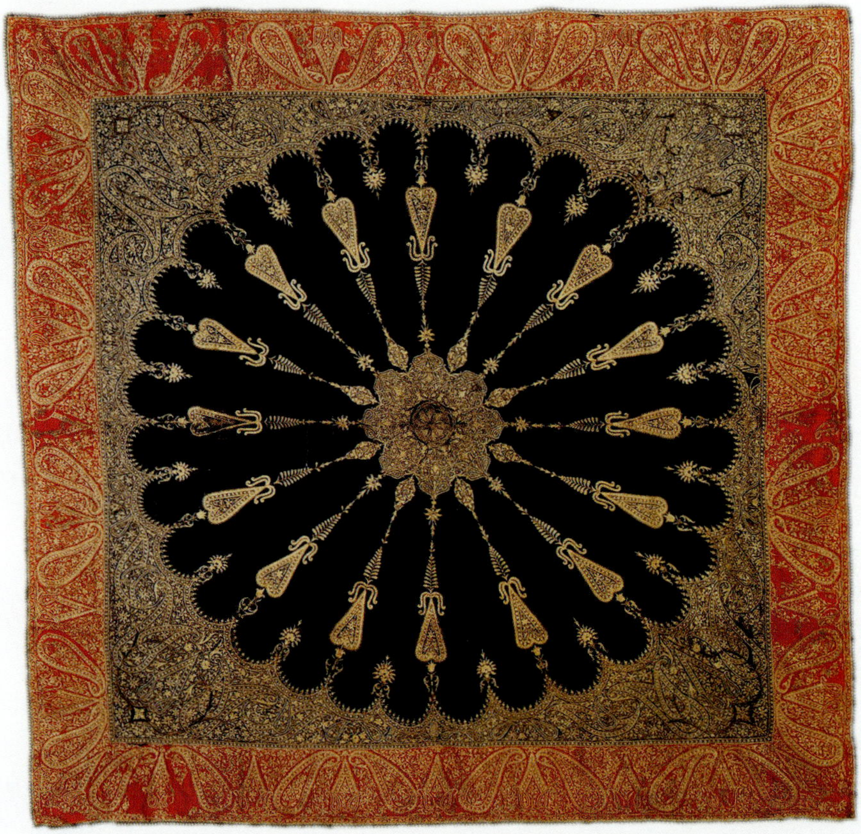

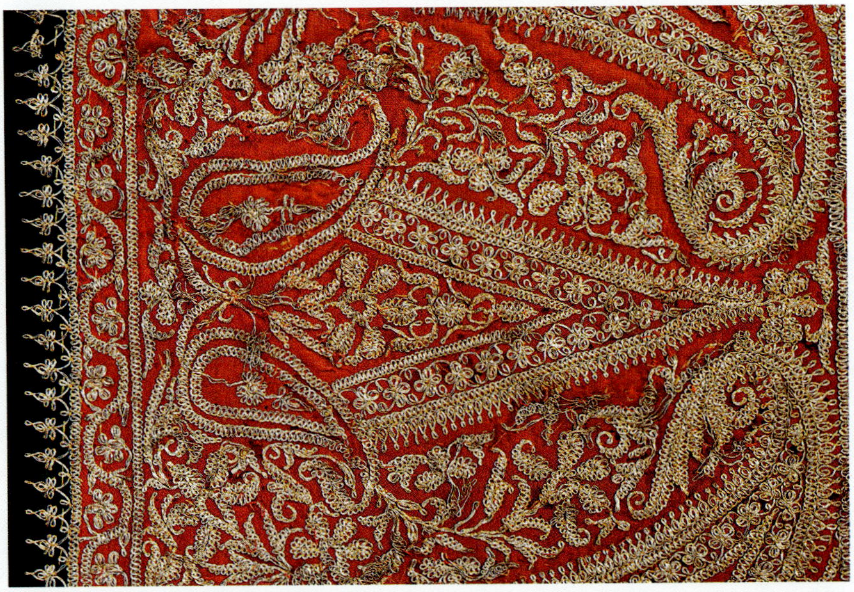

DORI-KA-KAAM

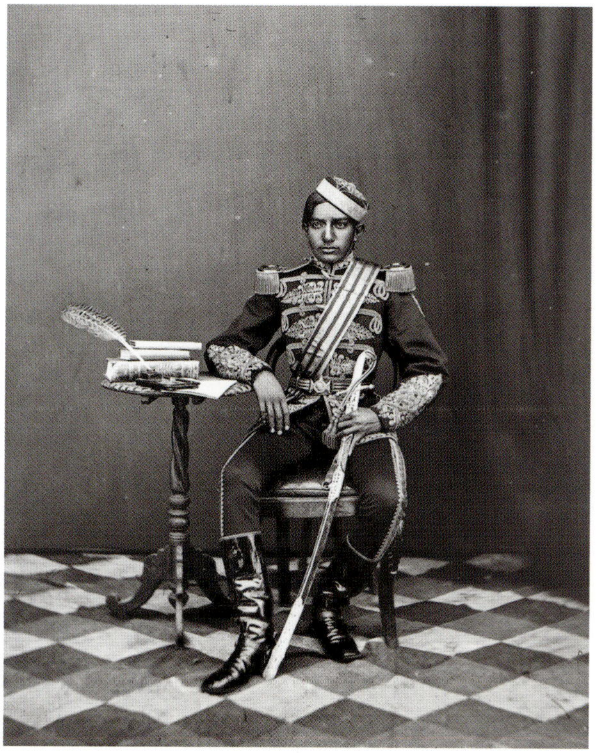

Man in an English style coat, ornamented with a thick golden *dori* on sleeves, front, and neck.
MSMS II M 2012.04.0040-0006

Facing page: Dori-ka-kaam
Embroidered Cloth (with detail)
Stitched with metallic threads or *doris* all over, this spread showcases the intricate technique known as *dori-ka-kaam.*
MSMS II Museum, Jaipur
Reserve collection

Dori-ka-kaam involves stitching metal threads or *doris* wrapped with cotton yarn to a fabric that has been made taut using a wooden frame. The thread used here is much thicker than those used for other metal embroidery techniques, resulting in far bolder and more dramatic effects. The secret of this craft lies in twisting the metal thread and the yarn tightly to avoid any accidents. If the twist is too taut, then the *dori* gets raised and creases begin to appear in the fabric after it is dislodged from the frame. To ensure that the wrapping is correct, a thread is passed through the *kangni* and *dabka* or cotton yarn and the two threads are tied to a nail. These are then hand twisted and stretched in a tight line to remove the excess twists. The two ends in a tied state are then wrapped around the wooden *fatila* (frame) to ease out extra twists with each wrapping. This ensures that the *dori* lies flat on the fabric surface after embroidery. The *fatila* also allows for the gold thread to be twisted, stretched or looped as required on the *karchob.* The ingenuity with which an artisan manipulates the *fatila* determines the splendour of his *dori-ka-kaam.* The flexible *dori* is manipulated to create a multitude of curvilinear designs.

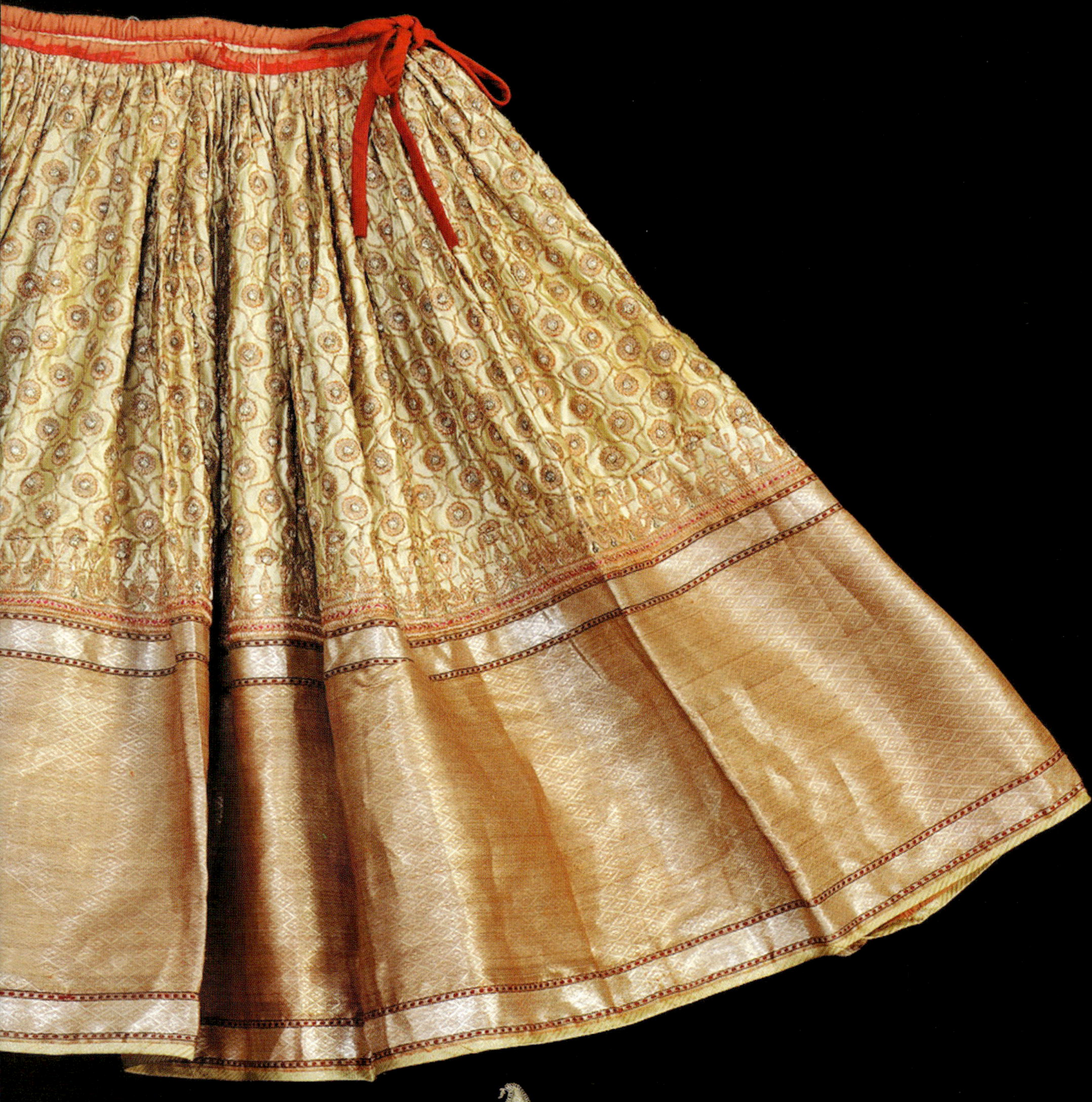

Dori-ka-kaam
Ghaghra
Yellow silk embroidered with metal thread in an all-over ogee design. The lower half of the skirt is plain, and bordered on both sides with a woven *gota*. There is a red piping and ties at the waist, and a narrow yellow *magazi* to finish the hem.
MSMS II Museum, Jaipur
Reserve collection

Caps with dori-ka-kaam

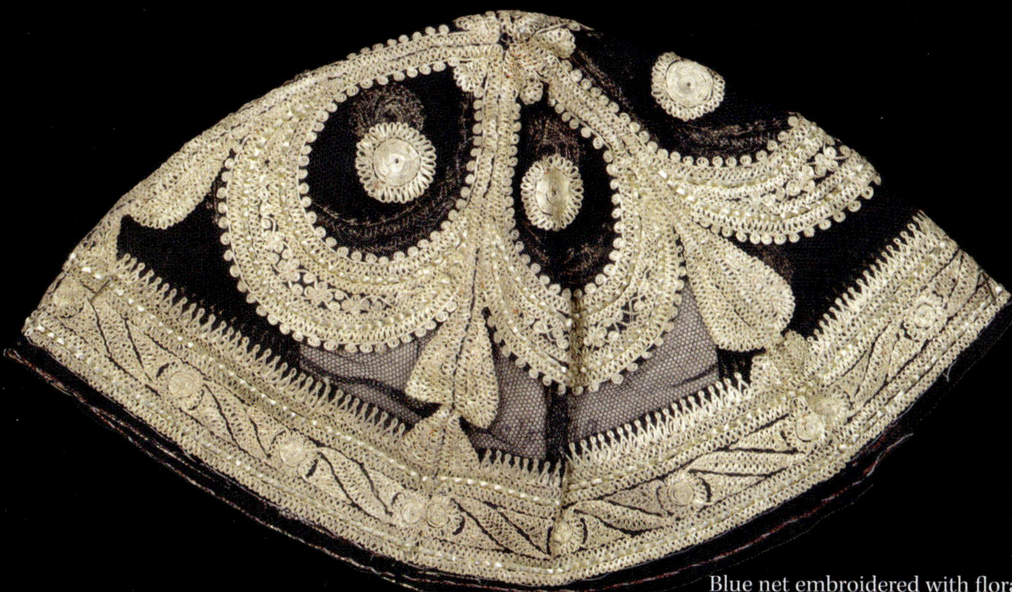

Blue net embroidered with floral motifs in gold thread. Use of metal wire is seen as embellishment.
MSMS II Museum, Jaipur
TC F-49

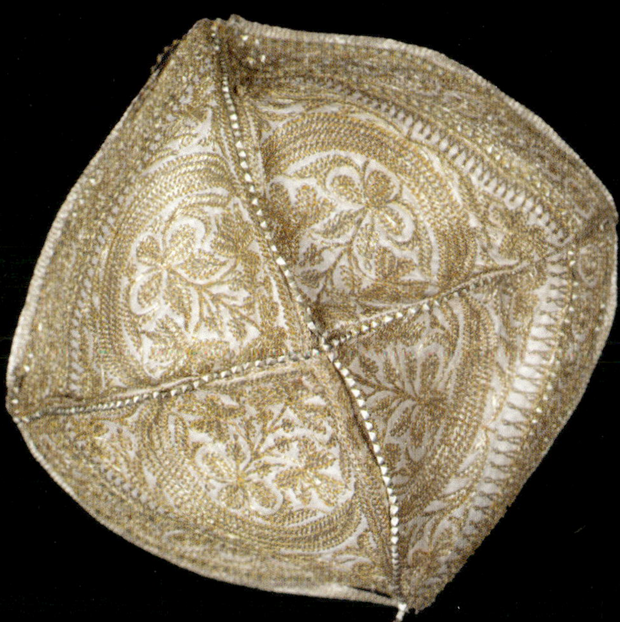

White cotton worked with gold thread. Four pieces are joined together and a metal wire is seen on the joints. A red border is embellished with circular motifs.
MSMS II Museum, Jaipur
TC F-23

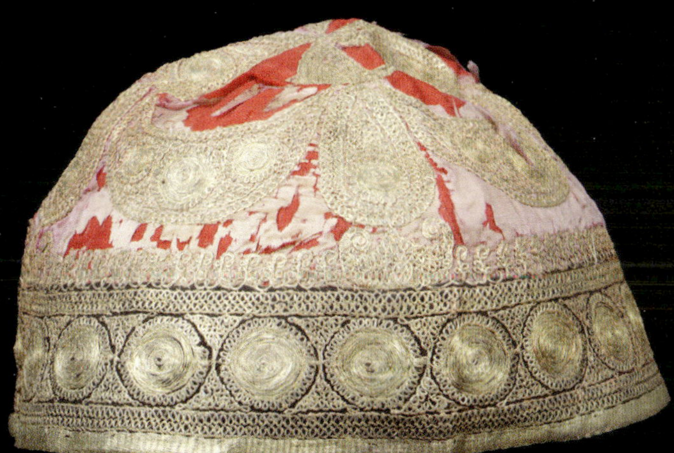

Pink silk with gold embroidery on leaf and moon shaped motifs. The border has circular patterns.
MSMS II Museum, Jaipur
TC F-47

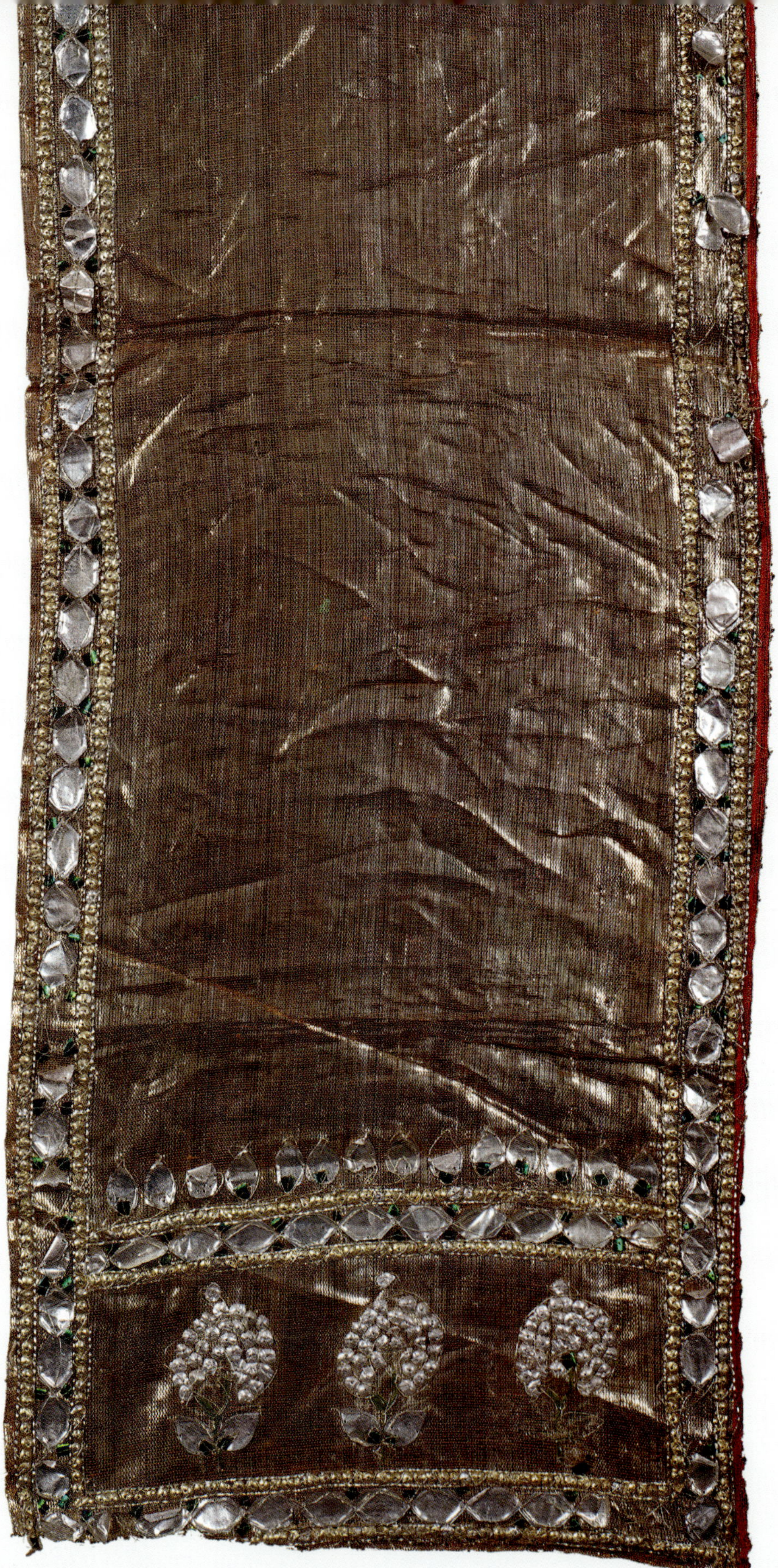

DANKA

This remarkable embroidery is roughly 400 years old and draws inspiration from jewellery making traditions. Historical records show that it was a Persian craft brought to Udaipur by Bohra migrants belonging to the region. It, thus, explicably remains a craft that is specific to Udaipur, in Mewar, Rajasthan.

The exclusivity of the craft is heightened by several factors. One is that the foils made of thinly beaten silver or gold sheets, called *danka*, which are stitched into the fabric and which form the core of this craft, have to be made with pure silver, or silver polished with gold. As gold and silver prices fluctuate, artisans only work on it when they have a definite order and advance payment. Stocking gold and silver sheets is an expensive option. Also, only a few people are proficient in the art of preparing the raw material required for the embellishments.

The luminescent foils, once stitched to the fabric, are enhanced with embroidery to give the garment the effect of sparkling jewels. Earlier, its use was restricted to royal clothing and its richness reflected the wealth of the wearer. Even today, it is largely used on garments made for special occasions like weddings. *Lehenga* (long skirt), *kurti-kanchli* (small blouse), *odhna* (long drape), turbans, *rumal*s (handkerchiefs), and saris are some of the the garments made. It is also done on *chaddar*s (coverings) presented

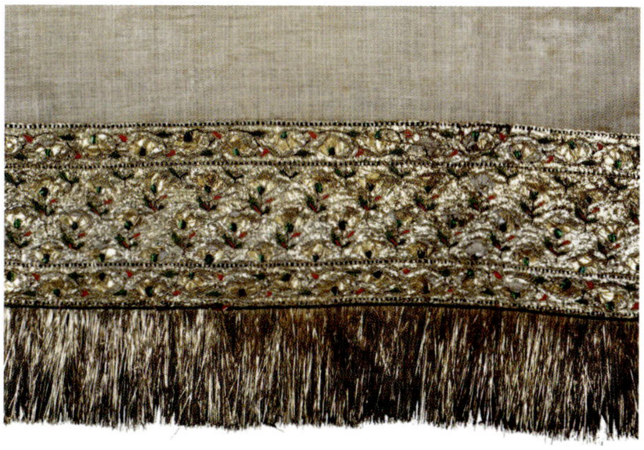

Danka
Patka
Off-white cotton edged with floral designs using gold *badla*, flat gold plates, beetle-wing in green and red, and green cotton thread. The borders at the two ends are wider, more elaborate, and finished with a *kinari*.
MSMS II Museum, Jaipur
LA.24

Facing page: Danka
Patka
Narrow silver coloured tissue piece with *danka* embroidery in green beetle-wing as a border all around. At one end is a second row of the border, and between the two are three floral *butis* made of *danka*, sequins, and beetle-wing.
MSMS II Museum, Jaipur
TC-628-75

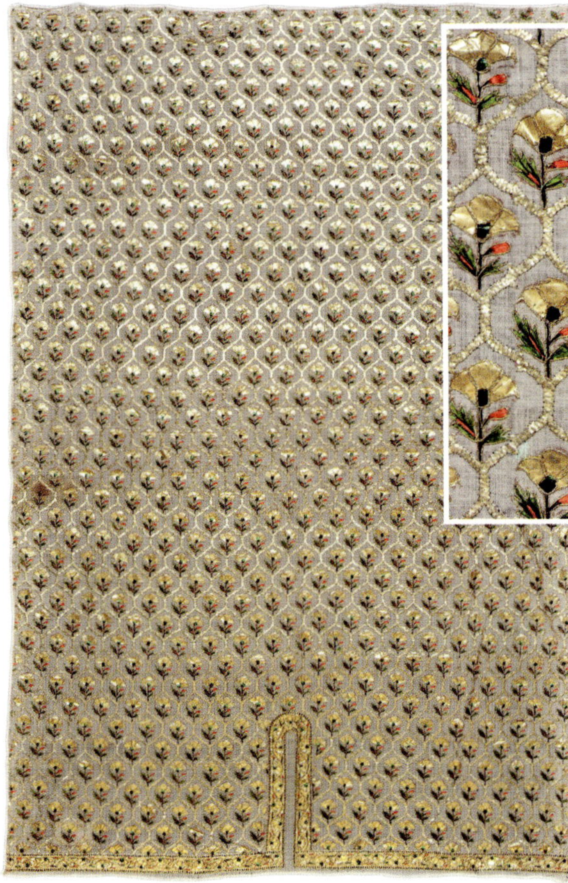

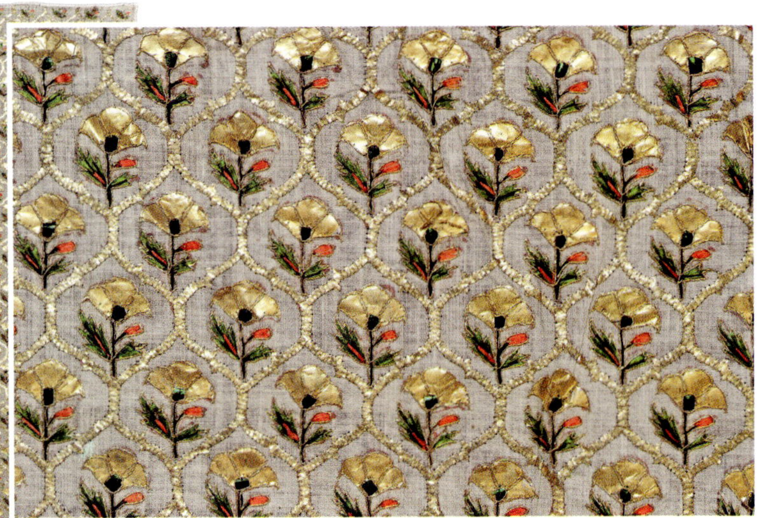

Danka
Robe
Cotton fabric custom embroidered with silk, beetle-wings, and metal thread.
MSMS II Museum, Jaipur
788.75

at shrines and dargahs by Muslims, especially during the month of Ramzan and on religious festivals, such as Eid.

The *danka* is fabricated using a small square plate of around 1.5 cm. The use of pure gold has been replaced with sheets of silver plated with gold. When made of a fine silver sheet, it is first heated and a gold foil is then pressed upon its surface. The silver sheets are of 98 per cent purity, beaten to form a smooth concave sheet. This process needs to be done with rigorous attention to detail, as the quality of a *danka* depends on how deftly the sheet is beaten to acquire the required gleam.

These sheets are then cut several times. First they are readied and trimmed into a size of 30 x 2.5 cm and galvanized in a gold mixed liquid, which lends the gold lustre to the *danka*. It is washed with clean water and polished using coarse sand. These fine sheets are then further cut with precision into rectangular pieces of 1.5 in, and then additionally chopped into rhombus shaped pieces. Each polished, delicate plate that finally emerges after this painstaking process reflects the idiosyncratic style of the craftsperson and his/her skill. These pieces are, unsurprisingly, highly valued and treasured by their privileged owners.

Danka embroidery is done in small workshops and it requires a wooden frame. These frames are either 6 x 3 ft, or 4 x 2 ft (length x breadth). Like other frame embroideries, it requires needles, crewel needles, and a spool to wind the *kasab* and silver thread on, all of which are locally available. The stencils for the design are prepared on butter paper and the marking is done on the fabric with chalk or white marking pencil after the fabric has been pulled on to the frame. Once the marking is over, the *danka*s are placed on the design with the help of a weak gum paste (wherever required) and then embroidered onto the fabric.

The technique used for attaching the *danka* to the fabric includes piercing the edge of the *danka* with a fine needle, and then drawing the thread through the fabric. About 7 to 10 strands of plied *kasab* or *badla*—a flat metal yarn wrapped around silk or cotton thread—is wound on a spool. This is then couched down along the edges of the *danka*. For an orderly look as many as 14 strands are used. The couching technique has to be done with a keen eye for perfection to protect the concave metal piece, which is fragile and prone to flattening. To secure it firmly, eight stitches in the shape of a knot are employed. Two stitches each strengthen the back, the corner, and the front. Round and flat metal braids, about a quarter of a centimetre in width, are used to accentuate the design. The chain and satin stitches fill the designs and the stem, and running stitches are employed for light stitching. It is common to see flat metallic sequins and *salma* in many *danka* embroidery creations.

The smooth and polished concave surface of the *danka* throws the refracted beams of light in all directions, giving the embroidered piece an ornate golden hue as if a piece of *kundan* jewellery has been embroidered onto the fabric. Some pieces bear resemblance to the inlay work on latticed screens or *jaali*s of the old *haveli*s of Udaipur.

Even though the designs are geometric, the liquid grace of the craft somehow makes it appear flowing and sensuous in its contours. This is in a large measure due to the artistry of the craftsperson, who is able to create an effect of movement and magic by placing small *danka* pieces with finesse. The traditional motifs include floral patterns (with eight, six, or four-petalled flowers), stars, creepers, peacocks, and paisleys. The fabrics traditionally used for embroidery were silk, velvet, and satin. Other fabrics put to use in recent times include chiffons and georgettes, also tissues and brocades that accentuate the beauty of the embroidery.

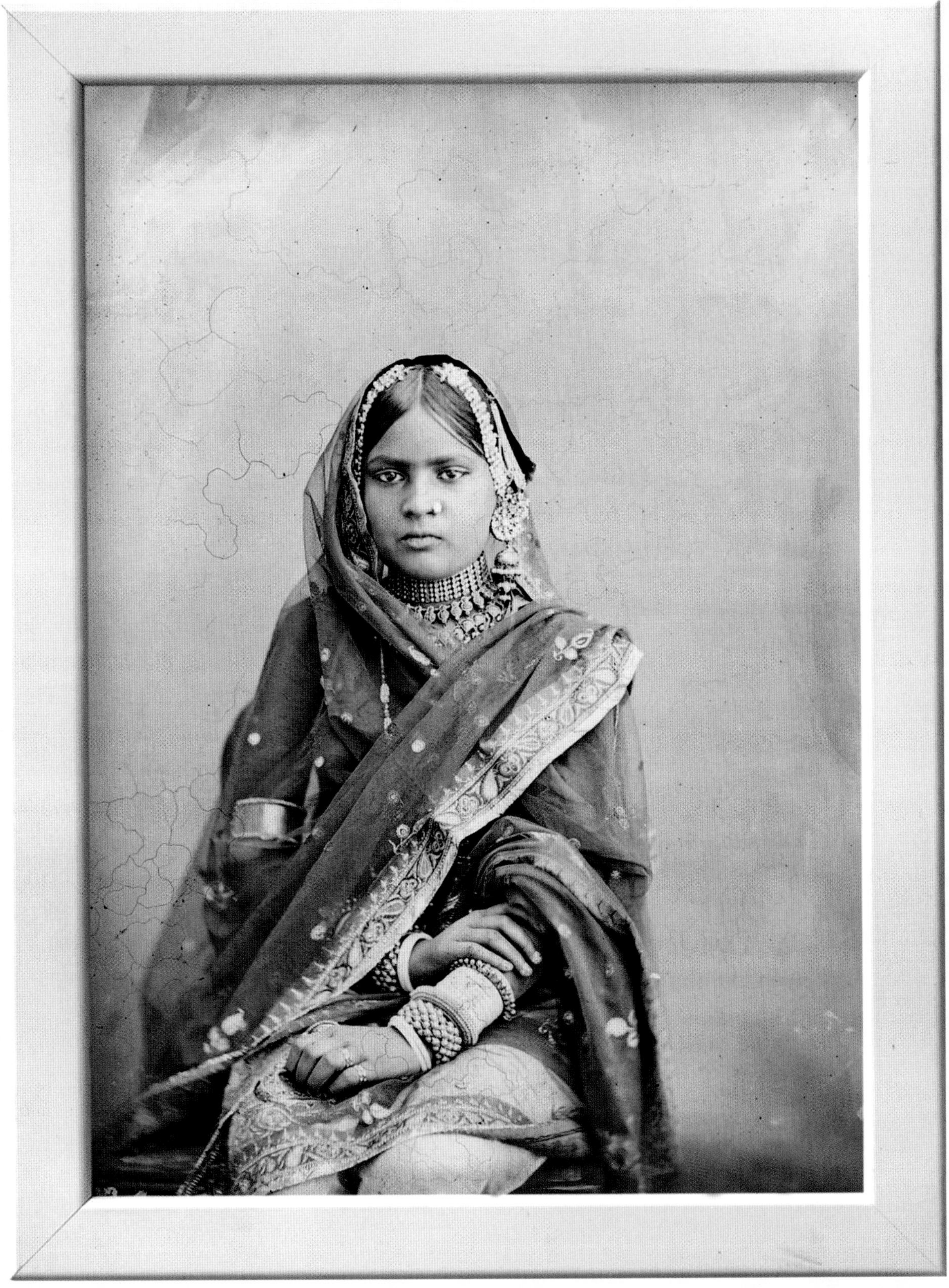

KAMDANI

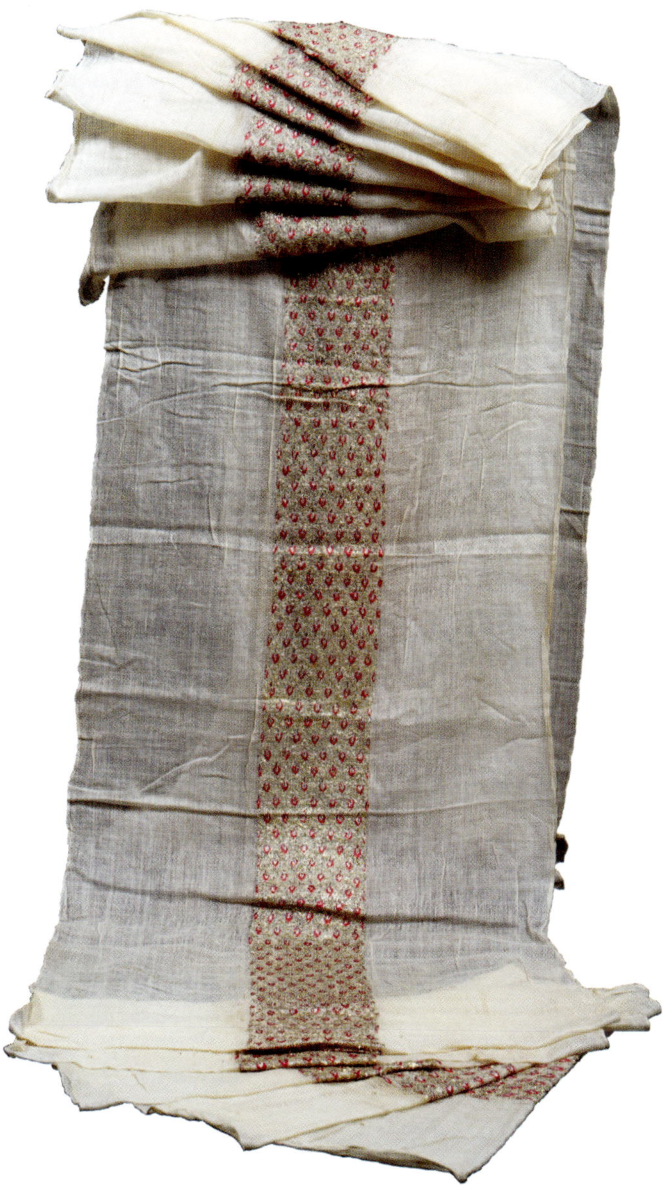

Kamdani as a craft is alive today in pockets of Uttar Pradesh (Sitapur, Aligarh and Rampur), in Delhi, Hyderabad, Mumbai, Ahmedabad in Gujarat and Rajasthan. For centuries, the nawabs of Awadh patronized this craft and Lucknow acted as a hub for artisans who perfected the technique. Records show that its popularity extended further north to Kashmir and to Rajasthan as well.

Kamdani
Pagri
White muslin with an embroidered panel running down the centre, in a network of flattened gold wire and floral motifs in white and pink silk thread.
MSMS II Museum, Jaipur
TC 883 75

Facing page: Woman in traditional attire consisting of delicately worked on *kamdani* dupatta and kurti.
MSMS II M 2012.04.0048-0002

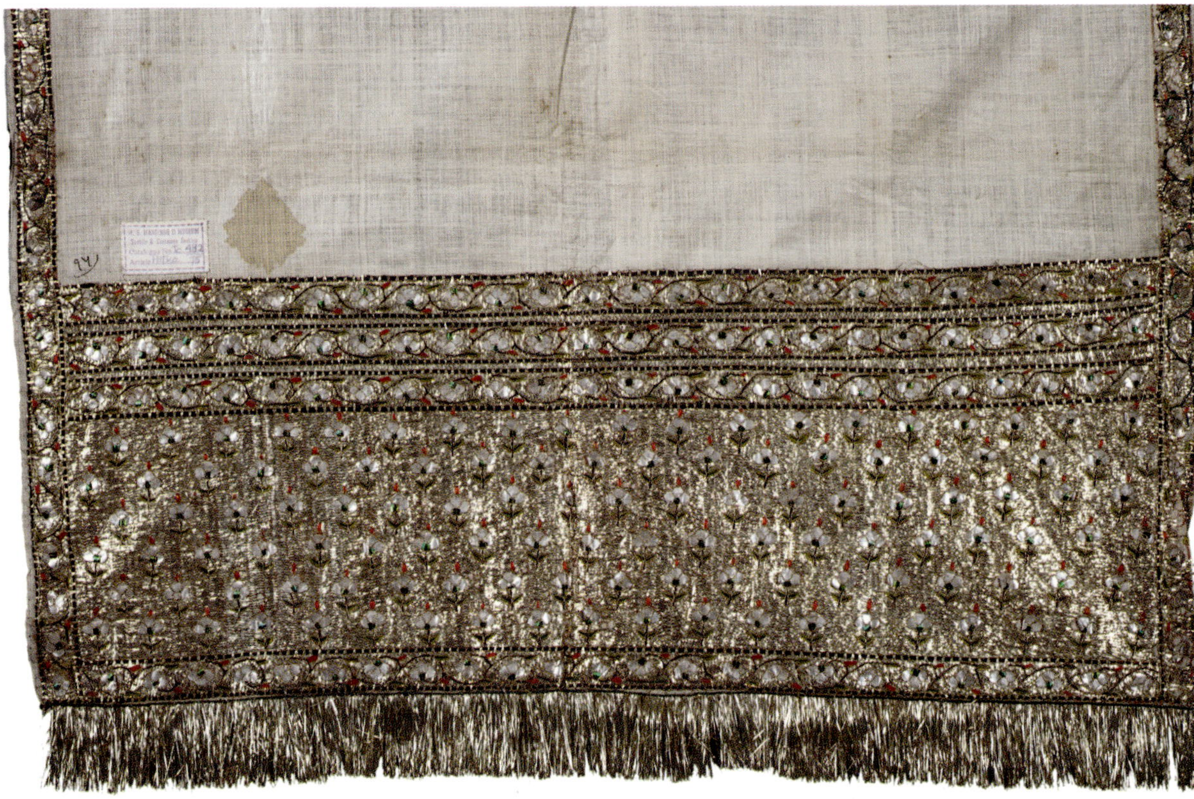

Popularly known as *mukaish*, *tarkashi*, *fardi-ka-kaam*, or *badla*, it is perceived as *shaahi kaam*, a form of handcrafted embellishment for royalty and the upper classes. Originally meant to be created only with pure silver and gold wires, today machine-made wires, in different colours and with varied metals (like steel, aluminium, and copper), are predominantly used.

The gold and silver was drawn and beaten flat to form the wire (*badla taar*). Today, manufactured metal strips, each approximately 2 mm wide and 30 cm long, purchased ready-made in bundles of 10–15 pieces here from Surat, are used instead. A special needle is used to work with the *badla*. Light, translucent materials, like georgette, chiffon, muslin, or net, are the preferred fabrics, as they accentuate the subtlety of *kamdani* work. An outstanding feature of *kamdani* is that the embroidery is executed with symmetry to produce an identical effect on both sides of the fabric.

The design is pierced on a butter paper pounce or *khaka*. Cotton swab dipped in kerosene and zinc oxide (white for coloured materials or *neel* powder for light-coloured materials) is used to transfer the design from the stencil onto the cloth. For a three-dimensional effect, called *vasli-ka-kaam* or *dhok-ka-kaam*, a piece of cardboard (or even x-ray film, these days) is carved in the shape of the motif, placed on the fabric, and covered with *badla* so that the base is not visible, yet produces a semblance of a raised surface.

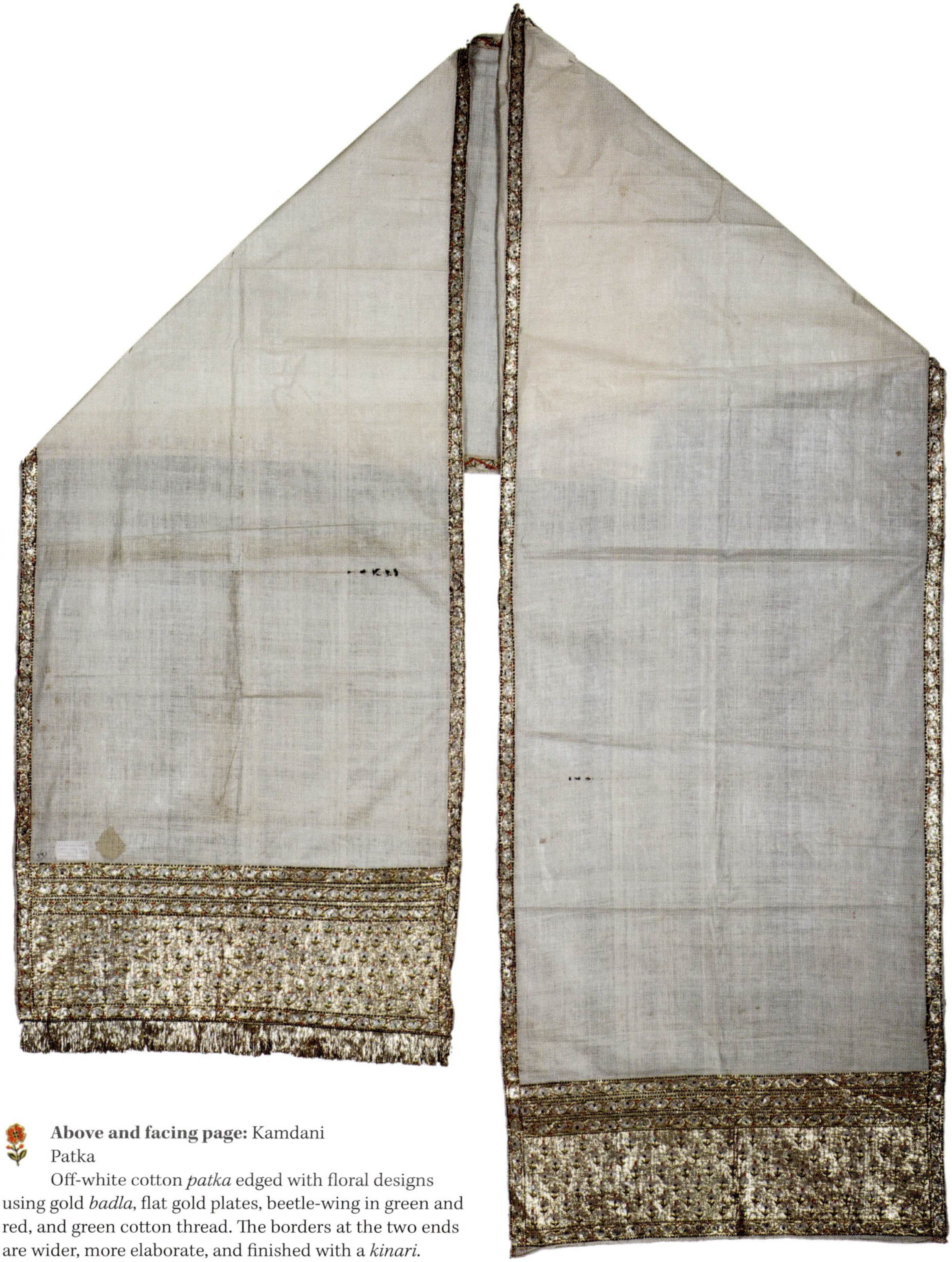

Above and facing page: Kamdani Patka

Off-white cotton *patka* edged with floral designs using gold *badla*, flat gold plates, beetle-wing in green and red, and green cotton thread. The borders at the two ends are wider, more elaborate, and finished with a *kinari*.

MSMS II Museum, Jaipur

TC.482.75

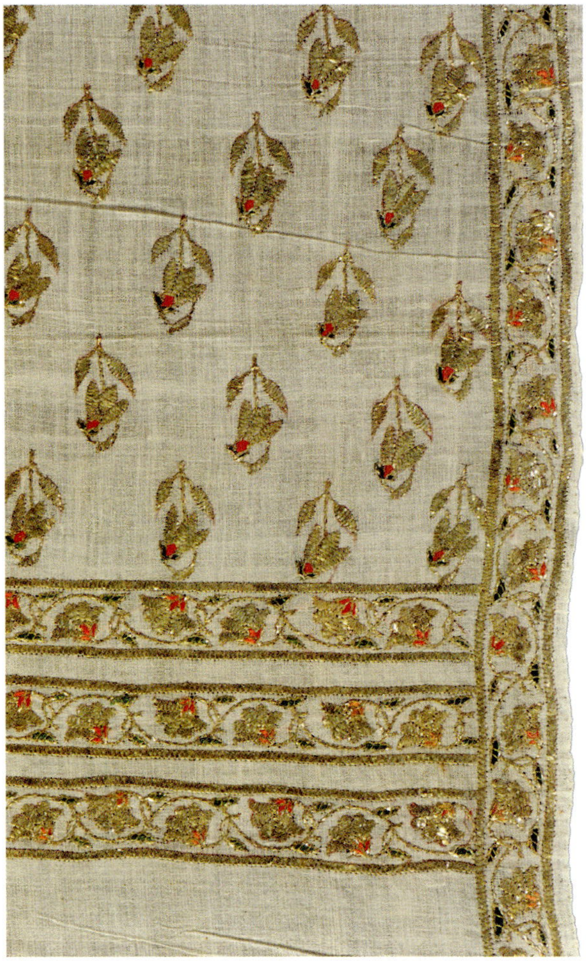

Kamdani
Sash
White cotton sash embellished with silk and flat metal strip.
MSMS II Museum, Jaipur
466.75

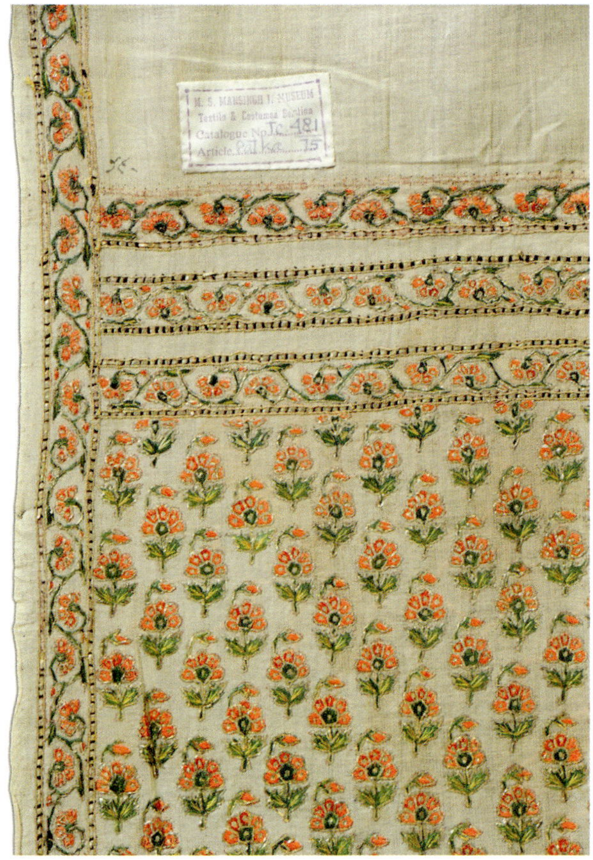

Kamdani
Sash
Off-white muslin embroidered in orange and green silk, gold badla, and dori, in an all-over layout of a small floral *buti*, and a narrow scrolling floral bel bordering the two ends.
In a corner, at the back, is inscribed in Nagari, the price of '20 rupees', and in another—'26 rupees' or '26 rupees, 1 Anna'.
MSMS II Museum, Jaipur
481.75

As the cloth needs to be held taut, the fabric is wrapped tight around the index finger and stretched between the other fingers. Then the *badla* is used almost as a needle at first. The next step is to run through an actual needle intertwined with a thread. An intriguing detail that emerges from oral records is that, earlier the fabric used to be pierced with porcupine quills or pointed sticks made of ivory, wood, or bone for openwork. As the metal strip passes through the cloth, knots or *fardi*s are created. A minimum of three stitches is needed for *teen sui-ki-fardi* (three-thread knot). For larger knots, the number of wire folds is increased, usually to about six times. *Fardi*s are executed at regular intervals and their density is

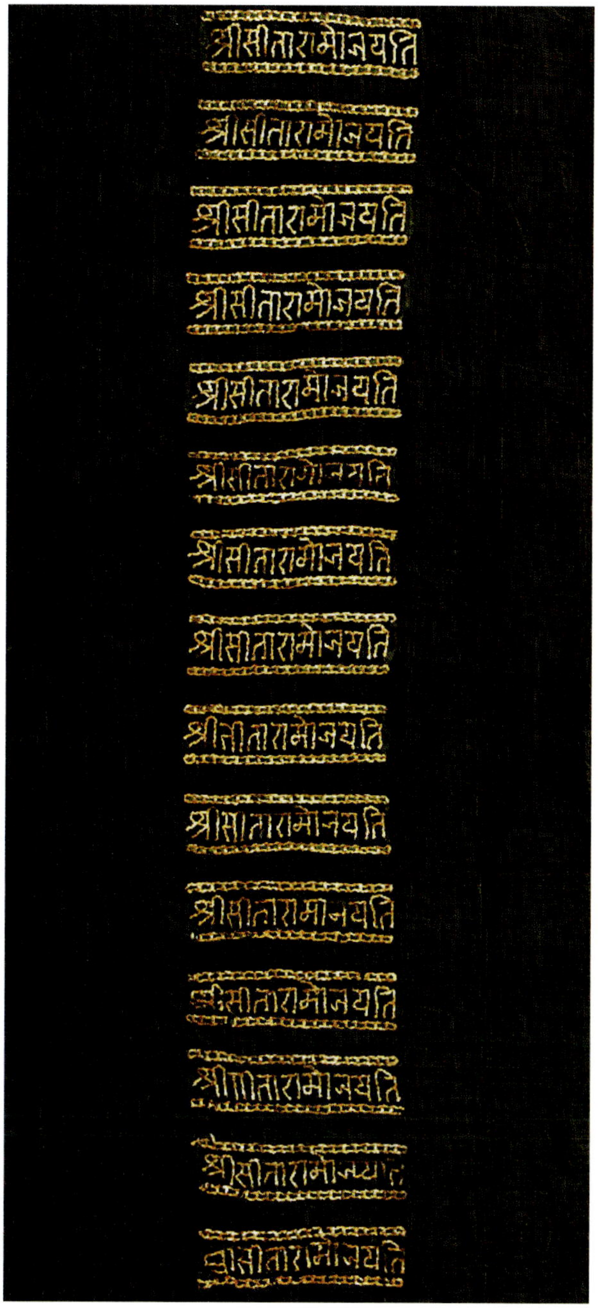

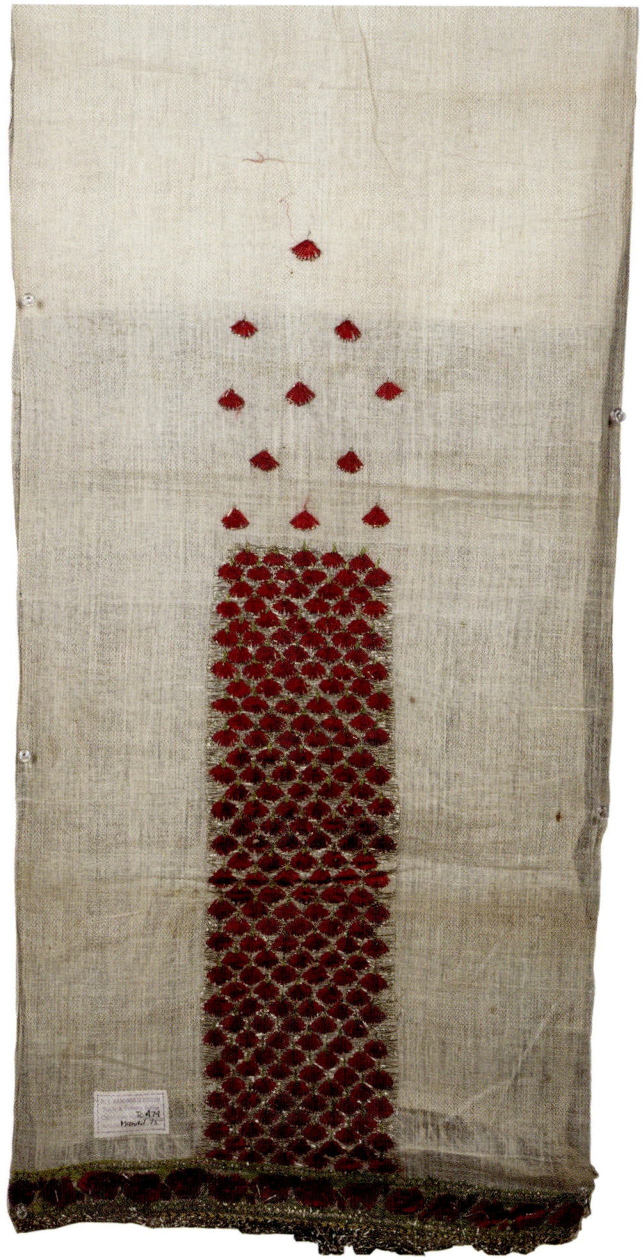

Left: Kamdani
Dark green muslin embroidered in gold *badla* with the word 'Shreesitaramojayati' in Hindi script between two narrow borders, repeated one below the other.
MSMS II Museum, Jaipur
Reserve collection

Kamdani
Headgear
White muslin *mandil* (headgear) embroidered with flattened gold wire and red and green silk threads, and edged with a floral bel and a *kinari.* On one side is a rectangular network of a red flower motif on a base of silver coloured metal embroidery, and a few scattered flowers at the inner end of this panel.
MSMS II Museum, Jaipur
474.75

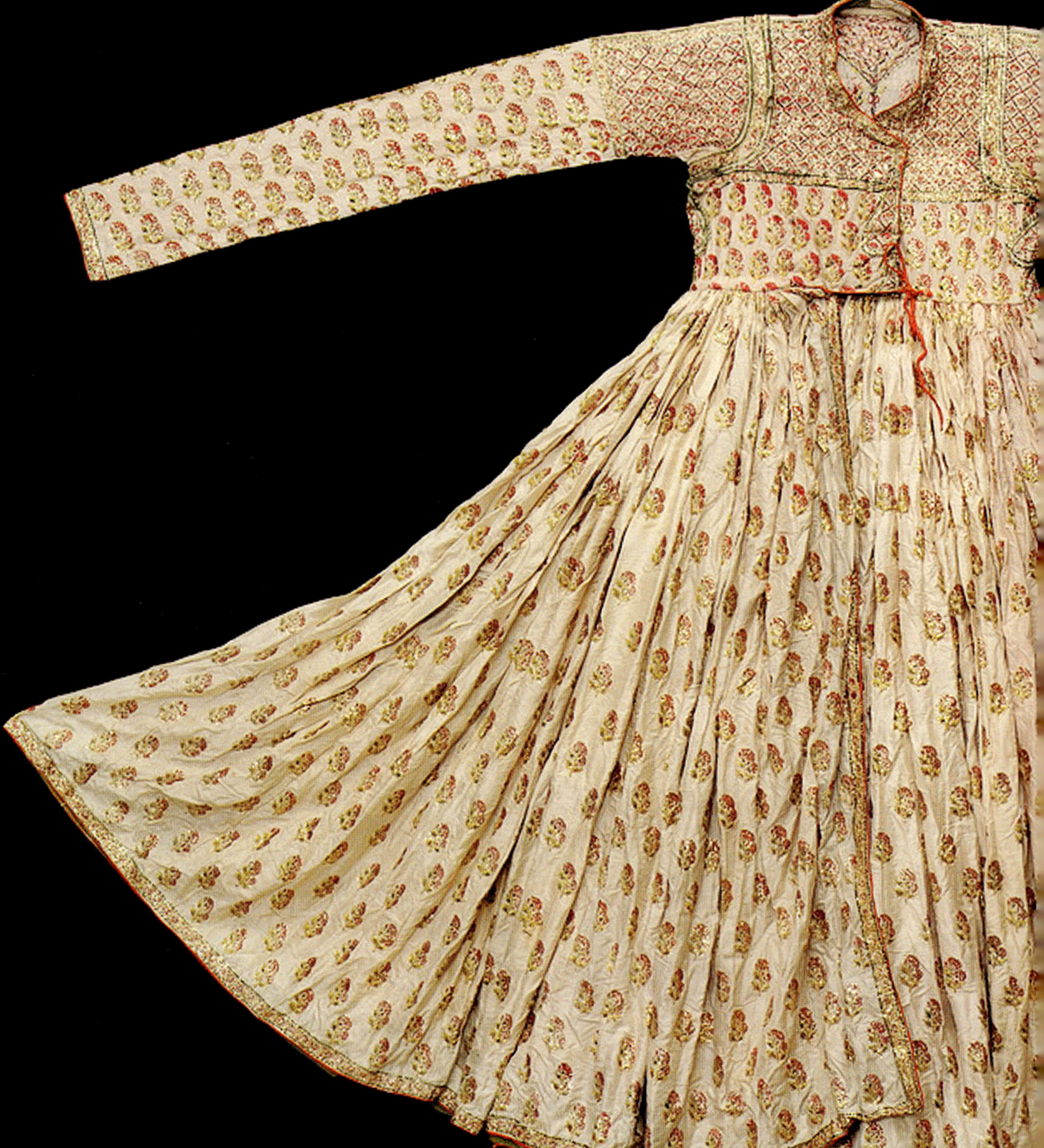

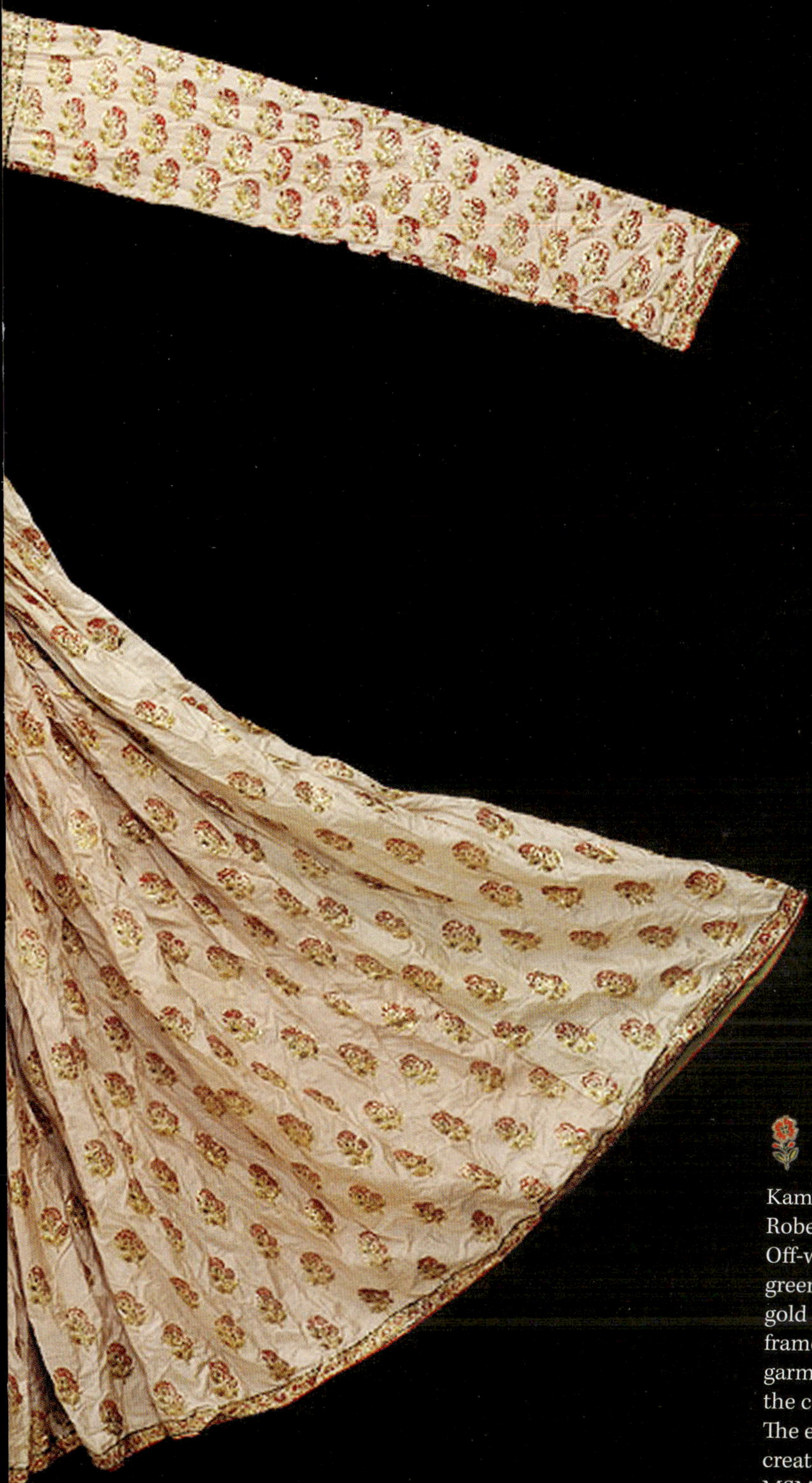

Kamdani
Robe / Jama
Off-white muslin with floral motifs embroidered in pink, green, yellow, and black silk thread, and embellished with gold *badla*. On the bodice are small flowers within a lattice frame, while a larger floral *buti* decorates the rest of the garment. A narrow scrolling floral border is placed along the collar, placket, shoulder, and lower end of the bodice. The embroidery has been engineered in three densities to create a graded design.
MSMS II Museum, Jaipur
555.73

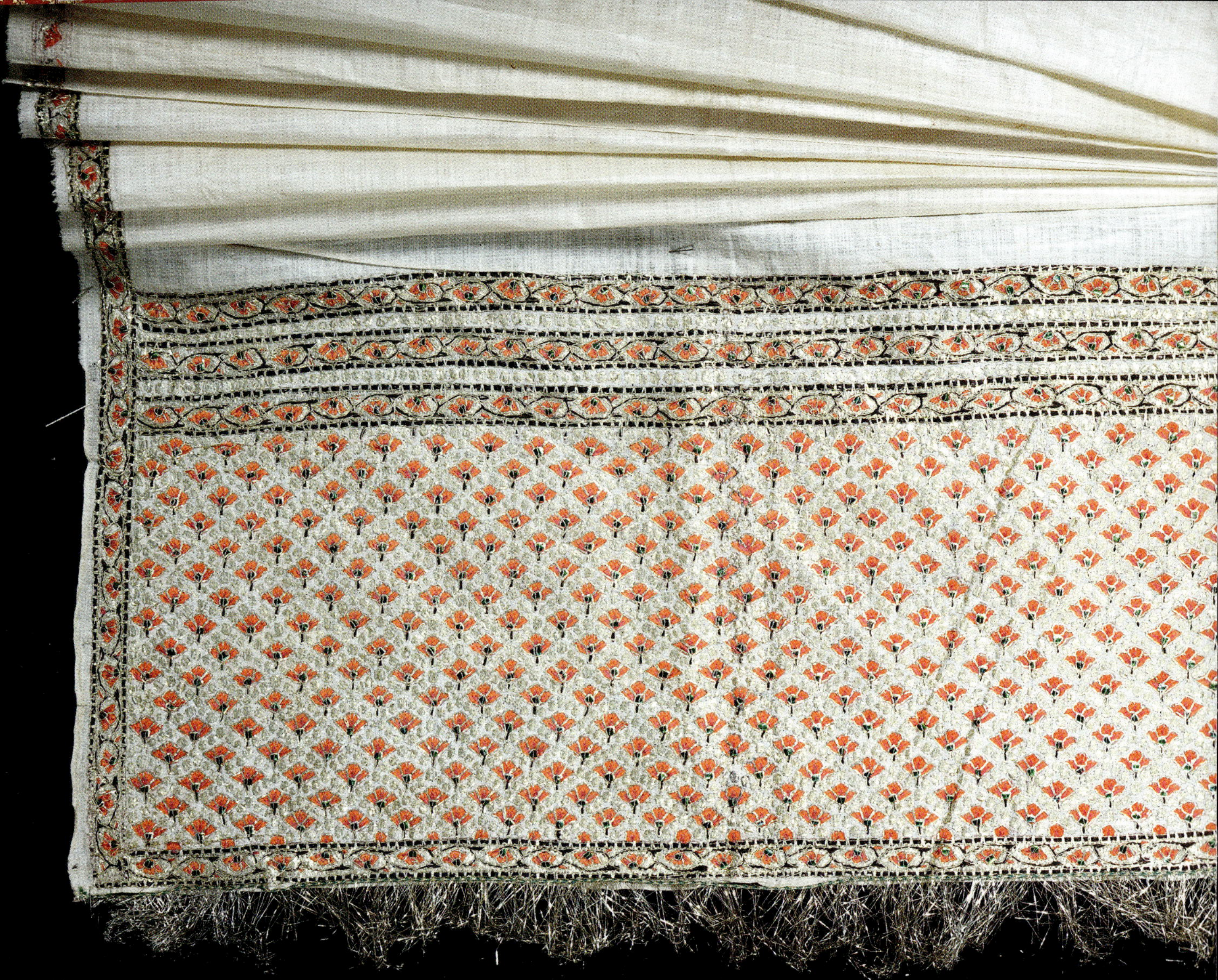

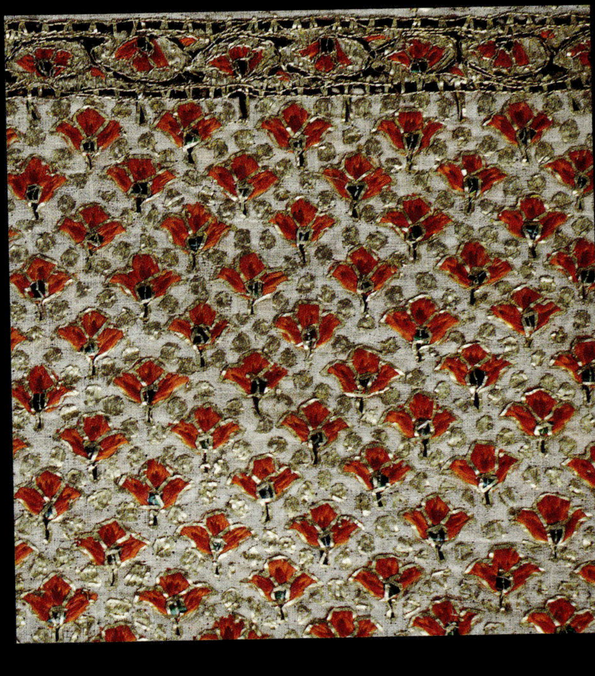

Kamdani
Patka
White cotton embroidered with a narrow floral scrolling border on the sides, one side further embellished with silver *badla* in orange and black thread and green beetle-wings. The two ends have a broad panel of a small flower motif, their inner edges finished with three rows of the scrolling border separated by metal dots.
A closeup of the same displays the embroidery in detail.
MSMS II Museum, Jaipur
484.75

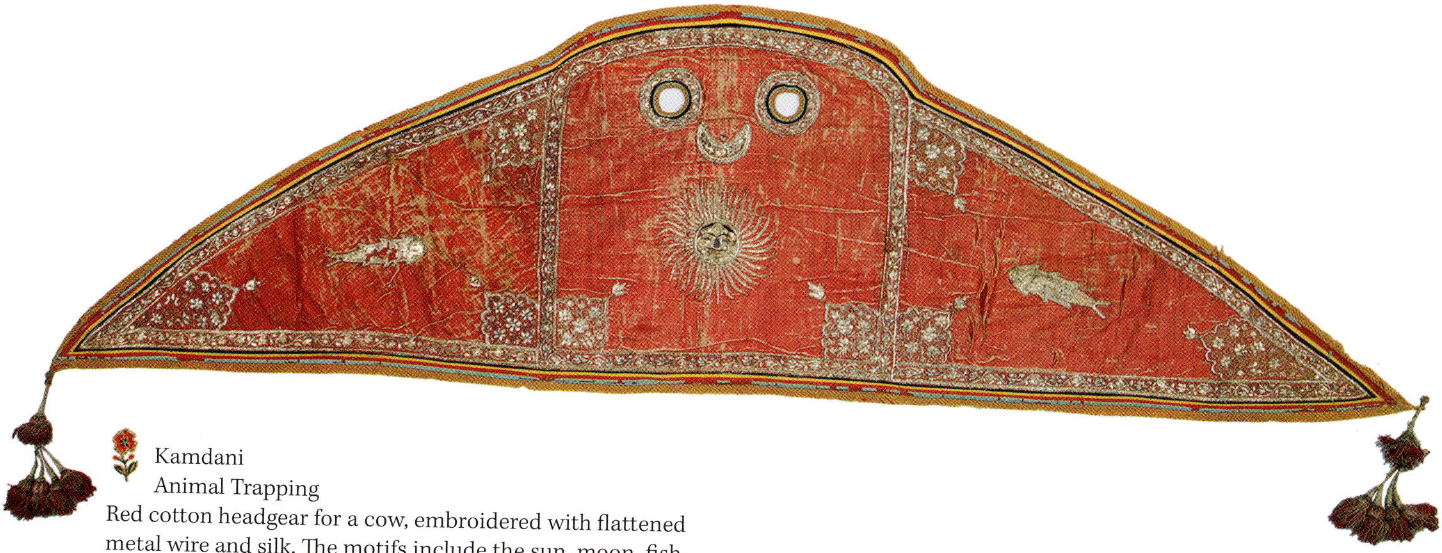

Kamdani
Animal Trapping
Red cotton headgear for a cow, embroidered with flattened metal wire and silk. The motifs include the sun, moon, fish, floral shapes, and a cartouche-like design at the corners. The piece is demarcated by golden embroidered borders, into a central square and two long triangles. The same borders, along with a piping of red and yellow *leheriya* fabric, are also found around the bottom of the cap and across its centre. In the middle, there are two holes (for the horns) embroidered around the edges, and at both ends are pompons made of cotton and zari.
MSMS II Museum, Jaipur
TC F 41

measured against *danas* (dots)—they could be 500 *danas* or 1000 *danas* (known as 'hazar buti' or thousand flower pattern).

An assortment of effects is accomplished in *kamdani* simply by filling the motif with *badla* wire in a different way: the *patta/patti* (where a straight stitch is used), *salami* (where a 45-degree angle stitch is used), *ornia* (where thin and fine lines are used), *chand* (a 45-degree angle stitch is used with a division in the middle), *dana* (a small stitch, also known as *taka/mukaish*), *murri-ka-kaam* (where there is a raised design in a rice shape), and *avala/tikki* (a circular motif, like an *asharfi* or coin, with an eyelet in the centre).

Badla, when used with sequins flanked on either side or as an eyelet, creates a resplendent and ornate look, particularly when combined with *chikankari* and *tilla* embroidery. In the final stage, the completed piece is placed right side down and adorned with a large cowrie shell or other smooth objects that mesh with the fabric. And, to give it an even tempered surface and a sheen, the metal is gently polished.

Designs and motifs of *kamdani* include floral patterns (*karan phool*, or flower with straight lines) and *munda phool* (flower with petals), geometric *jali numa* (lattices), paisleys, creeper designs, and animal and bird patterns. Fish and peacock motifs have found widespread acceptance and are often placed on borders, as well as *thali numa* (centrally) and as *bharaat* (fillers). The *fardi*, however, is at the heart of most endeavours and appear either as single dots, in clusters of dots, in lines, in zigzag, in circles, or in the shape of a diamond.

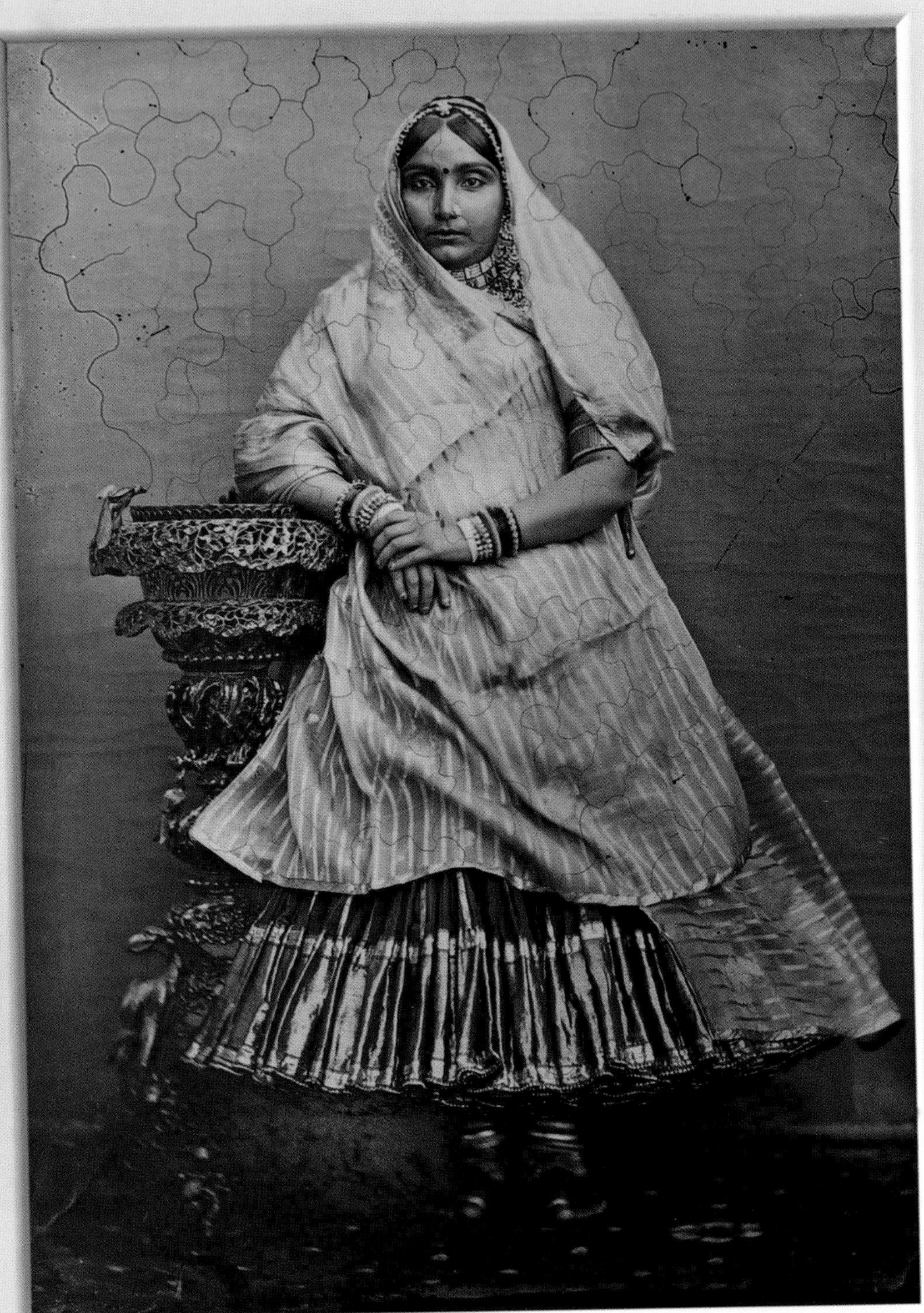

GOTA / LAPPE-KA-KAAM

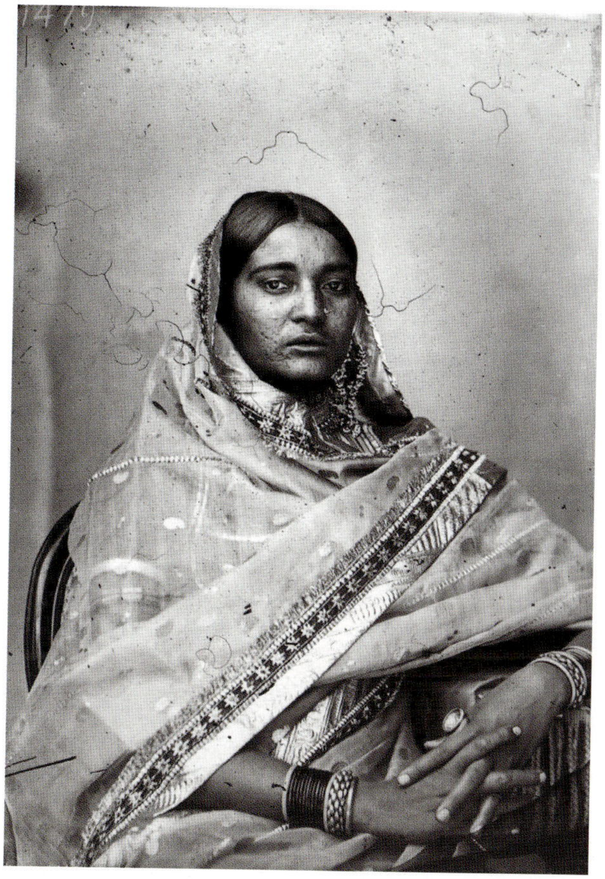

Woman in traditional clothing, draped in an *odhna* edged with *gota* appliqué.
MSMS II M 2012.04.0054-0051

Facing page: Woman in traditional attire, donning a *gota-patti* ghaghra.
MSMS II M 2012.04.0019-0005

Traditionally, *gota* is a strip of gold or silver ribbon that is woven, employing a satin, plain, or twill weave. Varying in width, these ribbons are usually made with silk or cotton yarn and, when embroidered, the embroidery is referred to as *gota-patti* work or *lappe-ka-kaam*. *Gota* is used to decorate *odhnis*, *kurtis*, *angarkhis*, turbans, ghaghras, as well as coverings, purses, caps, and other household products. Temple flags and embellishments to the dresses of idols of gods and goddesses are also embroidered using *gota*. Though pure *gota* is expensive, substitutes like synthetic zari have resulted in its widespread usage in today's fashion.

The craft is practised extensively in Ajmer, Jaipur, Shekhawati, Bikaner, and Kota in Rajasthan, as well as in the cities of Surat, Hyderabad, and Varanasi, and the states of Punjab, Haryana, Andhra Pradesh, and Jammu & Kashmir. Rajasthan is particularly famed for keeping this craft in practice, as on religious and social occasions and festivals, it is *de rigueur* for the people in the state to dress in their finest clothes, ornamented with *gota*.

The art of producing the *gota* requires an intrinsic knowledge of weaving techniques.

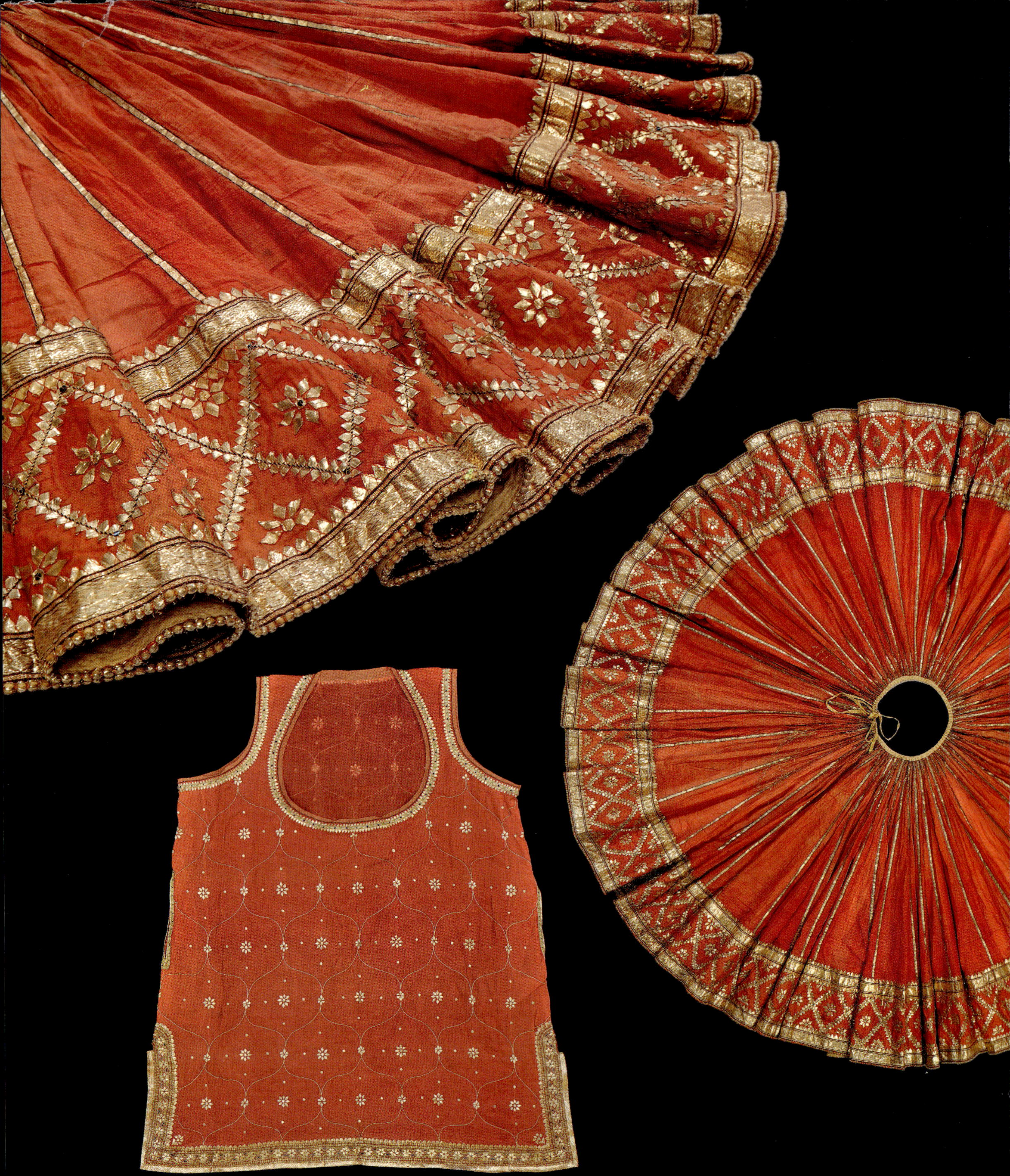

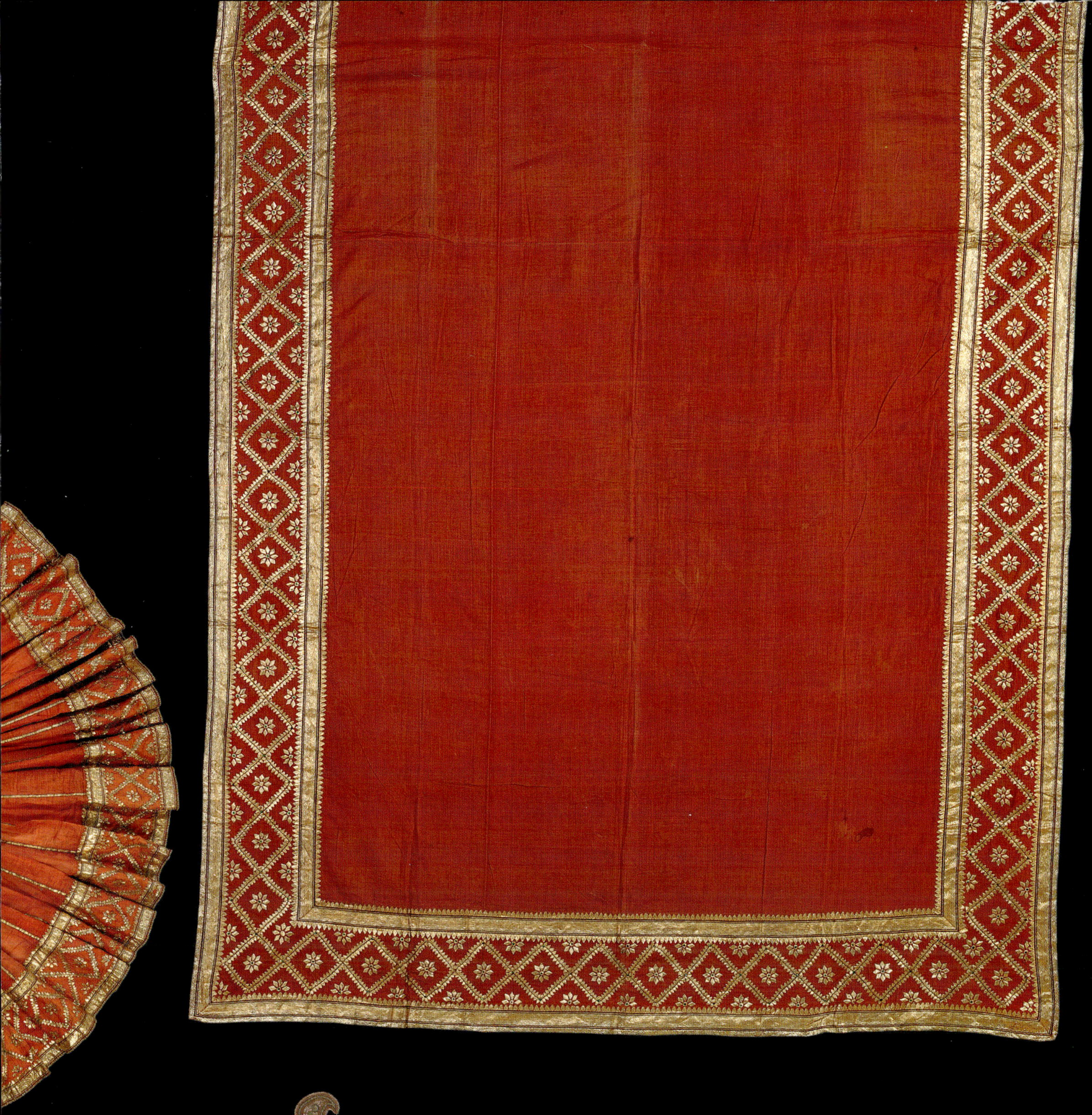

Gota Work
Matching ensemble
Cotton appliqued with metallic tissue.
Kurti (70 cm)
Ghaghra (78 cm)
Odhna (275 x 152 cm)
MSMS II Museum, Jaipur
J-44

These days, metallic yarn, called *badle-ka-taar,* is obtained in the form of bobbins from manufacturers for use in the warp, and weaving is done on a power loom. The use of pure silver and gold has been replaced with an alloyed mixture of copper and even metallized polyester film cut in a thickness of 0.25 mm, 0.4 mm, and 0.8 mm. The weft is made of cotton or silk thread in white or yellow and very often these days with satin or nylon. The warp-weft modification is due to both the escalating prices of gold and silver and the intrinsic merits of synthetic *gota*—it is resistant to moisture and its sheen is not susceptible to becoming dull like pure gold and silver *gota*.

It is mostly women who initiate the process of *gota*-making by winding the *badla* (yarn) on a *charkha* or spinning wheel, and making packets of yarns. Men then take over the baton and weave the yarn on a wooden handloom, a lace machine or a mechanized loom. A minimum of four warps are used; the maximum varies according to the desired width. Borders of thicker cotton yarn have been replaced by thinner cotton/rayon yarns. After it is woven,

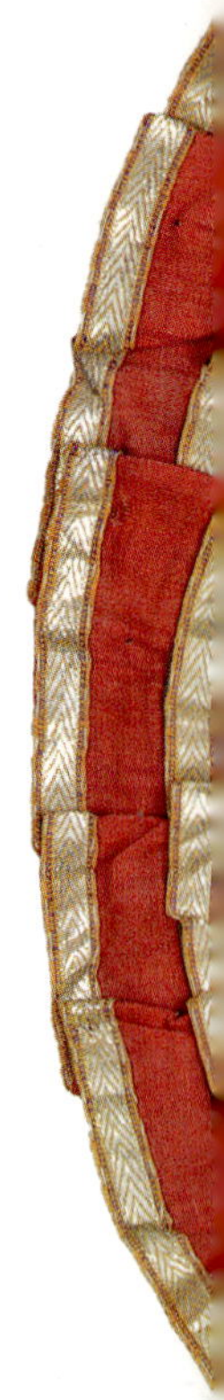

Lappe-ka-kaam
Thalposh
Circular dish cover with a reddish maroon velvet centre and dense embroidery in *zardozi*, silk, gold *gokhru*, and plain *gota* tape. A wide lightly gathered border is of six consecutive rows—red, yellow, black, white, and blue—each edged with gold *gota*. The piece is lined with red cotton.
MSMS II Museum, Jaipur
Tc.J.3

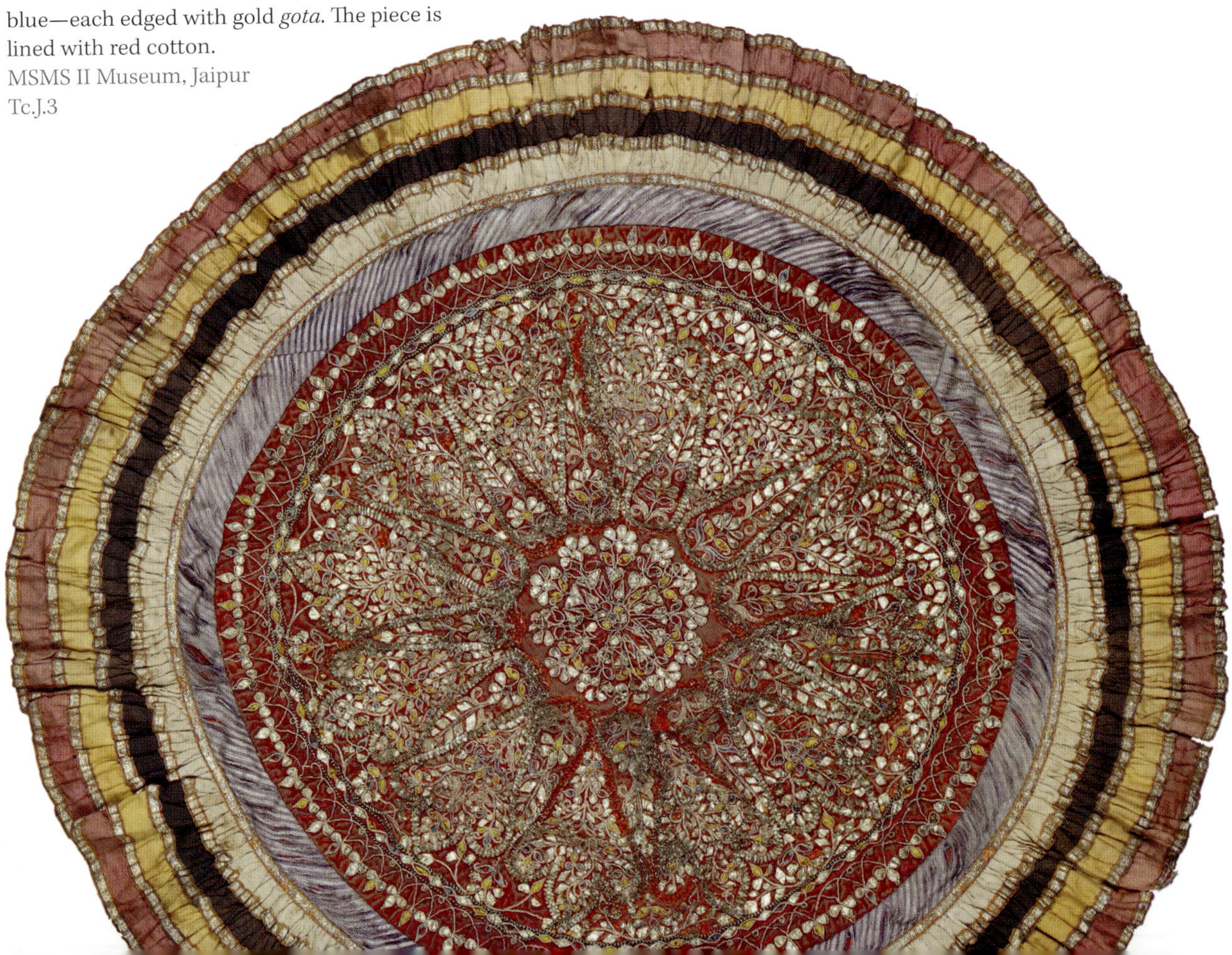

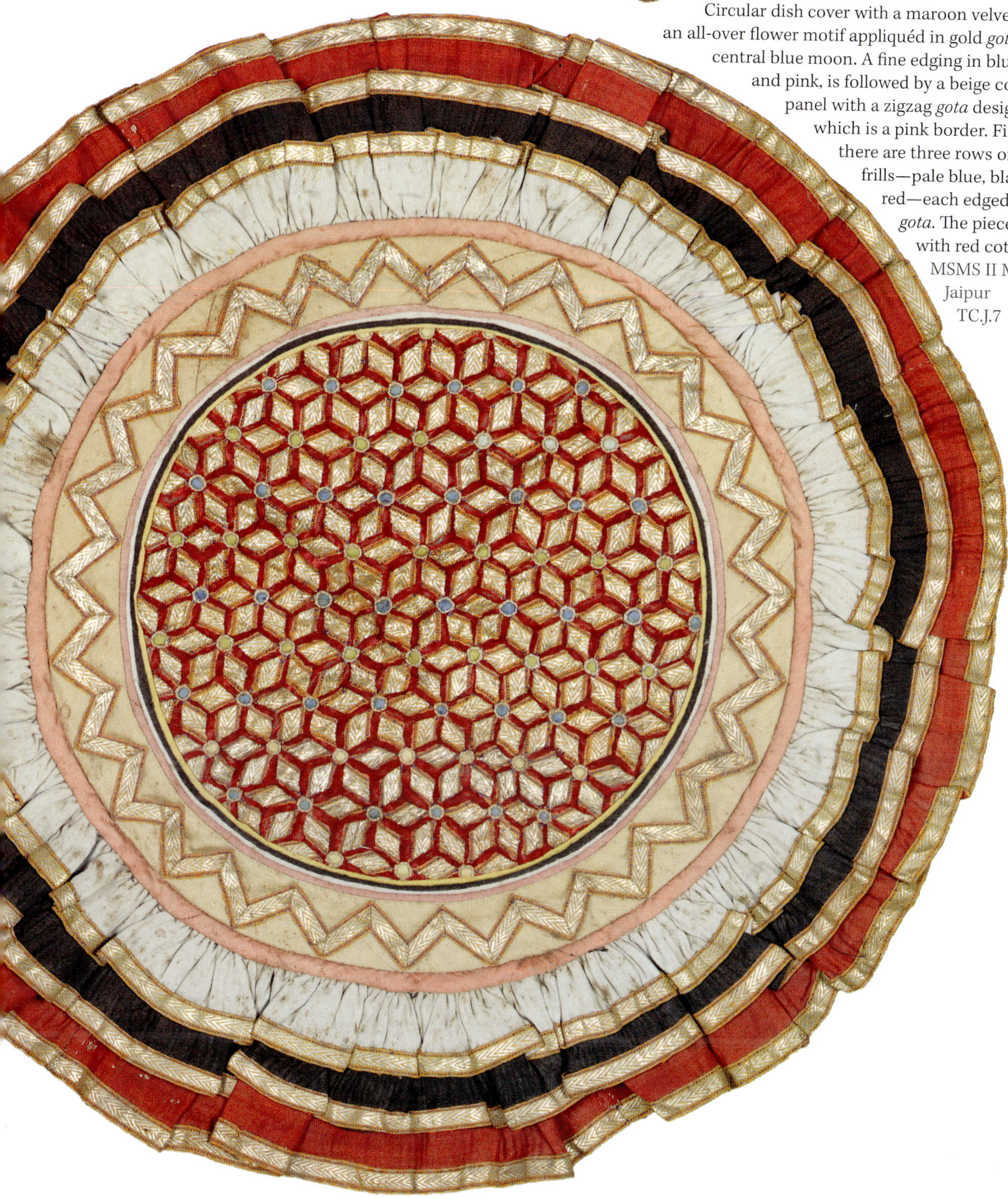

Lappe-ka-kaam
Thalposh
Circular dish cover with a maroon velvet centre, an all-over flower motif appliquéd in gold *gota*, and a central blue moon. A fine edging in blue, white, and pink, is followed by a beige coloured panel with a zigzag *gota* design, after which is a pink border. Finally, there are three rows of cotton frills—pale blue, black, and red—each edged with *gota*. The piece is lined with red cotton.
MSMS II Museum, Jaipur
TC.J.7

the *gota* is then wound by women on the *charkha* and finally packed for sale or use.

The number of *taar*s (warp ends present in the weaving) and the final width thus produced determines the kind of *gota* that emerges: *domasiya, teenmasiya, chaumasiya, panchmasiya, athmasiya,* or *solmasiya*. *Massa* is the traditional measure of weight. Thin *gota*s range between one-fourth and two inches. The thinnest *gota* uses eight yarns. *Aath tari* thus means 'eight ends': four *badla*s in the centre of the warp and four for the border. Depending on the final width required, the number of yarns could be increased to about 300–350 in the warp. While thin *gota*s are called *lappi*, broad *gota*s are known as *lappa, laffa,* or *chaura gota*. *Gota*s are also identified by the number of yarns in the warp; ones with 3–14 ends are known as *dhanki*, those with 14–18 ends are *siki*, with 22 ends *thappa*, and the ones with more than 34 ends are called *lappa*.

What adds to the allure of the *gota* is its many nuanced variations: *seekhiya* (simple tape); *lappa gota* (more than four inches broad with a twill woven tape); *siru gota* (striped with coloured motifs); *sal gota* (straight tape); *gokhru* (crimped tape); *lappa chaudani* (broad *gota* with a diamond-shaped design, that is, four dots placed as diamonds); *lappa naudani* (broad *gota* with a diamond-shaped design that has nine dots); *lappi* (thin *gota* about one and a half inches wide); *choti lappi* (half an inch wide); *nakshi gota* (thin with a chevron design); *kinar* (border); *gokhru* (*gota* twisted with a tweezer and then rolled to make flowers); and *lahardar gota* (*gota* with zigzag stripes woven on it).[1]

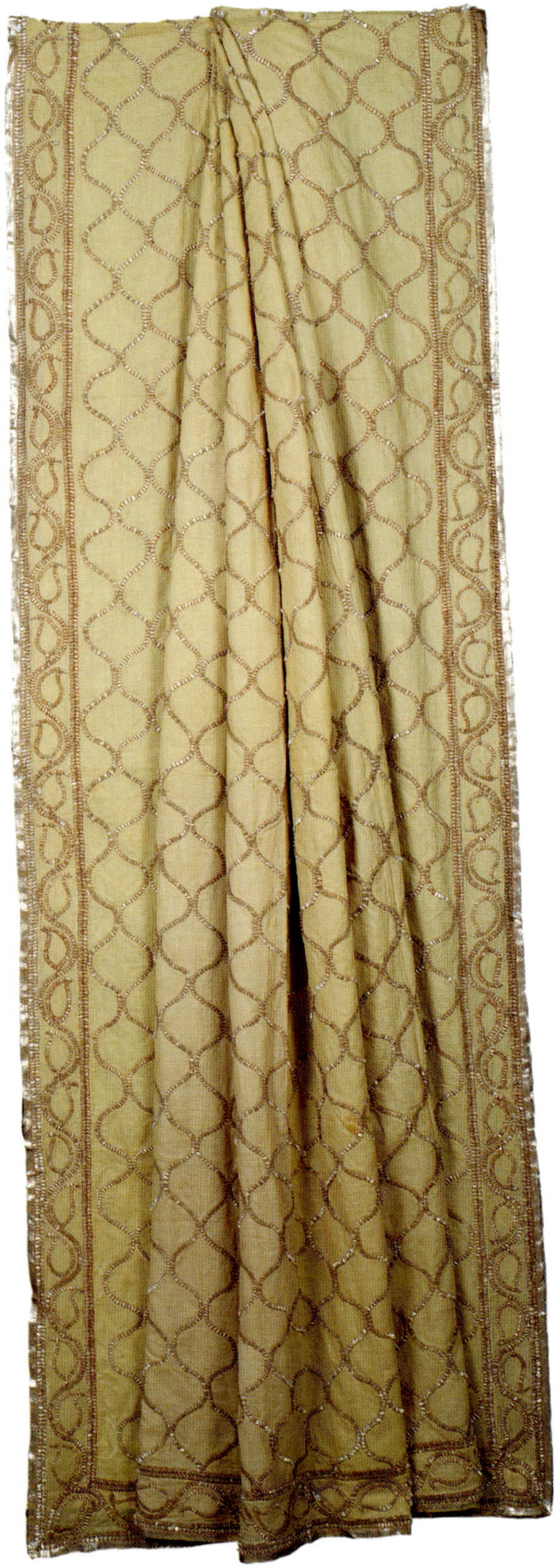

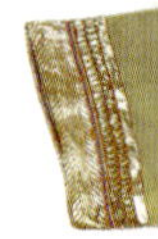

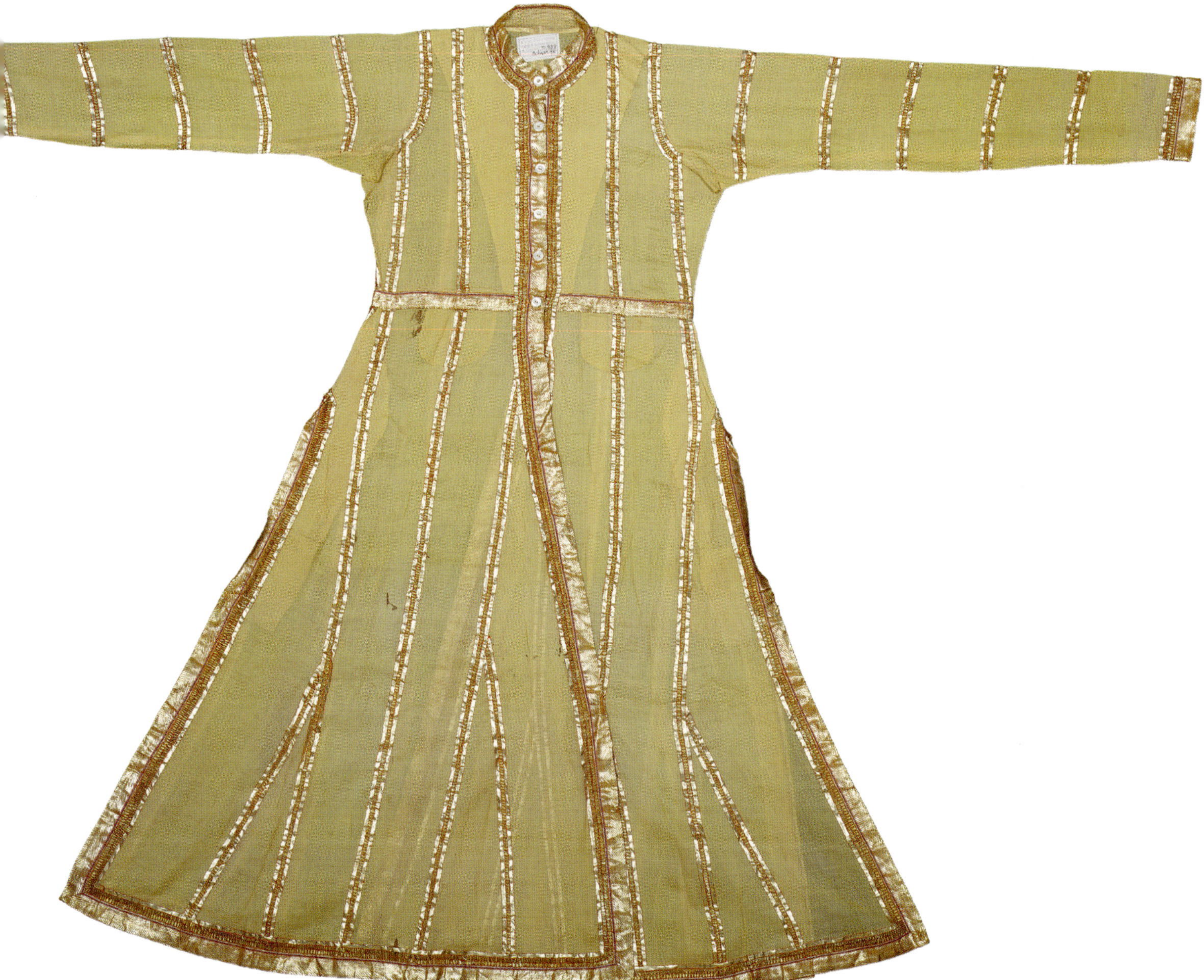

Facing page: Lappe-ka-kaam
Odhna
Yellow cotton with a gold *gokhru* in s-shaped lines forming an all-over lattice design. The border has a paisley scroll between two double rows of *gokhru*, and a metal gota tape at the edge.
MSMS II Museum, Jaipur
La.6.1

Lappe-ka-kaam
Achkan
Yellow muslin with vertical stripes composed of *gokhru* between two rows of *gota*, while the neck, placket, sleeves, and *daman* are edged with *gota lahargoda*, *chaumasiya*, and *gokhru*.
MSMS II Museum, Jaipur
TC.988.75

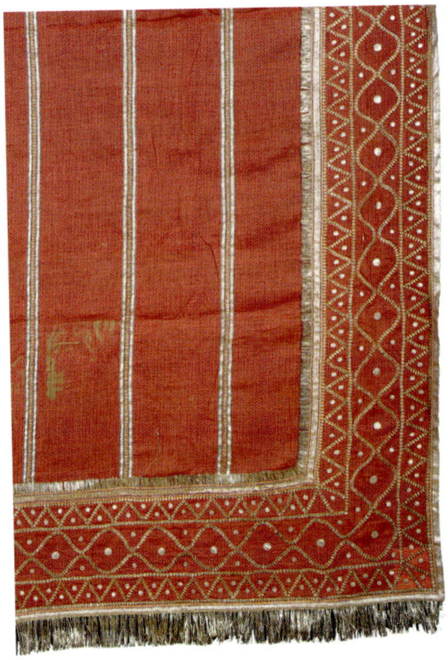

Lappe-ka-kaam
Odhna
Cotton appliquéd with metallic tissue (*gota*) and beetle-wings.
MSMS II Museum, Jaipur
TC.J.48

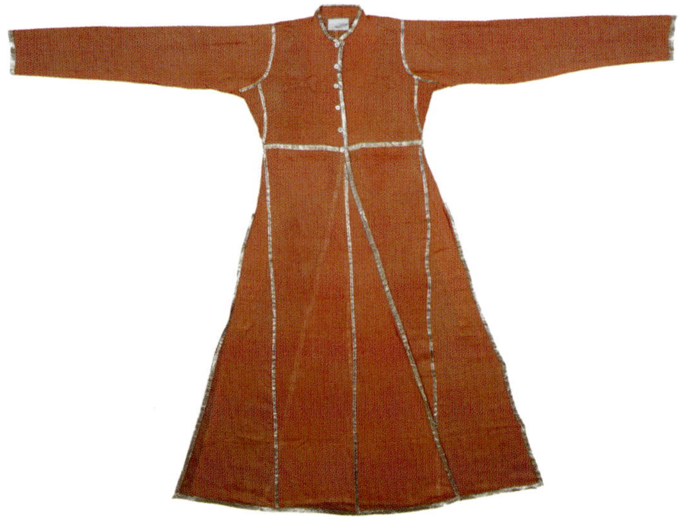

Lappe-ka-kaam
Angarkhi
Red cotton *jama* with silver *gota* edging on the neck, sleeve-ends, arm-holes, placket, waist, and slits. The garment is also stitched with *gota* from top to bottom and on either side of the placket, which is closed with buttons and button-holes.
125 cm (length)
MSMS II Museum, Jaipur
TC.986.75

Further variations occur when designs are imprinted on plain woven *gota*—the tape is passed between two metallic rollers, a plain and an embossed one—and the pressure indents the design on the *gota* surface. Among the more recognized designs are V-shaped ones, flowers (such as roses), leaves, and animal motifs. The embossing is done both on metallic and plastic *gotas*, the latter pressed over a heated plate rapidly, before it is embossed. This style is well defined and stands out with enunciated clarity.

Motifs and designs in the *gota* are manifold: flowers, leaves, stylized mango and heart motifs, animals and birds. In some cases, sections of the pattern are filled with coloured satin resembling the art of enamelling and hence referred to as *meenakari*. In others, stylized leaves, flowers, and birds are used individually or in clusters to add another dimension. Known as *chatai*, some of the more noteworthy patterns include: flower motifs, like *pan-ka-phool*, *jali-vala phool*, *kali-ka phool*, star *phool*, *champak-ke-phool*, *chhey patti-ka-phool* (six-petalled flower), *aath patti-ka-phool* (eight-petalled flower); *paan* (heart shaped); *kairi* (paisley); *mor* (peacock); *bankra* (lace-like band); *beejiya* (twisted); *beej bel* (creeper design); and *shakkarpare-ki-bel* (diamond-shaped border).

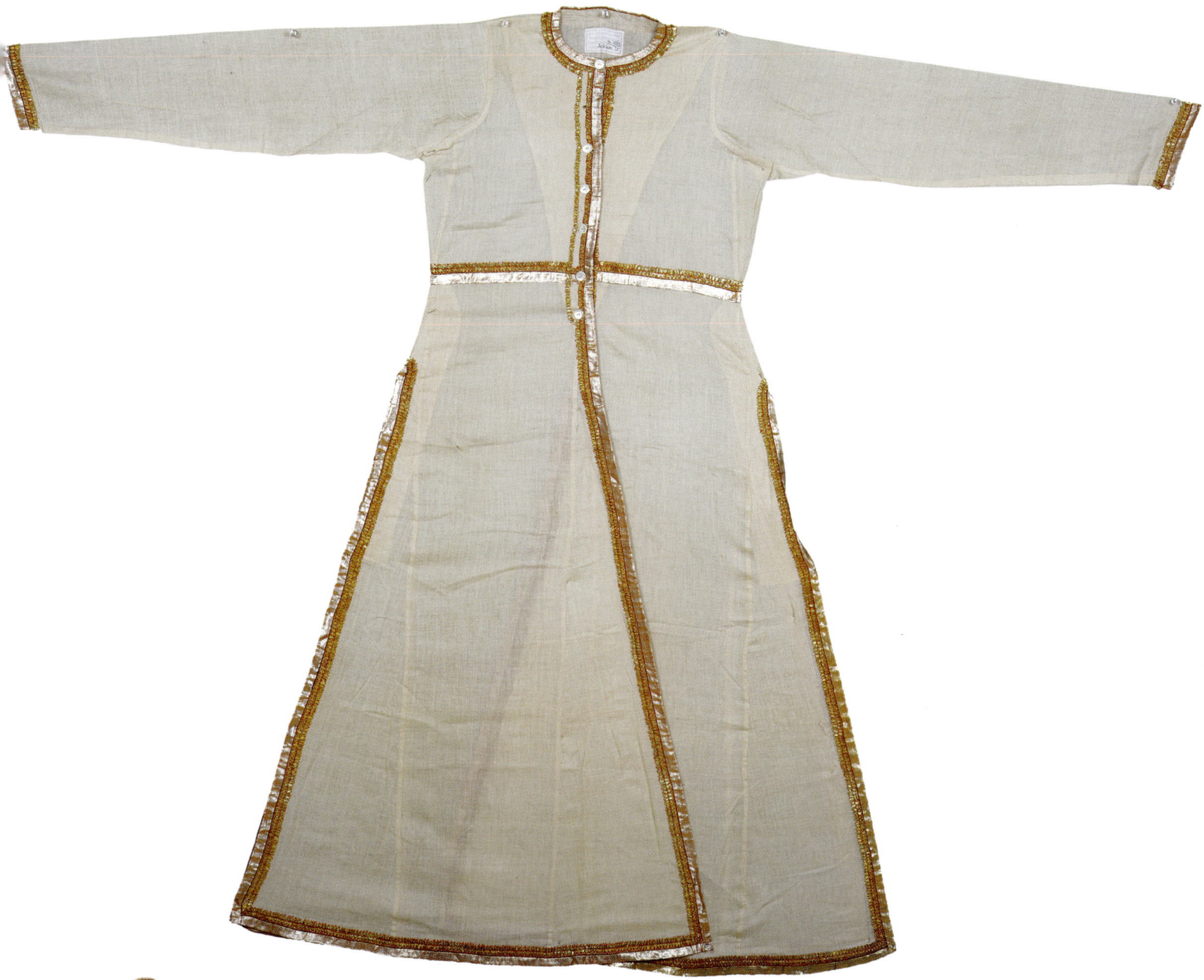

Lappe-ka-kaam
Achkan
Pale white cotton with an edging of *gokhru* and a *nakshi* and *lahargoda* type of *gota* on the neck, front opening, waist, sleeve-ends, bottom, and long side slits.
122.5 cm (length)
MSMS II Museum, Jaipur
TC.982.75

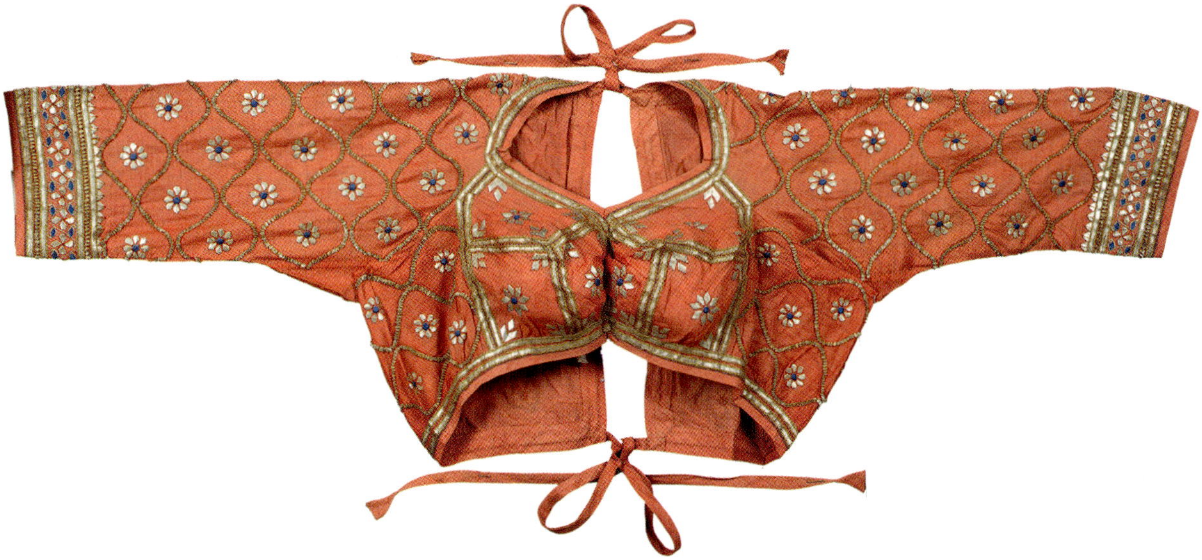

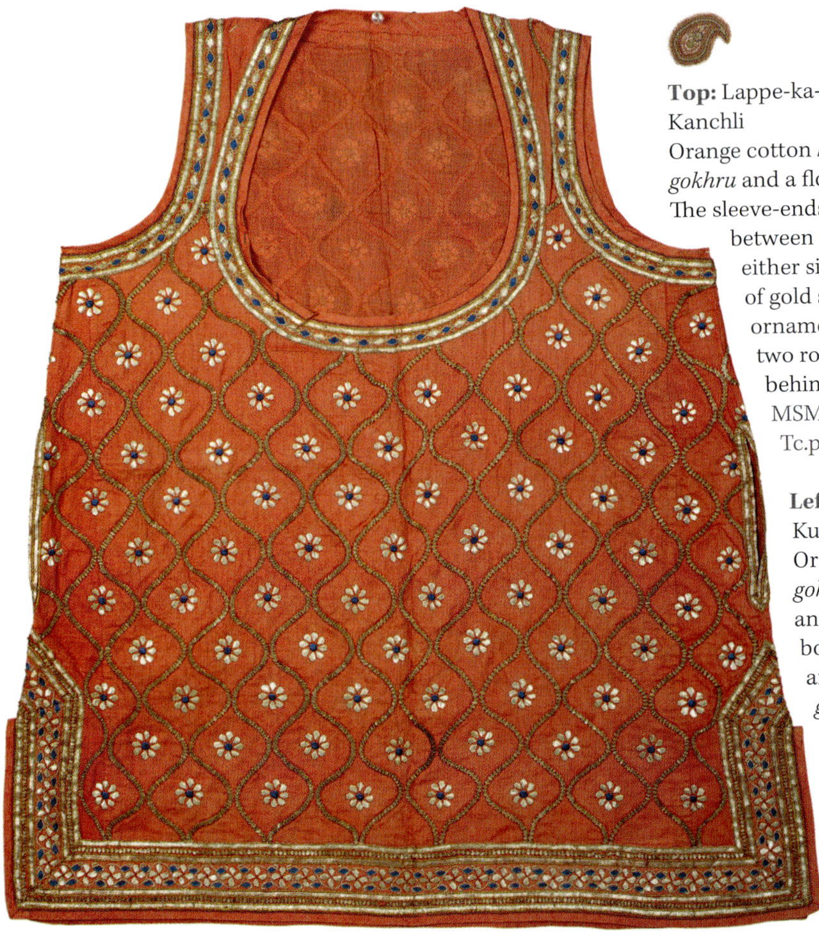

Top: Lappe-ka-kaam
Kanchli
Orange cotton *kanchli* with an all-over lattice *jaal* in *gokhru* and a flower motif appliquéd in gold and blue silk. The sleeve-ends are bordered with a floral scrolling design between two rows of *gokhru*, each with gold *gota* on either side. On the inner edge of the border is a row of gold sequins. The neck, bodice, and bottom, are ornamented and finished with *gokhru* between two rows of gold *gota*. The ties at the bottom and behind the neck are made of the base fabric.
MSMS II Museum, Jaipur
Tc.p.11

Left: Lappe-ka-kaam
Kurti
Orange cotton with an all-over lattice *jaal* in *gokhru*, with a flower motif appliquéd in gold and blue silk. The neck and armholes have borders of a scrolling design in blue and white silk between two rows of gold *gota*, while the pocket slits are edged with *gota* only. The bottom and side slits have a wider border with a floral scrolling design between two rows of *gokhru*, each edged by gold *gota* on either side.
70 cm (length)
MSMS II Museum, Jaipur
Tc.J.155.b

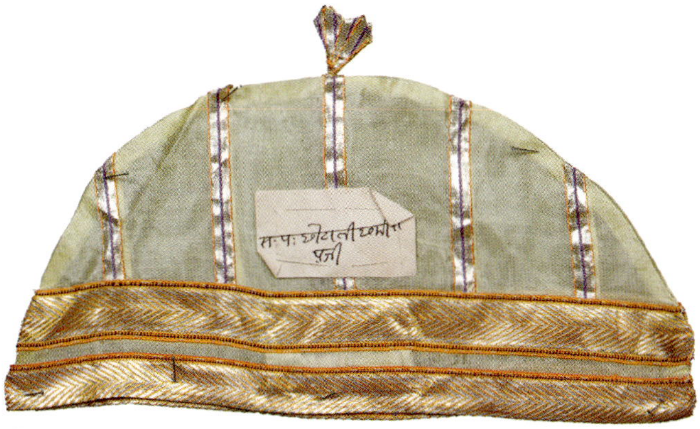

Lappe-ka-kaam
Topi
Lime green silk topi is embellished with vertical stripes of gold and silver *gota* and blue ribbon, which, together, also form a pompom on the top. The rim is bordered by two separated wider bands of gold *gota* with a chevron weave.
MSMS II Museum, Jaipur
TC.665.75

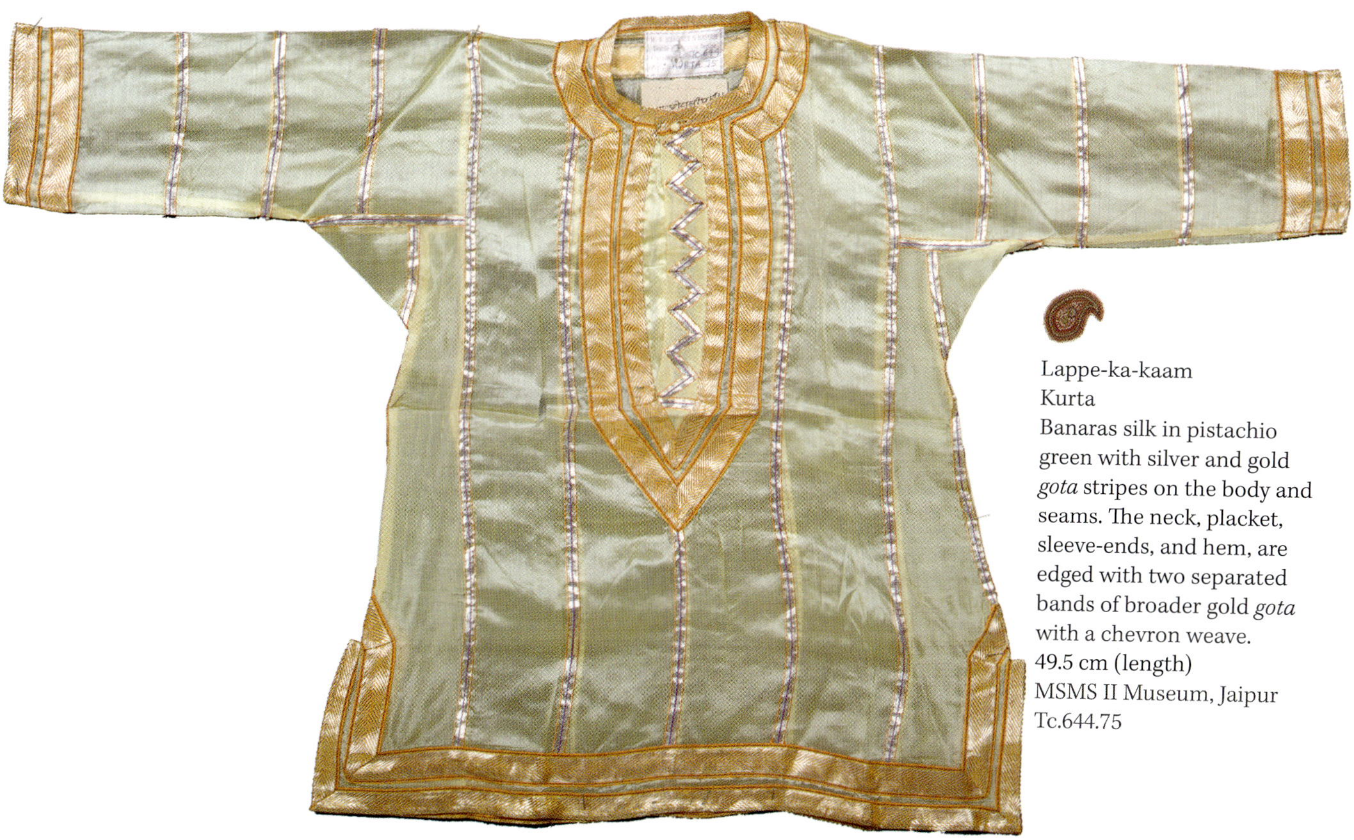

Lappe-ka-kaam
Kurta
Banaras silk in pistachio green with silver and gold *gota* stripes on the body and seams. The neck, placket, sleeve-ends, and hem, are edged with two separated bands of broader gold *gota* with a chevron weave.
49.5 cm (length)
MSMS II Museum, Jaipur
Tc.644.75

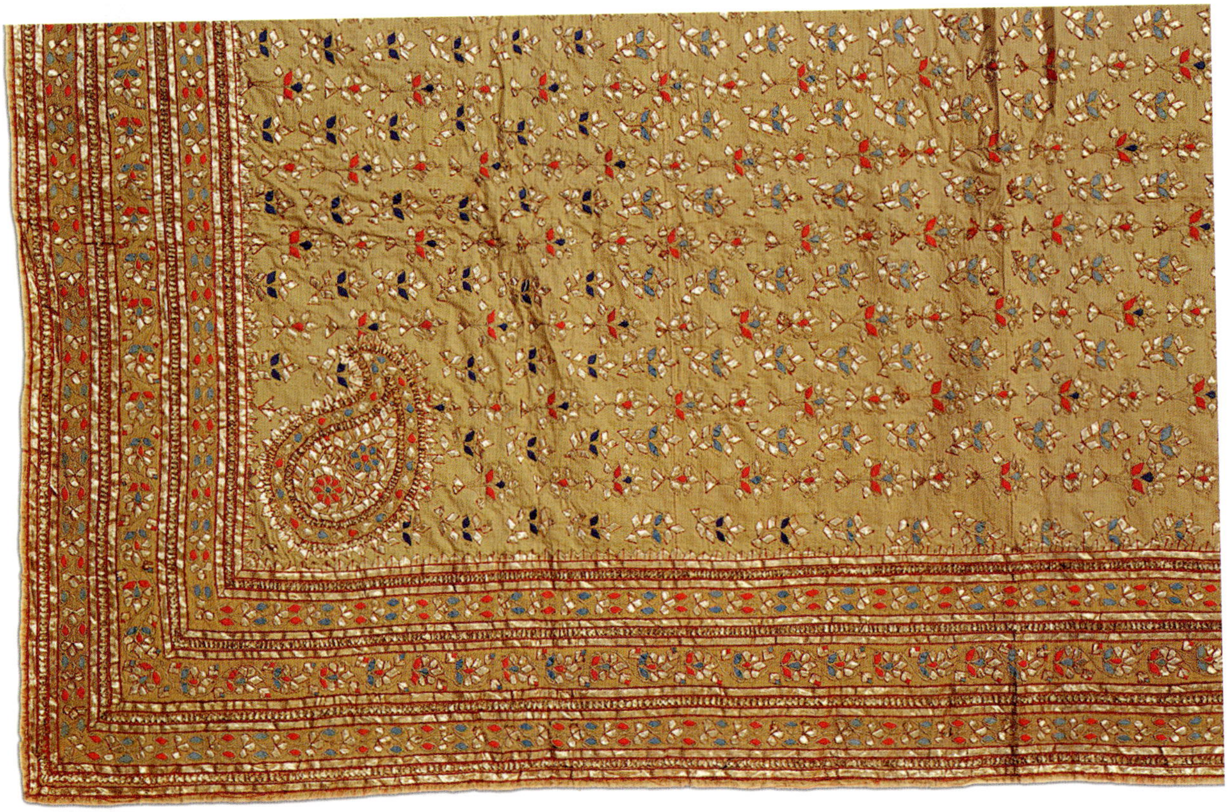

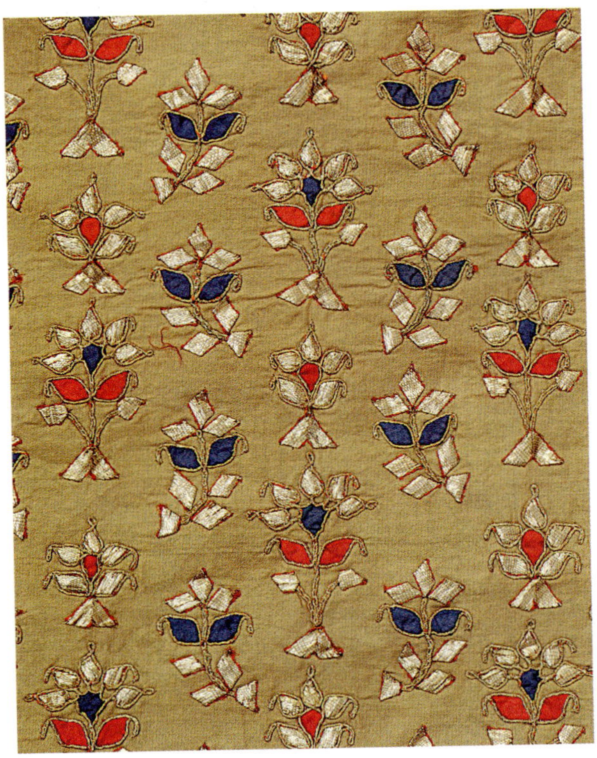

Lappe-ka-kaam
Odhna
Beige muslin covered with *bandhani* floral sprigs. It has an ornate border with a scrolling floral bel at its centre; and is embroidered with *gota* (two ways) and blue and green silk threads. The bel is edged on both sides with a strip of blue fabric appliquéd with small star-shaped flowers in *beejiya gota* tape, between two rows, each of twisted *gota* and *gota* tape. At the edge of the border is a flat *gota* tape with a diamond pattern followed by twisted *gota*, and along the inner side is a *kinari*, after which a zigzag appliqué of *gota* is seen on the body. The corners are adorned with a stylized paisley design.
(Left) Detail of the central field.
346 x 152 cm
MSMS II Museum, Jaipur
J 21

Gota is often attached to the borders or edges of fabric like lace, sometimes even twisted, spiralled, crimped, or made into single motifs, such as rosettes. It is usually women who work on the fabric through the appliqué technique, hemming, or by using a simple running stitch. Hand needles and presently 'aari' hooks are predominantly used to stitch the *gota* onto fabrics like muslin, satin silk, and thick cotton, and also to stitch the zari material on the edges with threads. They often fold the *gota* to make *pattis*, or diamond-shaped leaves, which are then pressed using a rolling pin. These *pattis* are used in turn to create designs of petals and leaves, animals and birds.

The *gota* embroidery is normally executed using a wooden frame. The base fabric is tied to the four sides of the frame using thick cords. *Khakhas* are first made and perforations with a needle are done on the design outlines. The design is then traced on the fabric, using chalk liquid. After tracing, the *gota* in tape or leaf form is placed and tacked using a running stitch; the thread colour is the same as that of the *gota*. These are then embroidered by a couching technique.

The edges of the *gota* are given imaginative finishes with an array of zaris (using an *aari* and thread). The finishing effects go under the name of *kasab, aari, dori,* and *dabka*. *Kasab* involves the appliqué combination of three or four threads; *dori* is made by plying *kasab* and cotton yarn; *aari* is a chain stitch done with a single thread of *kasab*; and *dabka* is a spring-like coiled wire made up of *kasab* threads.

Woven borders of different widths are also appliquéd to create various designs. Many experiments with zari woven yardage cut into designs have resulted in success. They are first appliquéd, then glued to a thin backing material to make it stiff and cut into required shapes. Cutting is done both manually and by using machines. Shapes vary from *tikkas* (circles), *pattis* (leaves), to *chauper* (diamonds).

While the tradition lives on, with many of its practising artisans savouring success, one of the reasons why old *gota* textiles are rarely found is because of the practice of transferring old *gota* to new fabrics when the old one gets worn out, or burning the fabric itself to extract the precious metals.

ENDNOTES

1. Vandana Bhandari, *Jewelled Textiles: Gold and Silver embellished Cloth of India* (New Delhi: Om Book International, 2015).

GLOSSARY

angarkha/angarkhi long-sleeved, full-skirted, stitched upper garment of varying length for men, generally open at the chest and tied in the front with strings; it has has an inner flap or *parda*
arka a type of flower
athmasiya width measure for *gota* or metallic tape appliquéd on cloth, 'ath' implying eight

badla type of metal embroidery with flat metal wire
badle-ka-taar flat metallic wire
bandha to tie
bandhani technique of resist dyeing practised extensively in Rajasthan
bandhej design produced on fabric using the *bandhani* technique; also name for the technique
begar alum mixed in gum-paste, used in printing
bidhan wheat flour thickener for printing paste
bilvapatra plant
buta large floral motif
buti small floral motif

chadar large sheet used for religious or ceremonial purposes
chakri circular shape
chalak type of metal embellishment
chand moon
chapai printing
chapakhana printing press
chaumasiya width measure for *gota* tape, 'chau' implying four
chaupel a kind of metal embellishment
chauper a board game played with dice
chikankari embroidery style—white on white embroidery
chikna a type of metal embellishment
chikna sunheri kora a type of metal embellishment in golden colour
chirai outline printing
chuna lime paste
chunri a drape for women to wrap around the upper part of the body

dabba-dabboo box
dabka a type of metal embellishment
dabu method of resist printing; also mud used in resist printing
dagala quilted upper garment
dana dot
danka metal embroidery done using a with a silver/gold metal plate
datta wooden mould which fits in a *sancha*; wooden block carved in bold relief
dhanki thin *gota* ribbon
dhatura a type of flower
dhavdi ka phool a type of flower used for dyeing
dhuniya a person who does cotton carding
dolidar dabu a type of resist used for block printing
domasiya width measure for *gota*, 'do' implying two
dori thread
dorukha two-sided

fardi dot; metal embroidery technique
fardi-ka-kaam/badla metal embroidery technique
fatila a wooden tool on which the gold thread is wrapped for embroidery
fitkari alum

gad wooden block carved in intaglio
gandadar zigzag pattern
gaund glue
gawarbali dabu type of mud-resist
geru local term for red fugitive dye
gota-patti/lappe-ka-kaam *gota* is a strip of gold or silver ribbon of varying width, woven in a satin, plain, or twill weave, with yellow silk/cotton and gold yarn, or white silk/cotton and silver yarn
gudri a type of quilt

harad a natural agent used for dyeing
haveli a mansion with historical and architectural significance
hina mehendi/ henna

ikat resist yarn, dyed fabric
indradhanush rainbow pattern

jaal or jali lattice
jaldar lattice pattern
jali numa lattice pattern
jhar buta small bush pattern

kalidar dabu a type of mud-resist
kamdani lighter style of gold embroidery
kangani/kangni shaped metal wire used for embroidery
kantha a style of embroidery using primarily running stitch
karan phool flower with straight lines; earrings
karchob wooden frame used for embroidery
karigar artisan
karkhana workshop
kasab metal wire
kasumba a type of flower used for dyeing
katori the shape of the metal piece used for embroidery; literally a cup
kesariya saffron
khaka stencil
khar river residue used to make emulsion for desizing fabric
khas special

khulla wooden blocks embossed with text
kinari border
kora embroidery material
kundan technique of setting gemstones in gold
kurti-kanchli stitched upper garment for women

ladoo (here) a round shape, resembling that of the sweetmeat of the same name
lappa/laffa/chaura gota broad *gota*
lappi thin *gota*
leheriya resist dyed fabric
likhai writing

marori a type of gold thread/cord; a style of embroidery
mend ki chapai wax-resist block printing
mitha tel a type of oil
mitti mud
mothra a type of *leheriya*
moti pearl
mukaish small dots of metal; *kamdani*
mulmul cotton voile
munda phool flower with petals
murri-ka-kaam raised rice grain-shaped design

nakshi tightly coiled thin wires
nalki shiny glass tubes used for embroidery
namavali object inscribed with a name
nashphal yellow dye obtained from pomegranate rind and turmeric
neel blue fugitive color
neelgar dyer
nua/nolia brass thimble used for tie-dye process

odhna/odhni woman's veil, usually worn in conjunction with a ghagra: drape garment which covers the head
ornia thin and fine lines
pagri/pagdi turban
palla/ pallu/ pallave end piece of drape garment
panchmasiya width measure for *gota* tape
panchranga five-coloured pattern
parda curtain
patka waist band
patta/patti leaf pattern
pattiya printing table
phool rangai dyeing with flowers
pichhwai painted or embroidered textile also used as altar cloth for the Hindu deity, Krishna
pomcha-piliya tie-dyed upper-body drape garment for women
potna smearing dye paste
prasad sweets offered in temples
pratapshahi type of *leheriya*

rajashahi type of *leheriya*
rangai colouring
rangkhana dyeing house
rangrez dyer
rangrez walon ka rasta the road of dyers
razai quilt
rekh line; a type of block
rudraksha a type of seed; also called the eyes of Lord Shiva
rumal handkerchief
rupehri silver

sada kora metal wire with single gold polish
safa a type of headgear or turban
safed kora dull flexible coiled silver wire
salaidar design with transverse stripes
salma zigzag coiled wire
samudralehar a type of *leheriya*
sangam a confluence of colours
saropa object inscribed with a name
sathiya religious symbol
satranga seven-coloured
shaahi kaam royal work
siki thin *gota* tape
sitara sequin
solmasiya a measure of weight, 'sol' implying sixteen
sunehri golden
syahi black printing paste

taar wire
tapai sun bleaching of cloth
tarkashi process for making fine gold wire
tatiyasthan a type of quilt
teen sui-ki-fardi flat gold or silver wire with a thread base used for embroidery
teenmasiya a measure of weight, 'teen' implying three
thali numa a round plate
thappa a thin *gota* tape
tikki/avala sitara
tili glass object used for embroidery
tilla couched embroidery using gold and silver thread forming circular loops on the fabric
trishul trident; prong

vasli-ka-kaam/dhok-ka-kaam raised metallic embroidery
vishnupada feet of Vishnu, a Hindu diety

zardozi metal embroidery done using gold and silver thread

ACKNOWLEDGEMENTS

This book has been a long journey of discovery of the beautiful and rich textiles at the Maharaja Sawai Man Singh II Museum.

It could not have been possible without the participation and assistance of a large number of people. Their contributions are sincerely appreciated and gratefully acknowledged.

I would like to express my deep appreciation and indebtedness towards the museum and their staff for their endless support, and their kind and understanding spirit during the period.

I owe a deep sense of gratitude to Princess Diya Kumari for supporting this research and for her cooperation throughout my study period.

I profusely thank Dr Giles Tillotson for the editing and photography, and for his kind help and coordination at the museum.

I would also thank my fellow researcher Rahul Jain for his prompt inspirations, and suggestions given with kindness and enthusiasm at every stage of my study.

I sincerely thank the photographers, Anchit Natha and Purushottam Diwaker, for their contributions.

I am also deeply thankful to Mr Bikash Dey Niyogi, Mrs Tultul Dey Niyogi, and Arunima Ghosh, and appreciate their help.

I take this opportunity to express my regards to my friends at NIFT—Jaspal Kalra and Manoj Kumar Singh, Ratika Baid, Amit Kumar, Shobha Kumari, Srishti Meherotra, and Shivangi Shaily, for their keen interest and constant encouragement.

Last but not the least, I would like to thank my family—Sundeep, Tanya, Kartik, and George, for their countless love and support. Without them none of this would have ever been possible.

INDEX